Human Dignity
Eleven Defenders of Human Rights
at Close Range

Arne Peter Braaksma

Pixel Perfect
PUBLICATIONS

Dedication

To those who dream of a better life in a better world.
To those who, understanding such dreams, speak truth to power.
To those in power, entrusted to make such dreams come true.

About the author

Arne Peter Braaksma, author of Nine Lives: Making the Impossible Possible, has worked as an editor in Britain and as a communication adviser and corporate journalist in the Netherlands. From Asian countries he contributed to various public and corporate magazines. This caused him to focus on human rights, the environment and (corporate) social responsibility. *Human Dignity* is a sequel to *Nine Lives* and presents stories of people whose lives reflect Gandhi's notion 'you must be the change you wish to see in the world.'

Table of Contents

Taking the plunge

'In reading the history of nations, we find that, like individuals, they have their whims and their peculiarities; their seasons of excitement and recklessness, when they care not what they do. We find that whole communities suddenly fix their minds upon one object, and go mad in its pursuit; that millions of people become simultaneously impressed with one delusion, and run after it, till their attention is caught by some new folly more captivating than the first. We see one nation suddenly seized, from its highest to its lowest members, with a fierce desire for military glory; another as suddenly becoming crazed upon a religious scruple; and neither of them recovering its senses until it has shed rivers of blood and sowed a harvest of groans and tears, to be reaped by its posterity.'

Charles Mackay in his Preface to Extraordinary Popular Delusions and the Madness of Crowds (first published in 1841; edition of 1852).

Throw a stone into a lake – into the history of any nation. Splash! The moment it plunges through the surface and disappears from sight, only the ripples speak of its passage. The cause is gone, but the effects are still lapping onto the shore. Now, what would happen if you could reverse this? Push back the ripples, forcing the stone out of the water. You would be holding the cause of the ripples in the palm of your hand again. By analogy, the contributors to this book are experiencing ripple effects, often acutely aware of the stone that caused them, but seeking to cause waves that move in the opposite direction.

Rather than piecing their perspectives together from afar, I decided to collect them first-hand, because these remarkable men and women are the living library of events that are unfolding as we speak. Obtaining stories straight from the horse's mouth offers greater insights than breaking news.

The causes of most people in this volume however are obscured by those who have opposing interests and spin facts into fable. But in the end, the truth will out, because it is more robust and enduring. Robust are also the endeavors of the contributors. Confronted with great challenges, they speak truth to power and tackle head-on what stands in their path. In this book, not fame, but the nobility of the cause is the determining factor. The advocates of these causes present us with testimonies that are authentic, constructive and significant beyond the borders of their own region. Where truth is suppressed, they speak up. Where all hope seems lost, they persevere, sometimes finding the last straw is nothing other than themselves.

Together, these testimonies form an uncommon odyssey across four continents. It offers rare, unpolished impressions of current affairs and the status quo with regard to human rights. Some chapters dive straight into regional issues, while others have a decidedly global focus. Not being eyewitnesses ourselves, how are we to grasp world events in these 11, let alone 217 countries and territories around the world? Who could? One thing however applies to all these stories: the local illustrates the global. The Inuit story illustrates global warming. The Sahrawi story illustrates that totalitarianism is alive and well. The Ecuadorian story illustrates why corporate social responsibility must be taken seriously – all the way to the courthouse.

Each of the contributors demonstrates bravery in the face of issues bigger than themselves. Thus, these chapters offer uplifting examples of staying true to one's beliefs and a feeling of hope and shared humanity. Last but not least, they reflect that an ordinary person can accomplish extraordinary things and can succeed against all odds in struggles that could have been yours or mine. The immediacy and the inside-out telling take you beyond the threshold of mere facts to the relevance of these struggles for all world citizens.

On my way to one of the contributors, an American customs officer asked:

'Business?'

'Yes.'

'What kind of business?'

'I'm a writer on human rights issues.'

'Human rights? In the US?'

'Yes.'

'Why don't you go to Chad?'

'Chad?'

'Or Sierra Leone. To write about blood diamonds and child labor.'

'Well, I might, one day.'

'Or China. So many human rights violations.'

'Yes, plenty of opportunity.'

'So, what brings you to the US?'

'Writing about human rights.'

'Human rights? In the US?'

'I'm here for the convention of Appalachia Rising this weekend and the march on the White House on Monday.'

'Appalachia?'

'Yes, Appalachia. There are serious pollution issues there as a consequence of mountaintop removal mining. The waterways, the groundwater and the ground itself are polluted and the people there are paying a heavy price for the way the coal is mined.'

'And that's a human rights issue?'

'Yes, it is.'

A pause and a frown.

'Well, welcome to the US.'

'Thank you.'

The fact that environmental pollution is not seen as a human rights issue is quite a universal misconception, as three of the chapters on the Americas demonstrate. Perhaps it only hits home when your husband dies from leukemia due to ChevronTexaco's oil spills in the Amazon, when your child suffers asthma in the Appalachian coalfields or when you cannot breastfeed your baby in Nunavut due to the toxins that blew over from industries thousands of miles away. More tangible than that the impact cannot be. Why is it so easy to grasp the connectivity of the internet and not that of the wind and the water? 'What you do to the land,' says Inuit elder Mariano Aupilaarjuk, 'the land will do to you.'

Aware or not, we always do something to the land and to each other. But this sense of connectivity is losing ground and so is the nobility of spirit that should go hand in hand with it. In 2010, the North Korean navy killed two South Koreans. Within a week, the issue was brought before the Security Council. Demonstrations in Egypt during the Arab Spring triggered responses from around the world almost daily. Contrast this with two stories in this volume: the Sahrawis, who have been suffering at the hands of the Moroccans and the Uyghurs, who have been suffering at the hands of the Chinese. For decades. Who heeds their voices?

This inaction may be due to the fact that news goes through a sieve. Spin doctors or 'perception managers' present the catastrophe in Iraq as a 'liberation' or appoint a man co-responsible for two wars in the Middle East as a 'peace envoy'. Language itself suffers so much 'collateral damage' that it wears out the key for the inverted comma. At the receiving end of such delusions, Iraqis, Sahrawis and Uyghurs experience real damage. There is nothing 'collateral' about it. As Mackay says: 'Popular delusions began so early, spread so widely, and have lasted so long, that instead of two or three volumes, fifty would scarcely suffice to detail their history.' Indeed. In other words: We get the news, but we don't get it. We dip in and out of a world that blurs the distinction between true and false. 'We should always be disposed to believe that that which appears white is really black, if the hierarchy of the Church so decides,' said Saint Ignatius of Loyola, the sixteenth-century founder of the Jesuit Order. He clearly didn't intend his words as a warning, but as an admonition to follow the precepts of the Church. A warning it is nonetheless. Four centuries later, George Orwell merged Ignatius' black and white:

> 'The keyword here is blackwhite. Like so many Newspeak words, this word has two mutually contradictory meanings. Applied to an opponent, it means the habit of impudently claiming that black is white, in contradiction of the plain

facts. Applied to a Party member, it means a loyal willingness to say that black is white when Party discipline demands this. But it means also the ability to believe that black is white, and more, to know that black is white, and to forget that one has ever believed the contrary. This demands a continuous alteration of the past, made possible by the system of thought which really embraces all the rest, and which is known in Newspeak as doublethink. Doublethink is basically the power of holding two contradictory beliefs in one's mind simultaneously, and accepting both of them.'

George Orwell, Nineteen Eighty-Four (1949).

One moment we're aware, another we're immersed in it. The last one to know it is in the water is the goldfish. During Germany's Nazi era, a man called Martin Niemöller realized that he had become immersed in perilous waters. He saw through the 'doublethink'. Having first supported the Nazis as a U-boat commander, he later denounced them as a pastor. After his release from Dachau concentration camp, in 1946 he addressed the inactivity of intellectuals and the purging of German society during the Nazi regime:

> 'They came first for the Communists, and I didn't speak up because I wasn't a Communist. Then they came for the trade unionists, and I didn't speak up because I wasn't a trade unionist. Then they came for the Jews, and I didn't speak up because I wasn't a Jew. Then they came for me and by that time no one was left to speak up.'

Martin Niemöller (1892-1984).

He connected the dots – the ripples. But what if you can't? 'The ideal citizen of totalitarian rule is not the convinced Nazi or the convinced Communist,' said political theorist Hannah Arendt, 'but people for whom the distinction between fact and fiction, and the distinction between true and false, no longer exists.' The 11 men and women in this book speak up, some of them under life-threatening circumstances. Their causes prompt us to think for ourselves, to speak truth to power and to see the connections between the local and the global.

In a classic tale of adventure from the 1920s, the hero Tros of Samothrace writes in his log: 'Though I know not whither I go, nor what I shall be, I shall go to no home of idleness. I shall be no gray ghost lamenting what I might have done, but did not.' Ripple effects occur in all waters – in any society. Where they are safe to navigate, most likely someone who was not idle spoke up before us. So, where shall I go? What shall I do?

Arne Peter Braaksma

ASIA/EURASIA

'Until one is committed, there is hesitancy, the chance to draw back, always ineffectiveness. Concerning all acts of initiative (and creation), there is one elementary truth the ignorance of which kills countless ideas and splendid plans: that the moment one definitely commits oneself, then providence moves too. A whole stream of events issues from the decision, raising in one's favor all manner of unforeseen incidents, meetings and material assistance, which no man could have dreamt would have come his way.'

William Hutchison Murray in *The Scottish Himalayan Expedition* (1951).

Michael Ward with William Hutchison Murray during the 1951 reconnaissance expedition route over the Khumbu.

Rebiya Kadeer - East Turkestan
Defending Uyghurs against Chinese oppression

'You can see people's dreams and wishes just by looking into their eyes,' Rebiya Kadeer knows. The 'mother of the Uyghurs' is determined that the Chinese Government should be brought before an international tribunal for its human rights abuses in East Turkestan. Starting off poor, uneducated, and divorced, her initial prospects were bleak. Remarkably, she became a businesswoman, social activist, and member of the Chinese People's Political Consultative Conference. The Chinese Government, however, imprisoned her for highlighting the plight of the Uyghurs. In exile in the United States she became the leader of the World Uyghur Congress. For a long time she was looking for a Uyghur leader, but her patience ran out. 'I then decided that I had to find that person within myself.'

Rebiya Kadeer in Geneva, 2011.
Photo Eric Bridiers / UN / Wikimedia
Commons.

'I want to be the mother of the Uyghurs, the medicine for their sufferings, the cloth to wipe their tears, and the shelter to protect them from the rain.' Rebiya Kadeer (1947), mother of eleven, and 'mother of the Uyghurs', is adamant that the Chinese Government should be brought before an international tribunal for its human rights abuses in East Turkestan.

Context

Yining, Xinjiang, is the place of a little-known massacre. It took place in 1997, just eight years after the drama that shook the world on Tiananmen Square in Beijing, China. Yining is the Chinese name for the city of Ghulja in East Turkestan, known to the Chinese as the Xinjiang Uyghur Autonomous Region. This landlocked Central Asian country is generally peaceful. So why did these terrible events unfold here?

Similar to the Tibetan Autonomous Region, its southern neighbor, East Turkestan is as vast as Alaska, constituting one-sixth of the area under the control of the People's Republic of China. But despite its official name, this new 'living space' for Han Chinese is in no way 'autonomous'. Fundamental freedoms and human rights are violated on a daily basis. This includes such extremes as coercive birth control – a Chinese form of ethnic cleansing – and reducing the native Uyghur nationality to a minority in their own country by a massive influx of Chinese settlers.

According to Amnesty International, more than 3,000 Uyghurs have been arrested since 11 September 2001. Among them are scholars, writers and journalists, who are labeled 'separatists', 'ethnic splittist', 'religious extremists' or 'terrorists'. China's 'Strike Hard, Maximum Pressure' campaign has little consideration for human rights or the preservation of the Uyghur national identity. Some believe that China's hardened attitude stems from their concern that since the breakdown of the Soviet Union there are seven nations with a Turkic-speaking population. As far back as 1962,when the Chinese Government spoke about the four plagues', it meant Kazakhs, Uzbeks, Kyrgyz and Uyghurs. But since glasnost (openness) and perestroika (reform or restructuring) these nations have all joined the UN, representing a power to be reckoned with.

Since the early 1990s, there have indeed been various small-scale attacks on Chinese targets in East Turkestan's cities. These were blamed on violent Uyghur separatist groups. More recently, Beijing claims that these attacks are fuelled by radical Islam. Now that China supports the US-led 'war on terrorism', it has linked the regional practice of Islam to al-Qaeda, creating a convenient cover for its own human rights violations. But Uyghur activists say that the attacks come from only a tiny minority and that most Uyghurs simply want to have the right to practice their own customs and live in peace.

In its '2004 Annual Human Rights Report', even the US State Department asserted that the Chinese Government 'used the international war on terror as a pretext for cracking down harshly on suspected Uyghur separatists expressing peaceful political dissent and on independent Muslim religious leaders'. The Chinese repression of the Uyghurs has simply been repackaged as a 'war on terror' that has the appearance – and no more than that – of worldwide acceptance, obscuring the difference between peaceful protests, civil unrest and violence. In the wake of violent attacks in 2008, the Olympic year of 'peace, friendship and solidarity', China has accused western countries of instigating terrorism, separatism and extremism in East Turkestan. It did the same in 2009, when riots between migrant Uyghur workers and Chinese in eastern Chinese cities cost the lives of several thousands of Uyghurs.

Earlier Chinese historians referred to East Turkestan as inhabited by barbarians. But these 'barbarians' were civilized enough to connect the Han Dynasty (206 BC-AD 220) with the Roman Empire by the famous Silk Road – or Roads in the case of East Turkestan. The region also welcomed Buddhism first, and then Islam, only losing its function as a Eurasian crossroads due to the advances of ocean travel since the fifteenth century.

Archaeological evidence shows that East and West were already linked three thousand years ago, and the famous Tarim Mummies unearthed in the early 20th century are distinctly Caucasoid in appearance. But those ancient links are gone. Shortly after the Second World War, East Turkestan was a poor nation, but with a great wealth of natural resources. Eyed by both Russia and China, it was eventually traded as a 'semi-colony'. Some Uyghurs believe their country was 'sacrificed' or 'sold for the peace of the world' when Stalin, Churchill and Roosevelt met during the Yalta Conference in 1945. The country passed hands, first from Stalin to Chiang Kai-shek, and then to Mao Zedong. Until the 19th century, China had never been in control of East Turkestan. What's in a name? The term Xinjiang was only first used in 1884 when the Manchus stationed troops there as a buffer against Russian encroachment. It means 'New Territory' or 'New Frontier', understandably a name that Uyghurs resent.

Whenever Rebiya Kadeer, the foremost champion of the Uyghur cause, entered the White House, she felt eager to talk about these things, but there never was time to do so. Jailed by China for 'passing on state secrets' and exiled to the United States in 2005, Rebiya was once so successful in business, that she was locally known as 'the millionairess'. As writer James Millward says, she is 'not an average woman'. She is also a fashion designer, philanthropist, anti-drugs crusader and a mother of eleven children. But it was the combination of being a staunch defender of Uyghur human rights and a member of the Chinese People's Political Consultative Conference that made her a liability to the Chinese Government. She has accused China of committing 'cultural genocide' against the Uyghur people, while it seeks to develop the rich energy and mineral resources (oil, gas, iron ore and uranium) of East Turkestan. The Chinese monopolize this 'second Arabia', while the Uyghurs continue to live on the threshold of poverty.

According to its 2015 World Report, Human Rights Watch claims that the political persecution across China is currently worse than it has been in the previous decade. Chinese authorities continue to detain, harass, and torture members of the Uyghur population. Human rights reforms were anticipated when President Xi Jinping took over in 2012. However, the situation has worsened, and persecution targets activists and their family members with unusual brutality. China refuses engagement with UN human rights mechanisms, and usually calls for 'political solutions', which never materialize. UN special envoys are not allowed to visit. Journalists have to sign an agreement stating they will not release unpublished information without prior approval. Thus, there is no news on East Turkestan or the Uyghur Autonomous Region. For the Uyghur population, that is bad news.

Although tears do not show on these pages, Rebiya had to suppress them while speaking of the fate of her country, her home and her family. One moment she speaks on Radio Free Asia, the next she addresses questions from an Australian journalist, easily picking up the thread of her narrative when she returns. Considered to be 'Public Enemy Number One' by the Chinese Government, she has recently published her autobiography Dragon Fighter. Her husband, literature professor Sidik Rozi, hands me a copy of Jung Chang's and Jon Halliday's Mao: The Unknown Story, in which he has marked passages relating to East Turkestan. It is 1 October, the day on which Uyghurs gather each year in front of the Chinese embassy in Washington to protest the occupation of their country. Waving the blue flag with a crescent moon mirroring Turkey's red flag, they call for the recognition of human rights and freedom.

Personal narrative — Rebiya Kadeer

After I left East Turkestan for the United States in 2005, the Chinese Government confiscated my remaining children's passports. It turned them effectively into hostages of the Chinese, and a pawn to exert pressure on me. I may never see my children again, but I believe I had no other choice. My son Ablikim is being shadowed and harassed on an ongoing basis. The Chinese police have even established a special unit called 'Office 307'. Its only purpose is to monitor my family members.

When I was a child, growing up in the north of East Turkestan, my family was not very rich and it was a very common family. My childhood was very peaceful and very happy, and courtesy and respect were most important in our household. The neighborhood was quiet and the people looked upon each other and their children in a very loving way. There was a feeling of great interconnectedness between the people and nature. Our city Altay was close to the mountains, surrounded by hills and rivers, trees and forest. It was heaven to me.

The things that impressed me very much then are the things that I miss very much now. In our neighborhood there were a lot of animals. The birds, from sparrows to nightingales, used to sing in the morning, just like a musical concert. There were also a lot of geese, ducks and chickens. Almost every garden and orchard had an abundance of flowers and the whole neighborhood was full of color. The grown-ups always smiled at each other. These things made the whole community pleasant, supportive and united. But later, I would be deprived of all three: the animals, the flowers and the smiles of our neighborhood.

Everyone enjoyed living in this peaceful environment. But an incredible change took place when the Chinese Communist regime came. Since the 1950s they forced our people into submission. They had a policy of banishing people to different places. Chinese soldiers came to our houses and rounded people up to gather their things and get onto big trucks. They deported people from our neighborhood to different areas of East Turkestan. We were spread out without knowing where we had ended up and without knowing each other's whereabouts.

The Banishment of Uyghurs – and the Settlement of Chinese

Who would doubt that 'population transfer' is taking place in East Turkestan? Over the last fifty years, the minority Han Chinese population there has shot up from 8 to 41 per cent, pushing the Uyghurs from the cities into the rural areas. And into poverty and ignorance.

Before 1949 there were only 300,000 Chinese settlers in East Turkestan. According to the official Chinese census of 2005, their number has risen to more than 7 million, while observers claim the figure is even higher. Annually, an estimated 250,000 Chinese settlers are moving into East Turkestan, and some sources claim that the Chinese authorities plan to settle 40 to 50 million Chinese in the region. Both 'banishment' and 'population transfer' sound deceptively friendly. The hard reality is painful: forced out of one's home, one's native country, and having one's social and cultural life disrupted and marginalized by newcomers.

Native Uyghurs are pushed out of the way by Han Chinese settlers. The steady flow of these 'immigrants' reduces the Uyghurs to outcasts in their own country, while their cultural identity and heritage are trivialized, their dignity denied and discounted. The fact that this is happening in broad daylight and on such a wide scale – it extends to Tibet and Inner Mongolia – without anyone sounding the alarm, is astounding.

But before the humans, they had already attacked the animals. The Chinese had a 'kill dogs policy' that also applied to cats. They took all domestic animals and killed them. Not long after this, they demanded that each household kill 10 sparrows a day. We had to hand over their legs as evidence. If we failed to kill ten, we had to pay a fine to the officials. Because of those policies, all the cats and dogs disappeared, the birds disappeared, and even the frogs in the creeks disappeared. The cows, horses, sheep and goats were all taken by the Chinese Government. 'You're not allowed to own any of these,' they said. 'They're evidence of your capitalistic views!' But after taking them from us, they simply passed them on to Chinese migrants. They trampled the flowers and plants underfoot and cut down the trees in our yards.

Occupied and banished
Wherever the Chinese central government officials spotted a house that they liked, they occupied it. People that used to be part of

Chiang Kaishek's Kuomintang that had surrendered, and retired soldiers of the communist Red Army could then move in. Their main purpose for doing so was to control us. Our whole neighborhood lost the ease that had existed before and people became more and more bewildered about what was going on. One day a classmate of mine was gone, the next day another. Due to the 'banishment policy', families disintegrated and became disconnected from each other. The faces of people became grim. Some said: 'We'll soon have to put up a fight!'

My parents started to speak in low voices, especially in the presence of strangers and outsiders. So much anxiety in their hearts! 'Don't let these words out of the house!' they would say, worried that my brothers and sisters overheard their conversation. All of a sudden, we had to be on tiptoes and live with secrecy. The Uyghur people used to be so hospitable, invite each other into their homes, and gather once a month to have music, folk dances, and merry-making. With the arrival of the Chinese, it all disappeared.

'You don't just belong to yourself, you belong to the people,' my parents used to say. 'Never forget to help others!' I thought of that even at school. When someone needed help, I would offer something. And there were a lot of people that needed help, for entire families were starving. 'Don't use the word Khitay, or in Russian Khitayski, in the presence of the Chinese,' my parents warned me. 'It may insult them. Use 'Hanzou' – that's the polite way. And if you see Hanzou on the streets, don't look at them. Cast your eyes down and go past them without speaking. If someone asks whether you are happy with the Chinese people that live near us, or what you think about the policies of the Chinese Government, keep silent. Never say a word!'

Each day there were trucks, and each day yet another family disappeared. My father and mother prayed for them to come back, not knowing that at some stage we too would have to leave. Our situation became very harsh, and my parents no longer allowed me and my brothers and sisters to go to school. I was too young to understand the Chinese 'banishment policy'. Their reason was simply to obtain fertile land for the Han Chinese immigrants. Their main target was city residents, because they are usually more educated than those in the rural areas. They 'banished' the local people to remote areas like the Taklamakan desert, so that they would not bother the Han Chinese immigrants.

One day, a truck stopped in front of our door. I was 13 then. 'I don't want to leave from here,' my dad said. He escaped to the Altay Mountains. The Chinese soldiers took my mother and all my brothers, sisters and other family members. For fifteen days we were on this truck that brought us to a village in Aksu Old Town County. Alternatingly, my brothers and sisters would sit in front next to the driver. 'Why are we hiding ourselves?' he said at one point. 'We should fight the Chinese!' While being deported, we still thought that they might bring us to some kind of home. But they unloaded us in the middle of the street, handing us a one-page document that stated 'these people are banished to Aksu Old Town County'. That was all. We had no idea what to do. My mother was extremely upset and went up to the driver. 'They asked me to bring you here,' he said. 'I'm just doing my job.'

The truck left. We were still in the middle of the street when it started raining. Fortunately, the villagers were very kind. They gathered around us and others who had also been 'banished' here. Without exception, they were poor and starving, and desperate for a piece of bread. Despite their own hardship, many villagers gave us whatever they had to spare. My
mother gave them something in return, a shirt or a picture. One man who had arrived on his bicycle stepped forward: 'If you need a room, we have some space.' He led us to their yard and showed us two rooms. 'Do you have money for the rent?' he asked. 'Yes,' my mother said. She had hidden a little bit of money. The Government had requisitioned the house from
the previous owner, so we had to pay rent to a government official.

A sacrificial marriage
My older sister, who had graduated from college, was assigned to the Aksu County school as a teacher. They simply informed her and

her husband that the rest of the family had been taken away. As they had some help from other people, they escaped the harshest conditions. My other sisters and I started going to school again. The schoolteacher repeatedly told us about Mao's simple upbringing. 'Maybe he doesn't have the understanding to rule a country properly,' I concluded, 'as he was only a simple farmer?' But what we earned was not enough for the whole family. 'If you allow Rebiya to marry my son Abdirim,' our neighbor said, 'that would help your family and mine, because he is working at the bank.' But I was only 16! I loved going to school, and I wasn't thinking of marrying and starting a family! However, I saw how much my mother was struggling to make ends meet. After resisting the idea for a few months, I decided that I had to make a sacrifice. 'My father is in the Altay Mountains and normally he would support us. But he can't. So if I can help by marrying this boy, I will.'

Both for arranging the paperwork and the marriage celebration, Abidirim gave me a lift on his bicycle. So now I was 'banished' to a new place and married! I had been really angry about the killing of all the dogs. But when my classmates started disappearing and my neighborhood fell apart, I became aware that something was really wrong. While my father was still there, I had asked: 'Why did these other people come to East Turkestan and do whatever they want?' But for the rest we never talked about it. It was just like a big man hitting a smaller man. 'We came to make you happier and more peaceful,' the Chinese said. But of course, it was completely the opposite. They just took our land, with no concern whatsoever for our lives. What could I do? How could I help my family and our people? I became absorbed in reading novels. At that time, the Chinese had translated many Russian novels, and many people knew Russian. There were also books from Soviet Central Asia, the Middle East and even a few western novels. But I especially enjoyed novels that aroused a sense of patriotism. Why didn't the heroes from these novels come to our land and liberate us!? There should be somebody that stands up and says: 'Let us be!'

Reading awakened a great love in me for our people and the desire to liberate them. It burned inside me like a fire. As I was still young, I imagined myself falling in love with the handsome heroes in the novels, and walking together for the liberation of our people. But what was it that I wanted to achieve? East Turkestan has its own rich and distinct history, its own language and its own literature. We are an independent state with every right to our freedom and independence, and our culture has even spread to other Turkic-speaking nations. But due to the oppression by the Chinese, we are lagging behind and we are losing some of our characteristic features. I can't stand that. Our people are very hospitable and kind-hearted and we love the arts. Therefore to me it's intolerable that people from another nation invaded our land to suppress us. Of course I know that the Chinese are humans just like us. But I wouldn't have been in the situation I find myself now, if they had dealt with us on an equal basis.

But let's return to my love for the liberation of my people. I realized that if I wanted to achieve anything, I needed a job and a position of authority to enable me to talk with the Chinese on an equal footing. 'You're not educated,' I heard wherever I went. 'You have six children. You don't speak Chinese. How could we possibly provide employment for someone like you?' Indeed, how would anyone listen to an uneducated woman that is raising her children in her own home? Even when I explained the Chinese oppression to my own people, they didn't understand. For a long time I was looking for someone, a Uyghur leader who would speak out loud the kind of things I was thinking about. But by the time I was 29, I realized I was wasting my time. My patience had run out. I then decided that I had to find that person within myself.

My first marriage failed. I openly criticized the Government in Beijing, and my husband could not handle the pressure. And as I would be outside making money on my own, according to our Islamic culture I would be under a curse. Therefore I felt I needed someone who thinks and feels the same as me, who understands and respects my dreams and wishes, and who has a strong patriotic feeling about our country. I wrote a list of 10 conditions, the criteria for my new husband-to-be. Again, my friends just laughed: 'Who on earth would marry you? You think about nothing but 'country, country, country'.

Look at us: we're all under the control of the Chinese. You're just one person. What could you possibly do about it?' Many Uyghurs feel strongly about their country, but they are afraid to expose themselves, even when they meet me face-to-face. And as I am the voice that articulates their plight, they respect me. The words I speak are other people's wishes; they cannot speak for themselves. On the other hand, none of them has ever betrayed me, nor have I ever betrayed them. That's why I have earned their trust and their respect. When I went hungry and had nothing, people provided me with meals and helped me. And because of the respect between us, people expect something from me, while I feel it is my duty to do something for them. At first I didn't know the cause I would be fighting for. It developed over time.

Businesswoman, congresswoman
When I started as a businesswoman, I was still a young girl. Then, it was no more than making hand-made shoes, sewing and selling clothes, to provide for my children. In the eyes of the Chinese, even that was illegal! Next, I took up selling rabbit and lambskin hats. This was before the Chinese Cultural Revolution that started in 1966. After that, I changed again. I made trips to the eastern Chinese provinces to buy silk scarves, shirts and cassette players. Sometimes they caught me, confiscated the goods and fined me. The law came to my aid however. In the early 1980s, the new motto for China's future launched by Deng Xiaoping was 'to get rich is glorious', and the Chinese Government allowed people to start private businesses.

My first attempt was offering laundry services, next serving noodle dishes, at first only for a hundred people. My business grew to 140 stalls in Urumchi, a leather factory in Kazakhstan, trade with several Central Asian countries, and even with Turkey. But I didn't forget about my country and had become aware of maintaining goodwill and public relations. I was young and attractive, and it was hard to be the only woman among all those businessmen. Many of them stared at me disrespectfully. Regardless, my sense of being a 'mother of the Uyghurs' was formed at that time.

I know my people through and through, and that once upon a time they flourished, while now their condition is deteriorating. Yes, the Chinese Government can brainwash young Uyghurs, and lie to the rest of the world. But our people are aware of their corruption and deception. On the street they refer to the Chinese politicians as kikesh, 'political stutterers'. Nothing can beat the fact that I have experienced and witnessed everything with my own eyes. This is why I have been working so hard over the last 10 years to let Chinese people know that we have to be able to live as equals, and treat the Uyghurs like the Chinese would treat their own people. In my offices and factories I employed Uyghurs who were in financial difficulty, and destitute farmers decorated the offices. There was a lot of drug and alcohol abuse. Uyghur youths were even abusing substances in my own building and the market stalls, so I decided to start a campaign against heroin. We used white-on-red slogans in the style the Chinese Government also uses. And to promote women's rights and economic security, I established the Thousand Mothers Movement. All along, the Chinese Communist Party was suspicious, always keeping a close eye on every non-governmental organization.

Knowingly or unknowingly, people started to listen to me. They witnessed the increase in my income, the respect I earned, and my greater authority in business affairs. Privately, I had plans for intervening in the Government, even though no one thought I could possibly do so as a woman, or as a businesswoman. But doing business in a very strategic way got me there. I became the director of the Xinjiang Chamber of Commerce and in 1992 I was chosen to become a member of the Chinese People's Political Consultative Conference. Now the second of my goals, a position of authority, was achieved. That's when I started talking to the Government about Uyghur people. I came this close to the Government, at which time I respected its policies. I encouraged the Uyghur people: 'The harassment that you suffered in the past was because of the top leaders at that time. Let's try to leave those things in the past, and try to live in harmony with the Chinese people in the future. Then things will get better.'

The cultural genocide was still going on, but I was looking for ways to resolve things in a different way. I thought that if I could win the hearts and minds of the Chinese, it would prevent them from forcing their cultural ideas upon our people. So at every party meeting, I stressed the same. 'Stability and harmony can only be accomplished by equality,' I said. 'The Han Chinese immigrants don't need more stability and harmony. It's the poor Uyghur people that are living under harassment that need it.' Thus I spoke for five years in East Turkestan before reaching Beijing. There, I thought, they can help solve the problem. I got the opportunity to speak my mind in the Chinese People's Political Consultative Conference. But not long after I was fired for doing so. I got a lot of money and the Chinese allowed me to continue doing my business, although they wished they could control it. But I was being deceived. After 10 years, I realized that my two terms of serving the Chinese Government had been wasted. In that year, 1997, the Ghulja Massacre happened. The problem wasn't that the Chinese Government didn't know us. It was exactly because they knew us so well that they wanted to wipe us out.

'Is he Uyghur or Chinese?'

The Ghulja or Xinjiang Massacre, 5 February 1997

When Rebiya Kadeer heard rumors of a massacre in the city of Ghulja, she could not believe her own ears. Could a peaceful demonstration of hundreds of young Uyghurs holding banners and shouting slogans for equal treatment indeed be cracked down in such an extreme manner? She decided – as a Uyghur and as a member of the Chinese People's Political Consultative Conference – that she had to go and see for herself.

'I arrived in Ghulja City in the morning of 7 or 8 February. Although most Uyghurs were too scared to talk, I managed to speak to dozens of families, almost a hundred people. An Uzbek elderly lady said that she had seen numerous Chinese military trucks piled high with dead or beaten Uyghurs going into the local Yengi Hayat – 'New Life' – Prison but had not seen people leaving. She said she was certain that nearly 1,000 Uyghurs had been taken into the prison, but that the prison could only accommodate 500 prisoners. Furthermore, she said she saw many military trucks leaving the prison that were filled with dirt. Many others I spoke with had also witnessed this. Many suspected that dead bodies were buried in the dirt and were being taken out to be disposed of.'

'The Ghulja Prefectural Police told me twice to leave and detained me. But I did not leave Ghulja. I simply felt it was my responsibility to bear witness to the events there and to gather information. I was eventually detained a third time. When I arrived at the police station they said: 'We've told you repeatedly to leave but you are still here. OK then, if you are so interested to know what happened here, look at this.' They then showed me footage they had filmed of the military crackdown in Ghulja in the preceding days. I believe their intention was to terrify me and to intimidate me into silence. I watched the footage in the police station with several other people, including the prefectural police chief.

'Chinese soldiers could be heard shouting: 'Kill them! Kill them!' One officer shouted to a soldier: 'Is he Uyghur or Chinese? Don't touch the Chinese but kill the Uyghur.' Later, eyewitnesses described how people were packed onto trucks so tightly that they had to lie on top of each other. Police officers reportedly sat on top of detainees beating them with sticks. Some of those lying on the bottom died of suffocation.'

'I have never seen such viciousness in my life and it is difficult for me to adequately describe the horror... Dozens of military dogs were attacking – lunging and biting at peaceful demonstrators, including women and children. Chinese PLA soldiers were bludgeoning the demonstrators – thrashing at their legs until they buckled and fell to the ground. Those on the ground – some alive, others dead, were then dragged across the ground and dumped all together into dozens of army trucks.'

The Ghulja Massacre has been a well-kept secret for almost a decade, but as the true story has emerged, it appears that these events were even worse than those on Tiananmen Square in 1989. According to Amnesty International, hundreds if not thousands of people were killed or seriously injured; others were beaten, tortured or disappeared without a trace. The Chinese authorities have not accounted for the lives lost and those missing.

Addressing the Government
The authority the Chinese Government had given to me was by intent only temporary. After they had finished off all these peaceful demonstrators, I believed they would finish us off too. Following the massacre, I wrote a report about all their hard-handed and unheard-of policies toward the Uyghur people. The Chinese all know these policies, but you'll find nobody that admits to it. Someone who dares to speak about it will simply lose their head. However, I was invited to come to Beijing and to speak with President Jiang Zemin. After meeting with the President, I put my concerns before the assembled representatives at the Chinese People's Political Consultative Conference. 'The Chinese Government has no interest in peace,' I said. 'You say there are only 9 million Uyghurs. There are almost 20 million of them. Why do you want to wipe those people out? Our country has a lot of natural resources. Why, if you want those, do you not respect the people that live there? What did they ever ask from you? They only want peace. And they have a right to their own ethnic identity, so why don't you allow them to have it? Just give them the right that God gave them. Let them speak freely and practice any religion they want. I am Rebiya Kadeer. I'm not your enemy, I'm your friend. I wrote this report because I want peace.'

I meant every word of it. But to them it was like a declaration of war. 'Please read this report carefully and follow up with the relevant actions immediately. There is no way you will succeed in wiping out our ethnic identity by killing us. I will await your decision, whatever my destiny will be.' At that moment, their response was very friendly. 'You're a heroic woman!' they said. 'You're an adventurous woman. You're a very good woman. You're so honest. We love you!' One however said something more worrying: 'We will await your changing hour, because your people love you too much.' I asked them: 'What kind of change are you waiting for? I'm doing a great job for you!' They made a promise: 'We will do as you say, read the report very carefully and solve the things you have addressed in it.' The meeting finished, after which I flew straight back to Urumchi. As I got off the plane, the Chinese equivalent of the FBI was waiting for me. They took me straight to the local party building, stripped me of all my titles – Member of the Chinese People's Political Consultative Conference, director of the Chamber of Commerce – and put me under house arrest.

I still had another copy of the report. It described in detail the situation in the villages, the fate of the peasants, the people that live in the Lop Nur region that is used for nuclear testing, including pictures. It should have been published outside of East Turkestan and outside of China, but I wasn't successful. In 1999, after two years of house arrest, a US congressional delegation investigating human rights issues came to Urumchi. I decided to meet them after government approval. But I was prevented from doing so, when PRC security forces detained me. They accused me of revealing state secrets to the outside world by sending magazines and newspaper clippings to my husband in the United States. The security officer questioned me.
'None of this concerns state secrets,' I responded. 'These newspapers are freely available. It only describes the suffering of the Uyghur people.'
'Name all the people that you spoke with about these sensitive topics.'
'I'm doing this by myself. There is nobody else.'
'Who are your closest friends?'
'Jiang Zemin, Hu Jintao, Li Peng...' I gave them a long list of Chinese officials that live in the Zhong Nan Hai district of Beijing that is adjacent to the Forbidden City, most of whom I had met as a party official.

'Who are your real friends?'

During a mock trial that was set up as an extravagant event with doctors, state attorneys, defense lawyers and some 30 police officers, a Uyghur judge insisted that I presented my defense. There was no audience and no legal representation. 'We will crush you like a snake,' the chief of police said to me. 'And I will emerge from prison like an eagle,' I replied. Like other Uyghurs, he had taken off his pride and dignity like an old coat. I was however under the impression that they would execute me, so I had to concentrate really hard. 'I have left behind all my wealth,' I said.' The violations of human rights that the people have suffered, I too have suffered. I have wanted to support my people, but in the end I've not been able to help myself.' In my view, the Chinese Government should wish that there were more citizens like me. I had helped maintain the stability of this province; I had supported the poor and orphans; and my international business had brought desperately needed goods, even benefiting the Chinese themselves. Instead of the death penalty, the court sentenced me to eight years. They led me away handcuffed and shackled.

I have never been tortured. But they did something horrifying. They brought in young Uyghur people and tortured them in front of me. It was extremely hard. Perhaps if I had been tortured at the same time, I would have been able to handle it. I also spent two years in solitary confinement, and what's worse, in total darkness. Only two years later there was light again. Once a month, or sometimes once in 45 days, all the inmates were brought into a public bathing area, and everyone had to rush washing themselves within half an hour. That included washing your clothes. Even when I was ill or my body was swollen, they never offered me help or medication. They give you water, but they don't care about your sanity.

My new room, where there was light, was called a 'labor cell', from where they take you outside to do labor. I spent long days sewing clothes. Next to me were other prisoners that fainted. After their recovery they were forced to continue working as if nothing had happened. This was in Baijiahu Prison, about 30 kilometers from

Urumchi. I was not allowed to speak, to look at anyone, or even to smile. Other prisoners were not even allowed to communicate with me in any way. If they did, their prison term would be increased or they would get tortured. Unless they require you to write something and give you pen and paper, you are prohibited from reading, writing, listening to the radio or watching television. They make life for political prisoners as hard as possible. It's all psychological torture.

'We're sure we'll kill you!' they used to say. I really thought they would. But at a certain moment I felt that the attitude of the guards was changing, and the war of words started decreasing. When I received a white comforter to keep me warm at night, I was sure something was happening. Next, I got a cleaner room. And then my children were allowed to visit me. They noticed I had become very quiet and morose. The changes were due to the fact that Amnesty International, Human Rights Watch and the Dui Hua Foundation had started intervening in my case. 'You seem to have a lot of owners,' the guards said. By that they meant people who were concerned about me. 'What is your relationship with the United States?' 'None,' I could honestly say. 'I just hope that the world will learn of the fate of the Uyghur people.'

Uniting Uyghur voices
My only wish was to escape, and get help from the United States for the Uyghur people. Human rights organizations kept track of my situation, I was awarded Norway's Rafto Memorial Prize in 2004, and finally, three years early, I was released in 2005. I immediately flew to the United States to be reunited with my husband and five of my children. Later, I became president of the Uyghur American Association and founded the International Uyghur Human Rights and Democracy Foundation. It's still very small and we don't have a lot of financial means. But the voices of the Uyghur people outside of East Turkestan are uniting and the concern of the international community is increasing. Ultimately I believe that one nationality cannot wipe out another from the face of the earth.

For many Uyghurs, escaping is made even harder by the fact that the Chinese confiscate the passports of Uyghurs. Some however who were tortured in Chinese prisons managed to do so. They settled in western countries, each with enough stories to fill an entire book. Even while they had a hard life, it is difficult for Uyghurs to leave their home and country behind. But had they stayed, they would have died. Fifteen years ago there were hardly any Uyghurs living in the West, but now there are more than 10,000 all over Europe, America and Canada, and another 20,000 in Turkey. In Kazakhstan, Uzbekistan and Kyrgyzstan together however, there are more than a million. After their independence from the Soviet Union, a lot of trade relations developed with China, and many Uyghurs came to Kazakhstan. West Turkestan became the independent nations of Kazakhstan, Uzbekistan, and Kyrgyzstan. But East Turkestan, where the Uyghurs live, is still not free.

People around the world should know that the Uyghurs are a unique ethnic nationality and that they are prevented from letting their voices be heard. The world knows about most other conflict areas, but the tragedy of the Uyghur people is that they are being buried under Chinese propaganda of 'security' and 'peace'. 'The suffering of the Uyghur people is even worse than that of the Tibetans,' the Dalai Lama once said. This is due to our geographic location, the fact that we are a predominantly Islamic nation, and because of China's strict control and persecution.

There is no instant solution. We are struggling for UN intervention to stop the Chinese from violating our rights. The first priority therefore is to get the UN and the western world to pay attention to our cause. We're working hard to collect documentation and writing reports that reveal the real situation – and not the fake stories that the Chinese are telling. The ultimate
goal is to solve the problem with the Chinese in a peaceful, non-violent way. We will try everything in our power to sit around the table with the Chinese regime to solve the problem. If the Uyghur people are not allowed the freedom they long for, the Chinese people can also not be at peace. Even the Chinese people that live in East Turkestan long for peace.

'The mouse that crosses the road will get hit by everybody until it's dead,' Chinese newspapers said recently, reporting about a party meeting. 'We will do the same with Mrs. Rebiya Kadeer.' You'll understand that contact with Chinese officials is impossible. Since 2007 they are brainwashing the Uyghurs about my life and their feelings for a free and peaceful East Turkestan. They distributed brochures to every household, forcing people to study them. People who don't participate in this kind of 'study' are considered as suspect in their ideology, and lose their jobs. Whether Uyghur or Chinese, everyone had to write a statement about me. Whoever didn't do so or didn't curse me, will be arrested. The party meeting reported in the newspaper vilified me, claiming that I didn't raise my children well. They are very patriotic. That may not be good in the eyes of the Chinese regime, but it is very good for our people. Ever since I was 9, I have been patient in dealing with the Chinese. It will last until I sit down with them to talk about the future of East Turkestan.

Demolition of a culture
Until then, they are continuing to demolish our culture. First of all, they are letting our people become poorer and poorer. Secondly, they are systematically lowering the level of education. Thirdly, they arrest educated people and those who have money under all kinds of pretexts and lock them up in prison. Fourthly, they are instilling a slave mentality in the remaining people. While I was still a member of the Chinese Government, an earthquake happened near Kashgar in Payziwat County in 1997. I organized a rescue mission of seven or eight trucks to bring food and medical supplies and help them to distribute these to the needy people one by one. When I arrived, there were only Uyghurs except for one person, the local Chinese leader. 'Sit over there!' he shouted at them. Even though there was plenty of dry space available, he ordered them to sit in a place where there was nothing but mud and water. I knew why. He was aware of my reputation as someone with a strong sense of our national identity. 'Stand up!' I shouted to the Uyghurs. It frightened them, but they all stood up. 'Stand or sit, but go over to the dry area.' I turned my face and cried. I was so angry at the Chinese leader that I said: 'You! Sit over there in the mud!' I let him sit there all day.

Telephone communications followed, and a lot of policemen and leaders arrived from Kashgar City. 'Why did you let this man sit in the mud?' I paid no attention to them. But this illustrates how Chinese ideology is turning the Uyghurs into slaves. Even back in 1954, when the Chinese found that the Uyghurs had bathrooms in their homes, they said: 'You're on your way to become capitalists, so we have to destroy your bathroom.' The Communists considered hygiene to be 'unproletarian'. Today, when Uyghurs from rural areas come into a bathroom, they don't even know how to take a shower. When you destroy a nation's educational system, their intellectual and business people, the next thing is to deprive them of their religious beliefs and ceremonies and their native language. 'Ignorance guarantees obedience' – that is the motto of the Chinese Government. They are systematically removing words that are 'not favorable to the socialist construction' or 'national unity', and replacing them with Chinese words. Our ancient language has contributed so much to Central Asian civilization. Now it is being threatened with extinction. The consequence of losing all those things is that it undermines your moral consciousness. Nothing is left to remind you of that.

On top of that, the Chinese are restraining the natural growth of the Uyghur population by coercive birth control: forced abortions and forced sterilizations. It contradicts their own preferential population policies for minority groups, but they do it anyway. In a town called Chapchal with a population of 180,000, only 100 women were allowed to give birth. And 40 Uyghurs working in the Chinese administration were fired, because it was found that their wives were pregnant. The worst part of it is the fact that they take many 16-to-25-year-old Uyghur girls to the inner Chinese cities. 'We will provide employment for you,' they say. In 2006 alone, 45,000 young Uyghur women were transferred from East Turkestan to inland China, where many of these future mothers were sterilized or ended up in prostitution. If they resisted, they were transferred to other Chinese cities, and severely punished.

The Uyghurs are not an aggressive nation. Yes, there are some militant Uyghurs that feel we are being too friendly toward the

Chinese and that they should be resisted with guns and explosives. But there are only very few. We would encourage them to stop that, because we don't want them or any of the Chinese to be killed. We continue to hope that we can solve this problem with the help of the international community and of democratic countries. The greatest help comes from the US Congress. Whichever president represents the United States, I hope it will be somebody who better understands the Chinese leaders, and who can deal with people who don't usually say what they really think.

For the freedom of East Turkestan, Islam doesn't have much importance. But Islam and our national customs are good for the moral grounding of our culture, and as the Chinese regime doesn't have such beliefs, it is changing the Uyghur people psychologically. China is a godless country. But when a person's manners are based in morality, it will make them loyal
to their own culture, their own people and their own country. We do have highly educated people and scientists, but even when they work very hard, they can just afford to put food on their plates and take care of their families. They too, are just very poor people, and even before your country, your family matters most. Those scientists could probably help to alleviate the suffering of the Uyghurs in the same way as I did through my businesses. But if there is nobody that stands out from the crowd, nothing can be accomplished.

Obstacles to overcome
You can see people's dreams and wishes just by looking into their eyes. And likewise they can see them in yours, hoping that you will represent their dreams and wishes accurately. That creates a natural leadership role, and it explains why I have people's support. As I'm getting older, I wish to train young people to take up the Uyghur cause, because the exploitation and the pressure exerted on the Uyghurs is intolerable. By working diligently, I hope to find the kind of people that may lead the next step in the struggle of the Uyghurs. But they only have real support when they naturally arise from the Uyghur people. One of my greatest examples was Ehmetjan Qasimi, a Uyghur leader during a short-lived period of independence in the 1940s.

Among Crafty Foxes

According to contemporaries, Ehmetjan Qasimi (1914-1949), the last President of East Turkestan, was a charismatic leader and an excellent political speaker fluent in Uyghur, Russian and Chinese. In August 1948, he was elected as the central committee member of the East Turkestan Democratic Union. Qasimi was convinced that independence was 'a desire not only of Uyghurs, but all the inhabitants and nationalities that live in Eastern Turkestan'.

The new republic, however, only lasted five years (1944-1949). Ehmetjan had to perform a delicate balancing act between the Soviet Union, the Kuomintang, and the emerging Chinese Communist Party. East Turkestan was treated as a bargaining chip and lost the 'Struggle for the Motherland' to 'crafty foxes'. Perhaps the most telling facts of Qasimi's life are the places of his birth and death. He was born in Ghulja, the city where the Ghulja Massacre occurred (see box above). He studied at Moscow's East Socialist Laborers' University in 1936, which is also the place where he met his fate.

In the 20th century, East Turkestan's Uyghur, Kyrgyz, Uzbek, Mongol and Kazakh peoples fought for independence, while China itself went through the transition from the Qing Dynasty to the Kuomintang and then to the Communist rule of Mao Zedong. In August 1949, East Turkestan representatives including Qasimi boarded a plane in Almaty, the capital of neighboring Kazakhstan. The plane was on its way to Beijing. The representatives had been invited by Mao Zedong to attend the All-China Conference that proclaimed the establishment of the People's Republic of China.

The plane never arrived. Instead, it landed in Moscow. Ten days later, the Soviet Union informed the Chinese Government that the plane had crashed near Lake Baikal, killing all on board. After the collapse of the Soviet Union in 1991 however, former KGB leaders revealed that Qasimi was among five Uyghur leaders that had been kidnapped, imprisoned and killed in Moscow on Stalin's orders, in accordance with a deal between Stalin and Mao Zedong. The truth isn't known, as both Mao and Stalin had the motive and means to dispose of Qasimi. Writer James Millward concludes that 'the answer may wait in an archive somewhere'.

In East Turkestan, people of Uyghur nationality are the largest group. The Chinese are much fewer in number, but they disregard our rights and those of other nationalities. The Chinese regime may have changed its ideology, but there is one constant: they have always felt hatred toward people of other nationalities. When you look at them however, they always have a smile. It is a fake smile, for in their hearts they never smile. But I don't think it is the same for Chinese people outside China. The Chinese Government is still using the Communist ideology to control its people, but in reality they have already been on the road to capitalism for a long time. It still is a low-level, state-regulated, and immoral kind of capitalism that doesn't measure up to western standards. But they simply want something different.

During a discussion with Sidik and some of my friends, the writer Abdurahim Ötkür once said: 'In East Turkestan it is impossible to oppose the Chinese Government. As soon as we raise our voices, we will all be exterminated. That won't solve anything. We also don't have any chance of organizing a mass movement. They will simply shoot us. Whoever wants to take up leadership must go abroad and work from there. Just between 1949 and 1972 I have witnessed about sixty major rebellions, in which approximately 360,000 people have lost their lives and almost half a million were jailed in labor camps.' I suffered in Chinese prisons as well. But prison life has strengthened me and I will never tire of working for my people. In moments when I feel lost, I remind myself of a fable my father used to tell me about an ant. Its message? There is no obstacle that cannot be overcome, no aim that is too high.

Soe Myint – Burma
Highlighting the struggle of the people

'I am going away. If we don't die, we will meet again,' said a note Soe
Myint left his parents when he left for the Burmese jungle. Due to
circumstances beyond his control he could not complete his studies
to become a military attaché. In 1988, oppression by Burma's military
junta led to bloodbaths, during which thousands died. Protests,
however, did not stop. For Soe Myint, this included the desperate act
of hijacking a plane to highlight the struggle of the Burmese people,
later founding Mizzima, a multimedia news agency. 'I had changed
from a student to an explosives trainer, and from a hijacker to a non-
violent activist and then a journalist!' Opposition leader Aung San
Suu Kyi was freed, but Burma's problems are far from over. 'The
struggle for freedom and democracy is never a lost struggle,' Soe
believes. 'We will win.'

Soe Myint in 2009

'The struggle for freedom and democracy is never a lost struggle. We will win.' Dreaming of a career in Burma's Foreign Service, Soe Myint (born in 1967) did not anticipate the changes ahead of him. Leaving his parents a note saying 'I'm leaving. If we don't die, we will meet again', he embarked on a remarkable journey to highlight the plight of the Burmese people.

Context

Two moments in the recent history of Burma are etched in the memories of its people. These are the calls for freedom and democracy of 1988, better known as '8-8-88', and the more televised and widely known Saffron Revolution of 2007. Still, the atmosphere of the country instills fear, smothers free expression and drains the spirit of its own citizens. Huge 'People's Desire' billboards admonish them to 'Crush all internal and external destructive elements as the common enemy'.

Through the prism of its very turbulent history, the desire to prevent the disintegration of the Burmese Union is to some degree understandable. Consider, as writer Thant Myint U says, the fact that there were 'three Anglo-Burmese wars, a century of colonial rule, an immensely destructive Japanese invasion and occupation, and five decades of civil war, foreign intervention, and Communist insurgency'. Burma's kingdoms and ethnic groups have never been truly unified. To this day, it is possible to explore the country's history by visiting its many former capital cities. In 2006, the Government announced the move to yet another location, Pyinmana.

Part of the tensions therefore do not relate to democracy versus dictatorship or rich versus poor, but to older rivalries. The term 'hill tribes' may seem innocent, but it is indicative of the fact that the ethnic Burmans consider themselves superior, having the duty to control and 'civilize' the Karen, Shan, and other nationalities that comprise almost a third of Burma's estimated 54 million inhabitants. Yet, it remains beyond comprehension how that could justify the never-ending human rights violations that the military leadership metes out to its own people.

The Burmese junta usually rejects criticism as political ploys to discredit the regime, and puts the blame especially on western nations. But perhaps their criticism only stands out due to the silence and absence of concerns raised by Burma's immediate neighbors. Some members of the Association of South East Asian Nations (ASEAN), in which Burma has participated since 1997, have expressed dissatisfaction with the slow pace of reforms. But as long as China, Burma's 'economic and military backbone', does not move, little else moves, and as long as economic interests prevail, many will close an eye to human rights violations.

Focused as they are on trade and investment opportunities, the policies of foreign countries often appear to the Burmese as self-serving. Both the United States and the European Union however have sanctioned Burma since 1997, exactly because of its severe human rights violations. Several major companies such as Coca-Cola and Texaco Inc. have withdrawn from the country. Another, Levi Strauss & Co., stated: 'It is not possible to do business in Burma without directly supporting the military regime and its pervasive violations of human rights.' While Amnesty International and Human Rights Watch paint a dark picture, other companies such as Total of France, and UNOCAL (Chevron) of the United States, continue doing business with the military junta. 'Totalitarian Oil' is what critics call them. In a cartoon in the book *Burma Behind the Mask*, a Total oil worker stands beside a pipeline, and a general stands beside a tortured prisoner, about to shake hands. 'Sorry, my hands are dirty.' 'Never mind, my hands are dirty too.'

'Sorry, my hands are dirty.' 'Never mind, my hands are dirty too.' (from Burma Behind the Mask, the Netherlands 1996)

The former State Law and Order Restoration Council (SLORC), now called the State Peace and Development Council (SPDC), governs with an iron fist. Government newspapers The Working People's Daily and The New Light of Myanmar are full of the latest speeches and decrees, but offer little solace for the pains of Burma's citizens. After the 2007 Saffron Revolution some businesses are returning, but the general conditions of the people have hardly changed. Moreover, without paying 'tea money' or 'lunch money' – euphemisms for bribes – it is hard to get anything done in business or Government networks, which in Burma overlap military networks. Transparency International ranks Burma as the second-most corrupt nation in the world.

Whenever the Government announces new development programs, many Burmese are alarmed, as this often means that they will soon have to 'contribute' their labor. For some, the drudgery of forced labor has become routine, to the point of believing that it is the way in which other countries reach their goals as well. They toil on road construction, military installations and tourist infrastructure. Burma however is signatory to the Convention Against Forced Labor, and is obliged to abide by its provisions. In 2006, the International Labor

Organization announced that it seeks 'to prosecute members of the ruling Myanmar junta for crimes against humanity' against an estimated 800,000 of its citizens at the International Court of Justice.

General Ne Win was Burma's great helmsman between 1962 and 1988. Not known for social reform, even his resignation was ominous. He looked straight into the camera: 'I want the entire nation, the people, to know that if in future there are mob disturbances, if the army shoots, it hits – there is no firing into the air to scare.' Having a great appetite for sex and being officially married to five wives, he looked the other way when his soldiers committed sexual offences, especially in ethnic areas. The generals consider this part of implementing the Mahar (Great) Myanmar policy. Rape as policy. So many women have become AIDS-infected by soldiers representing the military junta or Na Wa Ta, that AIDS is nicknamed the Na Wa Ta disease. Shunned by friends, infected young men often move into the monasteries. But as they shave their heads and share infected razor blades, the disease even spreads among monks.

As if daily oppression wasn't enough, immense devastation and suffering was caused in 2008, when cyclone Nargis touched land in the Irrawaddy delta. More than 200,000 Burmese were killed, one million were left homeless, and damages totaled $10 billion. The Government however complicated relief efforts by not allowing planes with medicine, food and other supplies, 'Unprecedented,' said the UN. Even a placard of a destitute family that read 'Help Us' was ordered to be removed. The cyclone is gone, but the junta is not. After her release, Aung San Suu Kyi won most seats in a parliamentary election in 2012. But the lower house remains under control of the government party and the military. Hundreds of prisoners were freed, but many remain behind bars, and hundreds still face charges.

Ethnic riots erupted against the Muslim Rohingya. In 2014, the secret Rakhine State Action Plan revealed that the Burmese Government aims for forced relocation. Even monks who played a role in Burma's struggle for democracy support blocking humanitarian assistance to the Rohingya, while ultra-nationalists stir up a climate of fear. 'After two years of steady if uneven progress, Burma's human rights situation was a car crash in 2014,' said Brad Adams, Asia director at Human Rights Watch. 'Burmese authorities and donors are sleepwalking arm-in-arm into an electoral disaster in 2015.'

Many Burmese are still finding refuge in neighboring India. In the Delhi suburb of Vikas Puri lives Soe Myint, the editor-in-chief of Mizzima News agency (mizzima is a Pali word for 'middle' or 'moderate'). International and part underground, it is highly inventive in finding outlets for news that the Burmese Government wants to keep hidden. Mizzima's work seems to exemplify Reporters Without Borders. At present, it employs more than 50 staff in Burma, India, Thailand, Bangladesh and China to provide the latest news. Additionally, there are many citizen journalists and video journalists who work underground. Soe, meanwhile, digs through piles of documents and photos to find his Operations Book, about which more later. Having witnessed and experienced Burma at its worst in 1988, Soe is well aware of the dangers. As a retired newspaper editor once said to him: 'If you haven't been in jail, you haven't been a reporter in Burma.'

Personal narrative – Soe Myint

We lived with the six of us. My father and mother, two younger brothers, one elder sister and me. My youngest brother now works in our Thai office in Chiang Mai, and is our news agency's managing editor. Another brother is in Burma, and my elder sister teaches in one of Rangoon's foreign language schools. My father and mother are now retired. I don't know exactly where they all are. The problem is that I do not communicate with them for safety reasons. If anyone would get in touch with them, the Government might cause them a lot of trouble. They did so in the past, so it's likely they would do it again.

There was only one year of difference between my brothers and sister, so when one went to school or university, we all went. We lived in a suburb of Rangoon called South Okkalapa. My mother came from Zayyawaddy, and my father from Okkan Township in Pegu

Division, both from paddy and crop-growing families. They migrated to Rangoon, got married, and started their life there in great hardship. My mother knew how to read and write, but not much more. 'You study, you study!' That was their main aim when we were young, as they knew the hardships of life without education. As a child, I noticed the poverty of people, especially when they came to my parents' grocery shop, and my mother sometimes lent them money.

I went to school in Yankin Township in Rangoon, where many government officers live and some of the ministers. My mother pushed us to excel. Consequently, we always passed our exams with distinction. After high school, I went on to study International Relations and Administration, which requires high marks for admission. As a child, I enjoyed playing football and swimming, but homework and helping in the household took greater priority. My dream was to become a military attaché in the Burmese Foreign Service. International Relations was a new subject, and the department was run by the wife of General Ne Win, the nation's dictator. My whole life revolved around becoming well educated. In tenth grade, I became a full member of the Burma Socialist Program Party (BSPP), the ruling government party. If you want to be in Government or move up in society, you have to be a full member, or Tin Pyae in Burmese. You might think I completely believed in the rightness of the military regime. But things were not that clear. I was simply interested in becoming a high-profile civil servant. When I tried to join the Defense Services Academy for officer training after passing 10th standard, however, I did not pass the entrance test. I was underweight, in spite of the many coins with which I had filled my pockets.

My parents hadn't come from a political background, and would only talk about what was going on in the township. Things nearby. But once I was studying, it was impossible not to become more aware of our Government and its policies. Opportunities to share views however were very limited. Basically this was only possible in the library or in the teashops. Writings on the walls of the toilets ridiculed the Government or criticized ministers. Some of my friends however were well-read, and even talked about the communist movement in the past, and an underground student movement developing now. Slowly, slowly, we came to know. I read the Government newspapers every day, but was mostly interested in the international news. Every day, late in the evening, I listened to the Burmese language broadcasting of the BBC. During those 50 minutes I was glued to the radio.

Suspicions of suppression
'The unitary system is the best,' we were taught. I also wanted to learn about the federal system, but we weren't allowed to study any other political systems. In fact, a lot of opposition had already been generated just by the fact that student unions were prohibited. 'Burma is a rich country,' we were told, so we were very embarrassed when we found out that it was officially recognized as one of the Least Developed Countries in 1987. What we learnt was only what we were given during the university courses. My parents wouldn't allow me anything else but advancing my studies. That remained my priority, until just a few months before the 1988 uprising. It was only during my second year in Rangoon University that a sense of suspicion began to develop about the military regime, and more and more students were becoming angry and frustrated about the suppression of the people.

The year before, 1987, the Government had announced the demonetization of the major currency of Burma. It immediately affected people's lives. There were students in our campus, who were living in a hostel as they came from different parts of the country. In one stroke, all their money was gone, and the Government provided no compensation whatsoever. It caused great disillusion among them. The Government had taken this decision, because inflation was very high, and huge amounts of money found their way to the black market and to goods smuggled across the border by the various groups of insurgents. They thought they could control all this. At home, all the money related to my parents' shop simply evaporated. Students started holding demonstrations and, being equally affected myself, I joined.

That was my third year at the university. For the first time in my life I realized that the Government didn't care about the people and only took action mindful of the military and the ministers. Alongside news about the poverty of the people and the demonetization, we heard about how rich the military leaders and ministers were. They even imported luxury toilets from abroad. The contrast was just too great. As with the funeral of U Thant in 1974, every student protest was suppressed and universities were shut down. Student movements in Burma have often played a vanguard role and many students have sacrificed themselves for democratic reform. Even Aung San Suu Kyi's father was a student leader once.

My parents didn't want me to get involved in politics. But now that they too had become seriously affected, my mother asked: 'Why did they do this?' She was a devout Buddhist, and got very worried about her children. 'You will go to a Buddhist monastery,' she said to me when I was about 19. In Burma, there is a religious tradition that if you're a boy, you are sent to a monastery as a novice, and when you turn 20, for a short while you live as a monk. This even applies to the men in the military. They all spent time practicing Buddhism when they were young. My parents knew the head monk of a monastery in Rangoon, so they sent me there. This happened every summer – we don't go on vacation, we spend time at the monastery.

After a while, the Government reopened the universities. Now there was even more unrest about the Government and what to do about it. Before 1987 it had been relatively subdued, but after we came back to university in 1988, people talked about it openly. The underground All Burma Federation of Student Unions (ABFSU) became very active. Even our nation's independence fighters had been leaders of this movement. But when General Ne Win came to power in 1962, he abolished the Student Union. It went underground, but its magazine Oway, The Voice of the Peacock, was still being distributed. 'Don't forget 7 July,' it said. That was the date on which General Ne Win had killed the students and dynamited the Student Union building in the Rangoon University campus. Literally. Criticism of the Government intensified.

7 July 1962

During the decade following Burma's independence in 1948, the country suffered from instability due to uprisings in the army and tensions among various ethnic minorities. Democratic rule ended in 1962 when General Ne Win led a military coup d'état. He became head of the Army, head of state, Chairman of the Revolutionary Council, and Prime Minister. Protests were ruthlessly suppressed.

When students of Rangoon University peacefully protested against 'unjust university rules' on 7 July 1962, Ne Win sent in his troops. About 100 unarmed students were shot, and the building of the Rangoon University Student Union was blown up. 'If these disturbances were made to challenge us,' said Ne Win, 'I have to declare that we will fight sword with sword and spear with spear.' He would rule for 26 years and pursue the Burmese Way to Socialism. This combined Soviet-style nationalization and central planning with superstitious beliefs, policies that writer Joseph Ball characterized as 'capricious, unpredictable and illogical.' Some dubbed it 'the Burmese Army Way to Capitalism' or 'the Burma Road to Ruin'. As Ne Win believed in astrology and numerology, he reconfigured the national currency, the kyat, to be printed in units of 45 and 90. The people however experienced looting of the economy by the military, total isolation from other nations and continued suppression of the minority peoples. A Newsweek contributor once described Burma's policies as 'an amalgam of Buddhist and Marxist illogic'. To further consolidate power, Ne Win and many top generals resigned, took civilian posts and, from 1974, instituted elections in a one-party system, ruling through the BSPP until 1988's nation-wide protests.

Escalating tensions

The students of International Relations had become keen observers of politics. Among each other, we spoke openly about all this, but not with our professors who are usually well connected with the BSPP. Some of my classmates became leaders of the student movement of August 1988. One is still in jail today, 20 years later. A few months before, in March, there was a fight between some of the local people and students of the Rangoon Institute of Technology (RIT). The fight was about the music that was being played in the teashop. The students liked Sai Htee Saing, a well-known Shan singer, and the locals something else. The argument turned physical, because the Burmese can get emotional and violent very fast. After a group of students disturbed a young local man's house, things escalated. His parents turned out to be local administrators and party members of the BSPP. Now, the locals were assisted by the authorities, the police intervened and fire engines dispersed the students with water. The students returned to the campus, organized a demonstration, and within hours riot police stood face to face with them. Many students were severely beaten and ended up in hospital. One student was shot dead during the night of 13 March. The news spread quickly.

There was a big puddle of blood, and a pile of bricks was erected where the student had been shot. Students were mourning, while the Government remained silent. 'Somebody has to be accountable for what is going on,' we said to the rector. 'No!' he said. 'Go back inside!' By now, the students were spreading pamphlets demanding a clarification for what had happened. I took some too. On the way back from RIT the next morning, the police had put up checkpoints. I passed through, holding the pamphlets secretly under my arm. They didn't find out. At the main campus of my own Rangoon University, I started distributing the pamphlets. I suppose that was the day I started revolting. Together with other students in my class, I wrote a letter to the supervisor of International Relations. 'There needs to be a public enquiry, and the truth has to be exposed. Unless these demands are met, we resign from the class, especially considering the fact that we, at International Relations, are seen by many other students as representing the side of the Government.' This all happened just before the 1988 uprising.

Some of my friends got in touch with the underground student movement and I interviewed them. The Government did make statements, but they were nothing but lies. Discussion began about what we had to do on a national level. The underground movement included communists and representatives of minority groups. This confused us actually, as we still considered those that lived in the border areas as bandits that rebelled, looted and raped women. Like me, Aung San Suu Kyi is an ethnic Burman. But I didn't see her take a strong stance on the issue of the minority nationalities. Later, when we were in the jungle, these 'bandits' became our friends, allies and fellow freedom fighters. Talking to them made us more aware of our country's situation.

The student protests spread in the campuses in Rangoon. The authorities closed down the universities quickly and sent the students away from their hostels to their homes. But, when universities reopened again, the students came out with more demonstrations and with larger numbers. Whenever we had rallies, I marched in front. On 13 June, we were marching along Pyay Road with maybe 3,000 students. We decided to come out of the Rangoon University main campus in marching to join the other students from Hlaing campus and RIT. Riot police blocked us just before we reached the American Embassy. Armored vehicles pulled up, and soldiers pointed their guns at us. We sat down, and started singing Kaba Ma Kyei, 'Till the End of the World', our national anthem. We were close to Inya Lake, at a place called White Bridge, where we used to sit around in the teashops. Still singing, we were hoping to get out of the blockade by the riot police.

Suddenly the students started running. A riot police car approached from behind, with police officers beating the students. I also ran. On one side was Inya Lake, on the other side houses behind high walls. Together with others I climbed over the walls, passing through the houses to Insein Road, which runs parallel to Pyay Road. Others had gone in the opposite direction, jumped into the lake, and were caught and beaten up or taken away by riot police. The ones I was with and that passed through the houses were helped by the inhabitants. They gave us water and snacks, but obviously all of that happened in a rush. Some of us succeeded in reaching Insein Road, where we started a new demonstration. At one point we tried to take over a bus, which we wanted to use to go to Pyithu Hluttaw, the House of Parliament. But riot police burst through with guns and shields, while we were throwing stones at them. There was no other choice but to let the bus go and try to escape.

I arrived back at the university campus. The streets were covered with stones and bricks, and slippers everywhere. It was eerily quiet. I went to the hostel where my friends stay. Some of them had been arrested, others had been beaten up. Radio announcements from the Burmese Service of the BBC confirmed this. Once again, after I arrived home, my parents sent me to a monastery. Within days, my head was shaved, and I was meditating and initiated into proper monkhood in June and July. I like meditation a lot, but after a month I returned home again. Meanwhile, the underground student movement remained very active.

Shwedagon Pagoda in 2009 (photo by Peter de Ruiter)

A sea of people
Some of my classmates were now leading the ABFSU. Its first public conference was held on the site of the old student union building,

dynamited by the army in 1962. My friends also met with Aung San Suu Kyi, long before she was under house arrest. She had returned to Burma to treat her ailing mother. They had a discussion with her, U Nu, the first Prime Minister of independent Burma, and other leaders. Aung San Suu Kyi then became involved herself. On 26 August she held a huge public meeting near Shwedagon Pagoda. From the stage, I could see a sea of people. It was her first big public gathering against the Government. She presented a new vision for Burma and openly criticized Ne Win and the rule of the military.

The Lady at University Avenue Nr. 54

'Were we to write about our experiences in the form of a novel, it would be criticized as too far-fetched a story, a botched Orwellian tale,' says Aung San Suu Kyi at the end of her book Letters from Burma. Prisoner of conscience, and prisoner in her own house, over the last two decades Nobel Prize laureate Aung San Suu Kyi (born in 1945) has been constantly subjected to arrests that are even illegal under Burma's own law. The job that would have been rightfully hers, that of Prime Minister of a democratic Burma, has been made impossible by various leaders of the military government.

When she was only two years old, her father General Aung San, the man who negotiated Burma's independence from the British in 1947, and father of modern-day Burma, was assassinated. As he was the nation's most charismatic nationalist, it became a national trauma. Married to Dr. Michael Aris, a scholar of Tibetan culture, Aung San Suu Kyi returned to Burma in 1988, after studying in India and Britain. Living separate from her husband, who was suffering from terminal cancer, he died in 1999. Efforts by UN secretary Kofi Annan, Pope John Paul II and other prominent figures left the regime unmoved. The couple was not allowed to meet again.

Influenced by Mahatma Gandhi's non-violence and Buddhism, Aung San Suu Kyi helped found the National League for Democracy (NLD) in September 1988, known by its flag with the Fighting Peacock. Put under house arrest the following year, she was offered freedom if she left the country. She refused. About her struggle against the military government, she said: 'It is not power that corrupts, but fear. Fear of losing power corrupts those who wield it, and fear of the scourge of power corrupts those who are subject to it.' The UN, ASEAN, fellow Nobel Prize laureates, presidents – heaven and earth were moved to sway the Burmese junta to free her. On the evening of 13 November 2010, Aung San Suu Kyi was finally released.

I participated in the protests through the Rangoon University Student Union (RUSU), and student magazine Pin Ma Yay See (Mainstream) appointed me as photographer. As I didn't have a camera, I borrowed a relative's Yashica. Each time after I had shot pictures of protests, hunger strikes or rallies, I took it to a shop downtown to have my films developed. Sometimes I was away from early morning till late at night, slept a few hours in odd places, survived on donated food, and moved on again. Often I had to run in the protests, so I kept losing my slippers. But there were slippers all over the streets of Rangoon. The protests spread from one township to the other, and throughout the country there were people on the streets. I was taking photos from 8-8-88 until 18 September to document all the events in Rangoon as much as possible. At that time, the people were completely joined in one arising, even groups from within the Army and the Navy. And when the Government announced that the demonstrators 'did not represent the silent majority of law-abiding housewives', the All-Burma Housewives Association joined the crowds clanging pots and pans.

At the same time, Rangoon was full of road blocks. There were horrible beheadings of people who were suspected of being government spies. Some were literally hacked to death. The city was full of rumors that Ne Win's spies had poisoned the water supply and had infiltrated the student leadership. Plainclothes thugs were secretly working for the military intelligence services. Everyone was a suspect. At 4 o'clock on 18 September 1988, the military declared martial law and took control. Security forces killed thousands of demonstrators, and General Saw Maung formed the State Law and Order Restoration Council (SLORC). The army beat up and arrested people accused of supporting the protesters. There was still a remnant of trust in me about the military, thinking that they would restore peace and tranquility. But when I rushed home due to a curfew, the streets were full of disturbing sights.

The day everything changed
The next morning, I saw soldiers of Regiment 22 that were clearing the blockades, stones and trees in the roads. At that time, except for some strategic or government areas, the administration and care of each township was in the hands of the people. The army forced whoever they saw to clear the roads for them. An army captain directed affairs, guarded by a soldier with an enormous gun. I went up to them and took photos, thinking: they're doing their job, I'm doing mine. My flash went off accidentally. This alarmed the soldiers, and one of them almost shot me. The captain with three black stars forced me down, but as he was very busy with ordering others around, he couldn't do anything with me. The soldiers continued clearing one township after the other. I was taken along with them in the first truck. The captain sat in front, and I was alone in the back, surrounded by the soldiers. For the rest of the day, I went along with them. That's when I saw all the brutalities. Everything changed.

As the soldiers moved, the protests were still going on here and there. Whenever they saw a gathering, they just shot. So while I was in the army truck, I saw my friends and fellow protesters being shot on the street. I had no choice but to witness it. They shot at people randomly, even people sitting in a teahouse. They were simply in a shooting mood. A few people were waving the flag of the Red Cross. They were also shot. Whatever they considered to be against them, they fired at. It was a pattern: driving, clearing, shooting. It became a real trauma for me for many years. Many of the soldiers didn't even leave the truck, but just pulled the trigger. They were basically brainwashed. 'These protesters are not students,' they said. 'They are communists. Did you see all those roadblocks?' At one point the soldiers had to have lunch, and I was having the same food as them. 'Aung San Suu Kyi is a prostitute,' they said. 'She got married to a foreigner.' What I witnessed shattered my faith in the Government completely. I went blank. It made me realize that the army will never take the side of the protesters or of democracy. I decided that I too would go to the jungle and fight them. That was the day.

Around 10 o'clock, they returned to their base camp, near to the place where they first arrested me. 'Don't ever get involved with protesting again!' the captain scolded me. He took away my camera, and I was very lucky not to be shot. Full of anguish, I arrived at my friend's home. Rangoon was totally under Army control. This also meant that I could not go back to the shop where they developed the photos, maybe 20 films. If the shop still exists today, these photos must be excellent documentary material, for in 1988 there were not many foreign journalists.

I went back to my parents' home and started planning to go to the jungle. I left sometime in October, meeting with many other students on the way. Only three years later did my parents find my note that I put inside my guitar: 'I'm going away. If we don't die, we will meet again.' Then they understood I had gone to the jungle. As for me, I had only ever been outside Rangoon to visit my grandparents in the birthplaces of my father and mother. I took the boat from Rangoon to the border with Thailand. On the boat, at night, you could see all the stars, and I was dreaming of revolution all the time. We didn't need any money, for we were given food and everything we needed. Our spirits were strong. First we arrived in Myeit in Tanintharyi Division, where I was told to contact a friend, and went from house to house to sort out my onward journey to Kawthaung, the southernmost part of Burma. Kawthaung is in Burma and Ranoung is in Thailand, with ferries in between.

There were maybe a hundred of us. From Ranoung, we set out for the southern part of Thailand in the Bilauktaung Mountains near Three Pagoda Pass. We went further by car. The person who helped us was the daughter of U Thant, the former UN Secretary General, and her husband, Dr. Tin Myint U. Several rich Chinese people in Ranoung gave us rice, dhal bat, dried fish, and supported us in every way. At one point I even saw Thai police escorting us on the way to the Thai-Burma border. Finally, we arrived at our destination in the middle of the jungle. Rumors about ships with arms and ammunition awaiting us were obviously untrue. There wasn't even any water there! We arrived in a village at Three Pagoda Pass that was totally destroyed, still smoldering, because there had been fighting between Mon and Karen peoples, as it is one of the main smuggling places of Burma. The village was economically thriving due to large fish ponds, marihuana sales in huge bags, fruits and so on. We, the students, liked the marihuana. They positioned us in between the fighting parties, to prevent further fighting. The day I arrived at the border was my 21st birthday.

Hardship and combat training
Thousands of students came from all over Burma. We trained ourselves with bamboo sticks. We were members of the All Burma Students Democratic Front, the Student Army. Our area was effectively under control of the New Mon State Party, and we enjoyed their protection. The Mon provided us with some M16s for guarding our camp. For a few days I was in tears, as I had never been exposed to such hard work, even to drawing water from the well. Those that provided us with basic military training were Burmese soldiers that had defected during previous uprisings. In our camp, there were about 300 trainees divided over 12 barracks. We did some shooting, but many of us found the training was lacking and that there were no proper arms and ammunition.

After some months, we were selected by another group that was led by U Aung, son of the former Prime Minister U Nu. They had some concrete support from abroad. I joined their arms and explosives training. Proper training! The American and Australian trainers had experience in the Vietnam War, and were hired as professional mercenaries. Our intention was to fight a guerilla war against the Government inside the towns and cities. I worked hard, and even became a teacher of demolition techniques. Small groups went back into the country to make contact with politicians and dissidents. They were arrested however, exposing everything that was happening in the jungle on the borders. We even suspected some within our group of being spies. Some of us got very frustrated and saw no future in the camps. At the same time, the Government started talking about elections, and put Aung San Suu Kyi under house arrest. General Saw Maung, the SLORC Chairman, gave fishing and logging concessions to the Thai military, agreeing with the Burmese military that Burmese students would be 'voluntarily' repatriated from Thailand.

Some of us went outside the camp trying to make money by producing bricks and charcoal, to buy M16s and other guns on the black market. We contracted severe malaria however. One of my friends even went mad, and again our plans were thwarted. In May 1990, the Government held free elections for the first time in almost 30 years. The National League for Democracy (NLD), the party of Aung San Suu Kyi, won 392 of the 489 seats, a vast majority. The military leadership however refused to hand over power. So among us, new ideas began to emerge such as hijacking a ship or a plane or demolishing power plants. Two students went back inside the country in 1989, one using my National ID card, and hijacked a plane from Burma to Thailand with the aim of highlighting the plight of the Burmese people. They wanted to land in Bangkok, but the Thai Government forced them to land in U-Tapao, which is used by the Thai and American air forces. Due to a lenient attitude from the Thai security services, they were sentenced to six years, but released earlier with an amnesty. They had only used firecrackers to simulate weapons. Following the incident, the Burmese Government searched my parents' house in Rangoon, but after a while they realized it was someone else. Yet, it gave us some ideas.

In late 1990, all the media talked about was the Iran-Iraq war and Burma just wasn't a topic. Seven of us moved to Bangkok, where we applied for refugee status with UNHCR. First I was treated for malaria for a month. After that, we started saving money, while going back and forth to the border for further training. We bought two or three AK47s, M16s, and practiced with improvised explosives, while staying in touch with the two hijackers in the Thai detention center. Three of us then thought: we should do a similar operation. We had some weapons, but we felt it would be wrong to use them, because we believed we had to sacrifice for a greater cause, and shouldn't hurt anyone. We stuck to that principle.

On 10 November 1990, our idea was to hijack a plane with the purpose of having a press conference about the situation in our country, assuming that we would be in jail for 20 years or die in the process. Our lives could be finished. But at least it would focus the world's attention on Burma. My English wasn't as good as it is now, but I wrote down everything in English in my Operations Book, and memorized it. We saved money, divided our responsibilities, and bought illegal Burmese passports under false names, mine being Ye Marn, Brave Energy. We could only afford two passports, so our third man would remain in Bangkok to hand out press releases and pamphlets. We chose a Thai Airways flight from Bangkok to Rangoon, which we would divert to Kolkata (more commonly known as Calcutta), India. This was because we liked India, it was a major neighboring country, and at that time India supported the Burmese movement for democracy. Bangladesh or China were not good options.

'We have hijacked this plane'
It was my first flight ever. The plane was enormous, an Airbus 300 with about 220 passengers. We brought along bags of food and energy drinks for the passengers, in case the hijack would take a lot of time and they would get tired. We also carried handwritten letters to the Burmese, Thai and Indian Governments, the international community, the Burmese radio services of the BBC and the Voice of America. I still have copies. We asked for: 1. To release all political prisoners including Aung San Suu Kyi and U Nu; 2. To withdraw martial law; 3. To cancel all military tribunals; 4. To bring an end to the civil war and restore democracy. And so on. We knew our demands would not be met, but it was all done to ensure press coverage. Back in Bangkok, my friend posted all these letters.

The flight from Bangkok to Rangoon was 45 minutes. Most passengers were Burmese, and there were some Japanese tourists and other foreigners. We had planned every step, and every word that each of us would say to the pilot, to the passengers and so on. We had filled a laughing Buddha statue with white soap, the color of most plastic explosives like Composition-4. In a shop in Bangkok we had found a switch that is used in cars for ignition. We connected the switch to the laughing Buddha with wires. That became our fake bomb. Thirty minutes before landing at Rangoon, we stood up, and spoke quite automatically what we had been rehearsing for months. My friend stayed in the passenger area, while I went to the cockpit. 'We are Burmese students,' he said. 'We have hijacked this plane.' He moved the women and children to the front, and the men to the back, so they wouldn't harm him, especially as both of us are only small in size.

The Japanese tourists didn't speak English or Burmese. But there was a translator, who had been in Burma during the war. He explained what was happening in Japanese to his fellow Japanese. As my fellow hijacker was holding the 'bomb', but needed to continue communicating with me, he asked some of the passengers to write messages. The stewardesses delivered them back and forth between him and me. 'What are you doing now?' 'I'm asking the pilot to divert to Kolkata.' On the plane were also reporters from SPAN, the bimonthly American-Indian magazine, to do a story on Burma. They got their story on the plane.

After I got up, I didn't have anything on me, except for flight path maps to show the pilot which route to fly. I walked towards the front of the plane, opened the door, and found the toilet, instead of the cockpit. 'What are you doing?' a stewardess asked. Naturally, I couldn't answer her 'I'm hijacking the plane!' I opened another door and found the cockpit. 'We have hijacked this plane,' I said. 'You go to Kolkata. This is the route. We will not hurt anyone or cause any problems, provided you do as I say. 'I was in the Burmese student movement, and many of my friends were killed.' The pilot was shocked. But he sympathized with the Burmese struggle. 'OK,' he said. 'But your route is too long. We will take a shorter route.' Immediately he diverted the plane. It was more than I had hoped for. On our way to Kolkata, the flight path is through the Bay of Bengal, well known for its air pockets. At one point, the plane suddenly dropped. My friend, who was holding the 'bomb', fell down, due to which the wires between the switch and the 'bomb' got disconnected. He got up quickly, and put it back together again. Apparently, nobody noticed.

'If there is any contact from the Burmese authorities, just don't respond,' I said to the pilot. As expected, the Burmese flight control asked: 'Flight TG 305, why are you not landing in Rangoon?' 'We're having some technical problems,' the pilot said. 'We're going to land in Kolkata, India.' Very clever; we were very lucky. After a while, the pilot shared family photos with me. 'After this is over, come and have dinner with my family.' Meanwhile, Burmese passengers helped us, and the air hostesses continued carrying messages back and forth, giving people the impression that there was a whole group of us. When we were about to land, I was not fully convinced it was really Kolkata, as I had never seen any city from above. Was the pilot lying perhaps?
'Are you sure that is Kolkata?' I asked him.
'Yes,' he said.
'Are you sure that is Kolkata?' my friend said to an air hostess.
'Yes,' she said.
We landed. 'Keep at a distance from the terminal,' I said to the pilot, for I was afraid that commandos would raid the plane. 'We just want to talk with representatives of the Burmese, Thai, and Indian Governments.' We knew the first two wouldn't, but perhaps the Indian Government would. We also wanted to listen to the Burmese Service of the BBC, because our third man had sent many messages to the media. But the pilot refused: 'No, you can't. But the media have already assembled at Kolkata airport, including the Home Secretary of the West Bengal Government.'

Highlighting the struggle
We had many lucky breaks. The West Bengal Government is run by the Communist Party of India (Marxist). They are very sympathetic to the Burmese democratic movement. 'So what is it that you want?' said the Home Secretary representing the Indian Government over the flight radio. While talking to them, my friend started releasing the passengers. For two reasons. They were tired and needed a rest,

for all the discussions took eight hours. We apologized to each one of them. 'O, son, you do what you do,' an old lady said, 'but I will get some sleep now.' The second reason was that, while we were releasing passengers, we wouldn't be attacked. This was serious, as commandos were encircling the plane. I spread more pamphlets, which the passengers passed on to the media. 'We will give up ourselves,' I said. 'And can we please have more food for the passengers? And repair the air conditioning?' We also insisted upon the safety of the Burmese passengers, knowing that they would be screened in Rangoon upon their return.

The police took the laughing Buddha 'bomb', but not the switch. They led us into a room full of reporters. But Indian reporters are very aggressive, and it was an incredibly noisy press conference. They were fighting, and tumbling all over each other without us understanding what they meant. I said whatever I had memorized from my Operations Book, but none of them got anything useful from it. The Home Secretary was sitting in the middle with us flanking him. In the end, the police intervened, taking us to room Nr. 4 of the airport hotel. There, a few national and international reporters made a video and took photos. It was quiet there and I could fully explain the Burmese situation. 'We're finished now,' we said, also because we were becoming very sleepy. That night we were put up in the airport hotel. The Government brought in a Buddhist monk who had connections with the Burmese embassy in India: 'Who are you?' We slept long after all this, and the next day we were all over the media. Burma's struggle for democracy was highlighted.

The time of our arrival was also the beginning of political change in India's coalition government. Rajiv Gandhi was no longer Prime Minister, but his Congress Party supported us. And the Congress Party was supporting new Prime Minister Chandra Shekhar, who was sworn in on the day we landed at Kolkata. The Indian Government was also the first that supported the Burmese democracy movement. The roots of this went back to the time in which Aung San Suu Kyi studied in India, and met with Rajiv and Sonia Gandhi in Oxford. Also, Than Than Nu, U Nu's daughter, was working for All India Radio, which actively supported the Burmese democracy movement, and she was very close to Rajiv Gandhi and the Congress Party. So we were very lucky that there were such close ties between people in the media and in Government who were sympathetic to our cause. In the morning, when we were taken from the airport hotel to the court, there were so many people in the streets that I thought there was a demonstration. At the court, we were garlanded and people asked for our autographs – the beginning of my new life in India.

'What do you know about India?' the Indian media asked. 'I know about Prime Minister Indira Gandhi,' I said, not realizing that she had passed away a few years ago. My knowledge of India was in fact very minimal. 'You can do whatever you like. We surrender and will cooperate with everything.' The Indian Government took testimonies of the pilots, the air hostesses and the passengers, after which we were put in custody in Dum Dum Central Jail in Kolkata for three months. In the plane, someone had advised us: 'You should ask for political asylum in India!' We didn't know what 'asylum' was, but many Indian Members of Parliament helped us, crowds of lawyers wanted to represent us, and human rights organizations followed in their footsteps with applications for refugee status.

We had only one set of clothes, so the lawyers called in tailors that took our measurements and provided us with nice shirts and trousers. There was a lot of support, even though the Government was very cautious not to say anything. George Fernandes, a well-known Member of Parliament and former Minister, as well as Rajmohan Gandhi, the grandson of Mahatma Gandhi, came to our aid, while Than Than Nu did her lobby work, and talked with Rajiv Gandhi and Prime Minister Chandra Shekhar. Finally, we were released on bail, and were taken to the office of the chief minister of West Bengal, Jyoti Basu. He was very supportive. 'What do you want to do, now that you are free?' 'We want to study and continue in the Burmese student movement.' The case was still pending, but we only had to show our face in court every now and then.

Activism and journalism

We moved to New Delhi and joined with some Burmese students who had already left Burma in 1988. For two years, I was general secretary of the All Burma Student League. I came to know about Indian politics, and Mahatma Gandhi's non-violent action still fascinates me. At this time, the early 1990s, the Indian Government and MPs still sponsored the democratic voices of Burma. 'I don't have any money,' Fernandes said, 'but you can run your office from my residence.' Seminars, press conferences, exhibitions, all this introduced us to Indian politics, and to non-violent political activities. While being active in the movement, I was encouraged to become a journalist and stringer for Burmese radio stations such as Democratic Voice of Burma and Voice of America that broadcast into Burma. Within a few years, I had changed from a student to an explosives trainer, and from a hijacker to a non-violent activist and then a journalist!

When we started Mizzima in 1998, there were only three of us: Thin Thin, Win Aung, and myself. We didn't even have a telephone line or a computer. On a laptop we wrote news and interviews, which we sent through to news agencies from internet shops. Now, with 50 staff, Mizzima is becoming a multimedia news agency with documentaries, books, and reporters in five countries. I spoke with Aung San Suu Kyi a few times. At first, somehow I wasn't so sure of her leadership. But after her house arrest in 1989, when released for the first time in 1995, she spoke to people, and I got really impressed. She had developed and matured and really spoke as a leader, something Burma hadn't had for a long time. She is very brave, and crucial to the solution for our country.

In India, I was able to travel to many places to lobby and organize meetings, exhibitions and films on Burma for the student movement. I took computer courses and courses in journalism and human rights. I was very fortunate to live in India with so many learning experiences, because when I left Burma I didn't know much about the essence of democracy, its challenges and weaknesses. It's a process. My lawyer Nandita Haksar offered us great help. She is a great activist and a committed lawyer, and her father was once an adviser to Indira Gandhi. Nandita became my guardian, and by now I have many Bapus, uncles and aunties in India. George Fernandes I call uncle. My book *Burma File: A Question of Democracy* was published and released in India, and became part of the campaign to demonstrate what I had been doing in Mizzima.

After we first arrived in Delhi, we used to have daily fights with rickshaw drivers, taxi drivers, neighbors and so on. 'What about this dead dog smell?' our neighbor said, rushing into our home when we were cooking dried fish. By that time, there were more and more Burmese students who came from the Indo-Burmese border to New Delhi to continue their struggle for democracy with non-violent political activities in India. But as newly arrived refugees, we didn't know how to behave. The only organization that supported refugees legally was UNHCR. But a few years ago, the Home Ministry started providing Burmese refugees with residence permits. UNHCR at that time provided some money for food and rent, but it covered our expenses in no way. We had no idea of building our lives here. 'You study,' the Indians echoed my parents. Finally I gave in, and studied Spanish. But was I not on a mission for the non-violent revolution of Burma?

Thin Thin, my wife, is the only one of us who finished her MBA studies at Delhi University. She is also an activist and supports the women's movement. In the beginning we had no money, and our life was a daily struggle for survival. Every Thursday, there is a market in West Delhi. Late at night, when most people have gone, a lot of garbage is left behind and we collected it so we could eat tomorrow. At one point my friend found a cabbage, but he had to fight over it with a cow that had taken it in its mouth just before. Both pulled, and he finally won. That was the kind of life we had. India gives you freedom, but doesn't give you food. We were lucky, however, to have some Indian individuals like my lawyer Nandita Haksar and her family who helped us in every way they could for our new life in India.

I was rearrested in April 2002, in other words after 9/11, when the atmosphere had changed. Just after I put the phone down for sending a news report to Voice of America Burmese Service in Washington, the West Bengal police came from Kolkata. 'You are under arrest for hijacking a plane.' This time it was very different from 1990, when the treatment had been first class. Then, we could play badminton, read Time magazine, listen to the radio and eat good food. Now, they treated me like a real criminal, humiliated me and threw me into a filthy police lock-up. Something had happened. The Minister of Foreign Affairs had been to Burma a few days before, where the Burmese Minister of Foreign Affairs had reportedly raised issues: 'Why do you allow hijackers to run a news agency?'

'Why did India give in to pressure from Burma?' My lawyer really fought a battle. To my own advantage, I had become a journalist by then, and had many friends in journalism and in the Government. 'You can just leave India,' one Indian official said. 'Our heart is with you, but our brain is with the Burmese Government now.' But we fought the case with the support of many Indians, Burmese and supporters around the world. Finally, I was acquitted in 2003, thanks to the intense lobbying for my case. The EU, chaired by the Netherlands, reprimanded the Indian Government: 'Why should you arrest someone who is working as a journalist 12 years after the case?' Neither Thai Airways nor any of the passengers filed any charges, and the Indian Government didn't manage to produce the crucial witnesses. Strangely, there was no evidence for violating the law against hijacking, while of course around the world people knew it had happened.

Rivers of saffron
Slowly, Mizzima became more known, and got support from international donors. Again we were 'lucky'. In September 2007 the Saffron Revolution happened, triggered by a demonstration of the 1988 generation of student leaders and then massive demonstrations by the Buddhist monks throughout the country. This time however, we were ready, with many of our reporters inside the country, and our underground office ready in Burma. Our people were armed with small digital cameras and mobile phones. Together with other news agencies, we were able to disseminate real-time news, images and interviews. It made Mizzima's work high-profile in

the public arena. But more importantly, the uprising reinforced my belief in the human spirit. We fear however the results of the 2010 elections planned by the military regime. If the election is rigged by the military junta, and neighboring countries recognize the results, it will strongly affect the Burmese in the Diaspora.

The Saffron Revolution

Stranger than fiction: Burmese soldiers were ordered to fight against the leaders of the religion that they live by themselves. Even the cabins of military vehicles display images of the Buddha. In 2007, the monkhood or sangha came face to face with the military regime or Tatmadaw. 'There are two powerful institutions in Burma – the military and the clergy,' said Soe at the time. 'The military has guns. But the monks have peace and the people's respect. By resorting to brutality, the military has lost the support of the monks. The military may be able to shoot, beat and jail the monks and the people, but they cannot do it for too long. The downfall of the military dictatorship seems at hand.'

Anti-government protests started on 15 August when the military junta removed fuel subsidies, causing the price of diesel, petrol and natural gas to rise exponentially within a week. Between 50,000 and 100,000 demonstrators gathered in the streets of Rangoon in September 2007. A dramatic shift occurred when the streets filled with rivers of saffron. Monasteries emptied, and the monks were cheered by crowds of supporters from the streets, from balconies and roof tops. Briefly, there was a glimmer of hope when Aung San Suu Kyi appeared at the gate of her house, accepting the blessings of Buddhist monks. They continued their way chanting the Metta Sutta, the Buddha's discourse on loving kindness. Police and troops however, brutally attacked people, killing many. Monasteries were subsequently raided and sealed, including Shwedagon Pagoda.

Video Journalism – The Making of Burma VJ
By Khin Maung Win

Like Soe Myint, Khin Maung Win was a student activist in 1988 joining the All Burma Students Democratic Front in the jungle. Four years later, he was one of the founding members of the Democratic Voice of Burma (DVB). For the award-winning film Burma VJ, based on real-time footage of the Saffron Revolution, Mizzima and DVB worked together.

'The DVB is the worst medium, as it most effectively distributes false news,' said Khin Yi, the Burmese police chief, during the press conference in December 2007. But our reporter was also there when the police chief was making these comments! That's how it was captured on Burma VJ. That's how we play the game with the regime. We had no idea there would be a Saffron Revolution! But when events started unfolding, we were well prepared, because inside the country we had set up a network of 30 to 40 reporters, all armed with handheld cameras and cell phones.'

Poster for the documentary Burma VJ (2008)

'We had also invested heavily in a high-tech communication system using satellites to beam information directly to different places. Unexpectedly, journalists from major mainstream media including Reuters, AP, AFP, The Guardian and many TV channels from across Europe gathered here in our Oslo offices, waiting for information from us. Sometimes, we uploaded footage of protesting monks or police brutalities directly to many TV channels around the world including CNN. People around the world could see those images within a few hours, despite the fact that the military regime had shut down telephone lines and the internet. Video files take up many megabytes, and in Burma internet is slow, so you need special tactics to be able to send it through. We used our own system. Our secret weapon.

'In Burma VJ you can even see a scene of a man filming from behind a wall, while soldiers are approaching and firing at people. After obtaining the footage, he has to very quickly hand it to others, who work round the clock to edit, compress and upload it as economical as possible. At the same time, they need to keep moving for security reasons. Meanwhile, we push them: 'We need this! We need that! Quickly!' Cameras are very small, but the soldiers check everyone, and the regime has its own people that film and take photos of journalists and protesters, which they submit to the military. Two sides film and take photos of each other.

'You might think it is difficult to get volunteers for this kind of work, but it isn't. Young people continue to resist the regime – students, doctors, plumbers, housewives. We offer the only free television broadcasts in Burma, and estimate that 10 million Burmese – one out of five – can watch these through their satellite receivers. They are mushrooming everywhere. Following the Saffron Revolution, the regime raised the license fees from 8 to 800 dollar per year. But they didn't implement it, knowing that a little spark can trigger big events.

'Satellite communication itself is secret, and done by small, advanced devices the size of a laptop. Uploading video files is expensive, seven dollars per megabyte. Just getting that one clip of the killing of the Japanese journalist out cost us 1,000 dollar. But the impact is incredible. It also has a preventive function. When soldiers realize there are cameras – even when they can't see them – they think twice. In 1988, they killed 3,000 people, and they could easily cover up their brutalities. No cameras, no journalists, no media. This time, everything was exposed, so they didn't get a free hand to kill people.'

Yes, I did that hijack drama in 1990. But I don't want anyone glorifying it. What is much more important, is to see the reason why, the desperation of ordinary Burmese citizens for a better life. Everything I have ever done is to do with the situation in Burma. Some of my university classmates chose to become diplomats, and are now working in embassies around the world. I, however, chose to revolt against the military government's systems of repression, and to stand up for the plight of the Burmese people. I faced many consequences, but there are so many people who are still suffering under the military junta after more than two decades. I am still doing what I believed in 1988, and will continue until freedom comes to Burma.

'Your struggle is a lost struggle like Tibet,' some say to me. I don't agree at all. The Burmese struggle is winning and will win. At some point the military government will no longer be there. We want the Burmese people to be treated like others in the free world with dignity and freedom. Maybe we won't achieve all this while we are alive, but the struggle for freedom and democracy is never a lost struggle! I hope one day to return home to a free democratic Burma, where all the nationalities can live together. That ideal keeps me alive. I want to be part of rebuilding Burma. We will win.

Tunnel Vision
By Khin Maung Win

'We have some very recent, very secret information that at first many people, including government representatives, didn't dare to believe. They only accept it when we show them the documentation. We're not guessing. This will become a big, big issue over the coming years. The information concerns tunneling projects in Burma with North Korean advisers.'

'The North Korean interest in Burma is simple. The country has been isolated by the international community, and needs friends. They're now helping the Burmese regime to build an extensive network of underground tunnels and emergency shelters, something they are expert at. Let me show you the evidence on my laptop. The Burmese regime is extremely worried about a possible invasion by the United States, as happened in Iraq. They're governed by fear. And as Burma's generals admire North Korea for being able to stand up to the United States, they want to cooperate with them, and be the same.

'In 2008, the number three man of the Burmese regime visited North Korea, and signed a Memorandum of Understanding concerning cooperation between the two countries that would cost many billions of dollars. North Korea provides Burma with the weapons and technology that they wouldn't get from anybody else. Why would Burma need to be like North Korea? The main reason for North Korea is to threaten South Korea and Japan. This gives them bargaining power. Burma might have a dream to be like North Korea by threatening neighboring Thailand with nuclear weapons. We have received many documents suggesting this dream.

'Look at this: a report prepared by the delegation led by the number three top man of the military junta last year. It was leaked to the media on purpose. North Korean advisers provide training, and high-tech tunneling equipment to dig through the mountains. Here is a promotion clip of the construction company. On photos taken inside the tunnels, you can see that the workers are using the equipment as displayed on the promotional video. Based on maps and PowerPoint presentations, we estimate that there are up to 800 throughout Burma, and especially in the border region with Thailand. One of the locations is designed to include an underground factory. It can hold 1,090 people. Excel sheets – the 'Myanmar Obligations Summary' and the 'Korea Seller's Obligations' – show the expenses: 7 billion dollars. And that is just part of the total projects. Most of the walls are 800mm thick. Every detail is there.

'Most dictators have a common philosophy. For the military regime to operate, it needs a common enemy. That's why General Ne Win waged war against ethnic groups, instead of solving the problem politically and bringing stability and peace. In fact, the regime considers itself to be in a perpetual state of war. Likewise, they need a foreign enemy: the United States and Thailand, which is seen as a puppet of the United States. Detailed reports compare the strengths of the Thai and Burmese armies and navies. Some documents actually speak about preparing for war against Thailand, about which we have informed the Thai Government.

'This tunneling work has been going on since 1996. We feel that it has to be exposed. Think of it! The regime is oppressing the people, and wasting the country's resources. And if Burma becomes another North Korea, that would be disastrous for China, Japan, South Korea and Thailand, and probably for the whole world. It has to be stopped!'

Martin Macwan - India
Advocating the rights of the Untouchables

'There is a different world that exists in this so-called democratic India,' Martin Macwan says. 'The enemy is something inside, not outside, and it runs from the poorest villages right up to the higher echelons of politics.' Having grown up in a hand-to-mouth existence, and having to clean the school in order to be allowed to attend it, Martin would later work as a librarian and literacy teacher. But when advocating the rights of the Untouchables, he lost some of his best friends during the Golana Massacre. Ever since, he has worked tirelessly for Navsarjan Trust, now active in more than 3,000 villages, demonstrating the power of civil disobedience and empowerment. 'Ultimately, every human being has a sense of spirituality that is more to do with values, ethics, understanding and vision.'

Martin Macwan

'There's a different world that exists in this so-called democratic India,' says Martin Macwan (born in 1959). In advocating the rights of India's Untouchables, four of his closest friends lost their lives. Macwan founded Navsarjan Trust, now present in more than 3,000 villages, which mobilizes social movement using anything from foot marches to court cases. 'Our approach is constitutional.'

Context

A man riding on his bicycle stops for no apparent reason. He gets off, takes his slippers in his hands, and starts walking. After 20 meters, he puts his slippers back on again, resuming his bike ride. He has successfully fulfilled the obligations of a Dalit – Untouchable – for passing the house of an upper-caste family, a custom that takes place in many parts of India.

A little further down the road, Dalits are building a temple. But when finished, they may never enter. All around the country, when a job is filthy, menial or undesirable, chances are high that it is being done by a Dalit. Anything from digging graves to handling waste and sewage, from other people's excrements to disposing of human corpses or animal carcasses, causing them to stink like death for weeks. Even the job of passing on bad news from village to village is the prerogative of Bhangis, a Dalit subcaste considered to be the lowest in the caste hierarchy. Although officially banned by the State Government, the word 'Bhangi' is very much in use, often by State representatives themselves.

India's Dalits or 'broken people' speak 19 different languages and are divided into 751 sub-castes. Dalit K.R. Narayanan became President of India (1997-2002), and even today, chief minister of Uttar Pradesh, Behenji – honored sister – Mayawati, aims to become Prime Minister, a position that holds more actual power than that of President. But despite these achievements, the vast majority of Dalits struggle to live a life of dignity. It is a social status you suffer, and not one to be cherished. 'India's Independence' might seem the obvious answer, when asking an elderly person: 'What was the most important moment in your life?' Not so for the 90-year-old village elder of Kheecha in Gujarat, the State in which Mahatma Gandhi was born. 'The day we were allowed to own land, even just a few acres. It gave us a freedom and dignity that we had never experienced before.'

Ever since India's Independence in 1947, legislation has targeted the elimination of Untouchability. 'Untouchability is abolished and its practice in any form is forbidden', says Article 17 of the Indian Constitution of 1950. The Untouchability (Offences) Act of 1955, the Prevention of Atrocities Act of 1989 and a range of other acts however have all failed to protect the dignity of Dalits, proving to be full of loopholes and very lenient towards those who break these laws. The abolition of manual scavenging alone demonstrates this. The Indian State has put forth myriad legal instruments to tackle it, but has been extremely slow to enforce it on the ground. Millions of rupees have been granted to rehabilitate 'sanitary workers', but through corruption and deliberate upper-caste obstacles, it has gone literally down the latrine. Squalor and destitution still are the markers of Dalit life.

Safai Karmachari Andolan, 'the movement to eradicate manual scavenging in India', and six other organizations revealed that the number of manual scavengers has actually increased from 588,000 in 1992 to 787,000 in 2003. Rather than accepting the leftover Victorian English term of 'manual scavenging', SKA insists on calling it *maila dhona*, Hindi for 'lifting shit'. Among the Dalits, and even among the 'shit lifters', there are many sub-castes. Vankars and Rohits dispose of the 'higher animals' like cows, buffaloes, and goats, while Valmikis only dispose of dead cats and dogs. The hides of buffaloes and cows bring in some additional income, whereas those of cats and dogs don't. Even the public sector, such as the Indian Railways, continues this practice. Still more surprising is the fact that the Indian State is the largest promoter of manual scavenging. It employs Dalits in inhumane and illegal practices from cleaning latrines in villages to maintaining centralized sewage systems in cities.

Orthodox believers see the caste system as 'the very spine of the Hindu religion'. The Laws of Manu (written circa 100BC) say that 'The Lord assigned only one activity to a servant: serving the other castes without resentment' (Chapter 1, Verse 91). Thus, a Dalit can never be wise or intelligent, even when they manage to climb the social ladder to the position of surgeon, architect or entrepreneur. 'You are born a Dalit. You live as a Dalit. You die as a Dalit, and you are buried as a Dalit. Segregated from the rest of society.' It reaches everywhere, and stretches from the most remote village right up to the Jawaharlal Nehru University in Delhi, giving rise to the dedication of the documentary India Untouched: Stories of a People Apart: 'to all those who deny the existence of Untouchability.'

In the hierarchical Varna system there are four groups, from high to low: Brahmins, Kshatriyas, Vaishyas, and Shudras. Dalits are considered to be so inferior, that they are outside of this system. Effectively, they are victims of the caste system, stuck in a vicious circle. Their traditional occupations lead to a poor economic status and child labor, and as education is mostly denied, their caste is automatically reconfirmed. 'Sit back. Do not enter the kitchen. Don't touch the vessels. Go and clean the toilet,' is what Dalit schoolchildren hear on a daily basis. Upper-caste children blow air and say 'phoo phoo' to cleanse themselves, if they touch them. Teachers don't want to touch their homework, so mostly it is never corrected. Having no land of their own, Dalits often migrate, always depending on seasonal labor. Girls and women experience gender bias. 'I'm double Dalit,' says a female hospital employee. 'A Dalit and a woman.' Dalits feel – and are made to feel – inferior.

'From the outside, India seems a democracy,' says Manjula Pradeep, director of Navsarjan Trust. 'But in fact, it is a castocracy. Caste is the most determining factor in all decisions.' Navsarjan, New Creation, is an organization founded in 1989 with the aim of empowering the Dalit communities of Gujarat. Its mission is to eliminate discrimination based on Untouchability practices, to ensure equality of status and opportunities for all, and to ensure the rule of law. In 1999, 2.5 million signatures were submitted to India's Prime Minister demanding the abolition of Untouchability and enforcement of national legislation.

Despite the fact that India's economy is growing rapidly, it appears not to benefit the Dalit. According to the International Dalit Solidarity Network, Human Rights Watch and Amnesty International's 2015 report that 'corruption, caste-based discrimination and caste violence remained pervasive.' State authorities fail to protect the rights of Dalits.

Manual scavenging continues despite laws that ban it. Dalits suffer malnourishment and lack of access to healthcare. Bonded labor and child labor continue as do extrajudicial killings and sexual violence against women. Human Rights Watch 2014 report on education was titled 'They say we're dirty.' Dalit children often sit separately or at the back of the class, while teachers refuse to correct their homework or deny Dalit children their midday meals.

'Untouchability is India's hidden apartheid,' says Martin Macwan, former Convener of the Indian National Campaign on Dalit Human Rights, and Navsarjan's founder. 'And in this era of globalization and human rights, no country can claim that caste is a domestic matter. It's a universal concern that affects 160 million people in India alone.' A major background role is played by the philosophy of Dr. Babasaheb Ambedkar's (see below) and his catchphrase: 'Educate, Organize and Agitate'. On the table in Macwan's office is a brand-new book that opens with a quote in Ambedkar's handwriting: 'Again, as the Buddha has said: the underlined passage is the most crucial. Satisfaction is the most important asset. He who has no satisfaction is always unhappy.'

One of the largest studies on Untouchability ever done – 1,650 villages; 98,000 respondents – confirms that the phenomenon is rampant. 'We used to do one step forward, falling four steps backward,' says Martin. 'Today we're falling only three steps backward. That's progress. Even the police, whether for us or against us, feel that we only take on genuine cases.' In a society where 'you don't cast your vote, but you vote your caste', Martin has become an influential advocate against caste-based discrimination and, in the words of the late Senator Edward Kennedy, 'a rare voice for tolerance, non-violence and effectiveness'. Over the last 20 years, he has kept his social activism true to its original intentions, but not without having to go through some agonizing experiences.

Personal narrative — Martin Macwan

'We have a football team, plus three referees,' we used to say. This was because I was born in a Dalit family with 11 brothers and sisters. Together with my parents and my grandmother, we lived in a community of 50 families on Shanti Faliya or 'Street of Peace' in a small town called Nadiad. It was in the state of Gujarat, just 55 kilometers from Ahmedabad on the main national highway to Mumbai. Our house was made of plastered mud and the floor was stamped earth.

I used to follow a herd of buffaloes and collect the dung. This we mixed with mud, which we used to plaster the walls, one of the first skills I learned during childhood. Every year before Christmas we used to plaster the walls again. In our one-room house, we all – boys and girls – slept in a row. In the winter we shared one common blanket. We had a hand-to-mouth existence, but never begged, because my mother always reminded us of human dignity. Sometimes, when my second youngest brother was crying during the night, my mother would take a glass of water, put some wheat flour in it, and shake it up to make it look like milk.

Two of my sisters died within two weeks after they were born. Due to falling oxygen levels, they became blue babies. My mother was working in a tobacco factory. For a few days per week I worked there too, and next to that I worked alongside my grandmother on the farms, starting at the age of eight. It was seasonal work to harvest a small grain called bajra, a staple food in our region that people use to make chapattis. It grows four feet tall like maize, and has to be cut at the roots. Then it dries for a week in rows, and you take the corn. It's very hard labor because the sun burns 42 degrees, and you're working from eight in the morning till six in the evening. I was paid one rupee per day. During the work you get a lot of grass on your body, and you turn all red, because it itches and irritates. Often you get very thirsty. But you can't decide to drink water by yourself, because of Untouchability. You had to put forward a request to the landlord. You hold up your hands to form a cup, and then they pour water without touching you, and without you touching the pot of water. Then you drink.

But the tobacco work was far more difficult. In Gujarat, almost 30 per cent of the tobacco of India is grown. When the crops are fully grown, the leaves are taken off and dried in large halls 100 feet long. Once you're inside, the doors close, but there is no ventilation. Inside, you break the leaves with a wooden bat, which creates a huge amount of dust. That's the reason why most of the children and women that work there have breathing problems, and many of them get tuberculosis. I had health problems all the time. Also, there was no childcare, so many mothers carried their babies. In the absence of water, when babies cried of hunger, mothers would rush out of the factory and breastfeed. But all the dust gets into the babies. Here we made even less: 75 paise, three quarters of a rupee for a day's work.

My father never went to school, but somehow managed to work on the railways, pipeline maintenance and textile mills. For the rest, the entire burden of the family fell on my mother and grandmother. Women have a greater ability to struggle than men. Men give up more easily. 'Never allow bitterness to overcome you,' my mother and grandmother said. 'That will take you nowhere!' They taught me to persevere. I was a very serious child, and spent a lot of hours alone thinking. Outside of the house there was a small platform on which I used to sit until late in the evening. I closed my eyes and took my family in mind, imagining how we could better survive. Next, in my mind I traveled along all the other families around me. I had a very strong community sense, and this habit developed when I was 11 or 12.

Dalit education
On the days that I didn't work, I went to school. The first school I attended was very near to my house and run by the British Salvation

Army. It was a makeshift one-room school. I was very inspired by a Spanish Jesuit priest called Father Herero. He lived a very simple, hard-working life, and hardly spoke. From early in the morning, after church, he would immediately go to the office, write, read, and visit villages. Then he got home, repaired his old car, washed his clothes, and climbed the roof of the school with hammer and nails to repair it. Very industrious, always smiling, no complaints.

One day however, the Catholic nuns came. 'Why are you not sending your children to our high school?' They had the best school in my hometown, called St. Ann's. 'We don't have money,' my mother said. 'Well,' the nuns responded, 'you're Catholics, so you won't be required to pay the fees.' My sister, me, and two other children from my street were sent to this school. Even after all these years, I can't forget how, when all the other children were playing, the four of us were given brooms to sweep the school floors, because we didn't pay the school fees. Every day I refused to go, and several times I ended up being pulled by a nun on one side, while I clung to my grandmother on the other. Finally they put me in a public school close to my home. There were a lot of poor children, but I liked it, because here we were all cleaning the floors. The teachers however were not very interested in teaching. Ms Taraben taught class three. Depending on the season she would bring a bag of mangos or lemons. She divided the class into clever and dumb students. The cleverest among them would teach the other clever ones. The dumb students were given a knife to cut fruits. Ms Taraben put her two feet on the table and slept for the rest of the day.

There was a boy called Ashwin, and he was a Patel, one of the middle castes, many of whom live in the UK and the United States. We used to compete to be the best in maths, but he could never beat me. Despite our competition, at school we were very close friends. But come Saturday or Sunday, it was a different story, because my grandmother was working on the farm of his grandmother. His grandmother showed us what to do, while Ashwin would just sit on a heap of grass watching. When I left the school, I lost contact with him. When I turned 17, and had completed my first year of college, my grandmother took me to the house of the Patel's to hand them an invitation for my eldest sister's wedding. Ashwin's grandmother immediately pulled up a chair. 'Now you sit here,' she said, and then she started weeping bitterly. These two grandmothers had always shared their woes and pains. Caste hadn't been able to divide them: 'Your grandson was working on my farm, but he is now in college. But my grandson is still at the farm, because he never studied any further.' She couldn't understand this, as a Patel should have risen to a better place in society. She wept and wept, and then put her hand on my head to bless me.

For a while, I attended another Jesuit school close to my house for class 4 and 5. After this, I was put in the Jesuit missionary school run by Catholic priests. But when my parents found out that I was bunking school, I was forced to stay in boarding, even though it was close to home. I didn't like it there at all, the teachers always complained, and we had to wear uniforms. Just before reaching the school there was a garden. I would sit there most of the day, collecting plant leaves, and talking to beggars. 'Where is Martin?' the teachers asked, and sent a squadron of boys to get me. I ran away home, but as my father threatened to kill me, I also ran away from home. Eventually I was found, sitting in a temple in the middle of the night. I never found out why I didn't want to go to school anymore. Perhaps it was because my dreams about life were so different from what was taught at school. Also, I was very worried about my mother and grandmother, because I realized how much they suffered to manage the family.

Poverty is almost automatic if you're born as a Dalit. More than 85 per cent of them don't own any land. My father's father had migrated from a small village to the town. It fits the pattern of Dalit history. It's a history of migration. Ahmedabad was once the Manchester of India, because there were 95 textile mills. Thousands of poor people used to live around those mills, but when they closed down, many of them had to move again. I never saw a person from my village that started a business. I was the first child from my street to go to college, and the first that ever traveled abroad. Even today, in my hometown you'll still find mud houses with tin roofs, as if nothing has changed in 50 years. The Dalits are landless, because corrupt Hindu canon laws prevented us. So there are structural reasons why poverty is so persistent among them.

At boarding school, the food was obnoxious. In the morning we used to get one burnt chapatti and a glass of tea. We cooled the tea by pouring it on the plate, and back in the glass. At lunch we got two burnt chapattis. The chapattis had a lot of uncooked whole wheat that gave us stomach aches. Sometimes, from a window on the third floor of the building, the priest would call us to do some work. We could see that he had a banana or an apple in his hand or a sandwich. The priests would always have an omelet, bread and toast, butter and cheese, chicken or fish and so on, while we children were stuck with whole wheat. So even though I had previously been impressed by Father Herero with the simple lifestyle, I started hating the notion of religion, and the indignity that we were subject to. And children need more nourishing food! But the priest in charge would say: 'I know what you're eating at home. Far worse than what you're getting here.' One time he challenged us. 'OK, when you come back after your vacation, we will measure whether you gained or lost weight.' When we came back, we ate a dozen bananas just to increase our weight. The priest found out, so he said: 'All right, I will take your weight in the evening. No, in the morning!' You won't believe how religious we boys were about not going to the toilet!

Vow of poverty
I failed my school exams twice, because my attention was failing. But during my vacations, I would read a novel a day – Tolstoy's short stories, Run, Baby, Run by Nicky Cruz, and many others. When I finished my school in class 11, despite my dislike of organized religion and sitting through mass, I had the urge to become a priest. I think it was more the inspiration Father Herero gave me. 'Yes, I already thought that one day you might come,' the priest said. I was seen by all the other children as a very serious boy, a thinker. Anyway, I was sent to St. Xavier's College in Ahmedabad as a novice, to prepare for the priesthood. But within days I had a confrontation, when a priest explained the philosophy behind the three vows: obedience, poverty, and abstinence.
'Any questions?'

I raised my hand.
'I understand the abstinence and the obedience. But I can't understand the
vow of poverty.'
'What do you mean?'
'My mother was a tobacco worker all her life. Even today, she's still working. After working for so many years, she's still wearing the same sari as when I was a child. In spite of all that hard work, she's still poor. But I see all of us sitting here, including you, the priests, wearing precious robes. I don't see even a drop of sweat on your bodies. We have all the best food. And still we say that we are poor. I can't accept that.'
'No, no,' they said. 'It's poverty of thought.'
'I don't understand. To me poverty is a daily reality of whether you're getting enough to eat, and of human dignity. How do you explain that I have access to all the facilities of the priesthood, while continuing to think that I am a poor person?'

I studied and started going to church. But I often went to the slums near my college. During church service I taught children how to read and write. Soon there were reports about 'the black sheep of the seminary'. In any event, things came to a point when my elder sister was getting married. It was summer time and I went home. My family still had to ration food, we could hardly afford new clothes or firewood, and my brothers and sisters only had one shirt to wear. You could read the poverty from their faces. 'Don't worry,' my mother said. 'We might be able to get some credit from the man who provides us with firewood.' But transportation cost one rupee. To save it, I borrowed a cart, and pulled it myself. 'Look at him,' people in my street said. 'A college boy, but still pulling carts!' My father had gathered just enough money for my sister's marriage and to cook a meal in the evening. In those 24 hours I wondered: will I be able to take care of my own family, while trying to save the whole world?

I rushed back to Ahmedabad. 'I'm leaving the order. I can't do it. My first responsibility is towards my family, my younger brothers and sisters.' That night, when I was at home again, I wept a lot. The four walls of our house contained no more than some planks with utensils and plates – nothing of any value. Earlier, we used to have many brass and copper utensils. 'We had to sell them to survive,' my mother explained. I got two jobs. One as a librarian at St. Xavier's college for 150 rupees per month. Next to that, I started as a literary teacher at an evening school for the slum people. Here they paid me 100 rupees, so altogether I got 250 rupees per month. Occasionally on Sundays I also did somebody's accounts. I gave up having breakfast. Anything that I could save, I gave to my mother. It meant a very big support for my family. I went on to study psychology at the same college. I used to rush to college, have a quick lunch and 45 minutes of rest. In the afternoon I worked in the library, after which I played volleyball or basketball with my fellow students, had a shower and went to the evening school to teach. After dinner, I would study until the early morning, getting only five hours of sleep. I read much more than required, and graduated in 1980, when I was 20.

During that time, the formation of my ideological beliefs started. Some of my professors had given up their jobs and had chosen to work in rural development. It was a group consisting of a Catholic, a Zoroastrian, a Muslim, and a Hindu. They had started a program in the 1970s based on the theory of 'achievement motivation' by American psychologist David McClelland. He had done some very successful experiments with businesspeople in the south of India. Participating in the program moved me to tears. 'What happened?' they asked me. 'I don't know. I remembered my parents, my childhood and all that.' Still, I only had two pairs of pants and two shirts. One pair of pants was torn from behind, so I stitched it. To hide the stitching I wore an extra long shirt. 'A new fashion?' people wondered. I didn't want to spend money on clothes, because I wanted to send every rupee to my family. Among the other participants there were many who were in their thirties and older.

Casting off blockages
Both the professors and the students found that there are social blockages that don't allow people to achieve, because of poverty and the mindsets they grew up with. Around 1972, after one of these workshops, one of the students had asked: 'Why don't you come to my village?' The professors visited the village, and for the first time

they were exposed to the prevalence of the caste system, and the poverty of the village of Pandad. I too went along. It totally opened my eyes about the caste system. Then they said: 'Why don't we do something with the poor people in the village?' So many of them were engaged in a mix between motivation and agricultural workshops. There, the college professors noticed that in group meetings everybody sits together, but they eat and drink water separately. It sparked a debate. 'Can we set up an institute for rural development that does not discriminate on the basis of caste?' So in 1977 they set up Behavioral Science Center (BSC). It was based on David McClelland's achievement motivation, Sigmund Freud's concepts of the role of the unconscious, and Paulo Freire's work of 'conscientization' in Brazil teaching literacy.

Cleaning the streets, Hyderabad, India, 2007 (photo Peter de Ruiter)

Occasionally, I used to accompany these professors to villages to help them carry out surveys. I decided to join them in BSC immediately after my graduation, but they suggested that I should join a new upcoming youth organization in my own district. I agreed and joined Ashadeep Youth Center. It was 25 kilometers away from my hometown, but I was paid 500 rupees. It enabled me to save a lot of money, but it was not enough to take care of my six brothers and sisters who were still at school, to clear the debts my family had incurred for survival, or to continue my law study. Poor families like us also had to save money to handle possible future uncertainties. I had to take a train from my hometown for 20 kilometers, and then a bus for another five. But I walked those last five kilometers to save those extra rupees. It was challenging work, because there was nobody else in the staff, except for the director who didn't accompany me to the villages. But in one year I set up youth organizations in 69 villages. On the afternoon of the fourth day I returned home from a tour, and ran to the farm. It was an extremely hot summer day. My grandmother was walking with a big bundle of firewood on her head. 'No,' I said. 'You don't have to carry all that.' I took the load from her, and brought her home. 'Tomorrow you don't have to go to work. I'm earning money now.' She had tears in her eyes. 'Enough,' I said. 'You have done enough.' It made a big change for my family, and everyone had a really good meal. My second desire was that my mother wouldn't have to work. But that had to wait for some time.

When you're poor, usually self-interest prevails and often the parents are neglected. So somehow, a year and a half after joining BSC, these changes made me into a role model in my hometown. My next assignment was to set up a cooperative in the remote district of Banaskantha in north Gujarat, an area with refugees from Pakistan due to the 1947 partition. A lot of Hindus were sent back and there were horrible stories of rape and murder. They lost all their property and even the land that the Government had given them as part of the rehabilitation package. It landed in the hands of local money lenders. I went there for one year. It was a seven-hour journey by bus. To cover the last kilometers, I was provided with a tractor, because it was desert, and except for a state bus there was no other way to cross it. After two hours I reached the village, by which time my back was half broken.

Experiences of extremes
The people lived in small huts, and didn't have a place for me to stay. I slept under a tree, which was very hard due to the desert heat during the day, while the nights were extremely cold. One winter

night it was so cold that even when I covered myself with three blankets, I was still shivering. The village head worried that I might die. They took me to the house of the chief, but it wasn't big enough, so they put a bed in the stable. I had to cover my face, because the buffalo and the camel would sniff at me, urinate right next to me and splash their tails in my face. When I opened my eyes in the morning, all the animals were staring at me. All the parents went to work during the day, leaving the children at home. To quench their hunger and thirst, they would chew on the bitter fruits of the neem tree.

One Monday morning, while brushing my teeth, I saw that a young man of maybe 20 was weeping outside his house. 'What happened?' I asked him. 'Enough now,' an elderly man interrupted. 'Get out, and go to work!' he said to the young man. The young man got up and went to work. In the evening, everybody came home from the farms, so I asked the elderly man why this young man had been crying in the morning. 'O, his son died last night. It was only a small child, and he needs to go to work again.' This young father had just lost his child, but the whole day had gone by as if nothing had happened! Here, parents didn't treat their children with love, simply because they had so much bitterness in their life due to the trauma of their flight from Pakistan. No dialogue, no peaceful coexistence. To them, their lives seemed to have no relevance.

Then, for six months I was sent to the extreme south of Gujarat to work with the tribals in Bharuch. They were all part of a milk cooperative, but didn't have enough bargaining power. In our team, a veterinary doctor explained to them how to increase the fat percentage of the milk, how not to get cheated by the middlemen and how to care for the buffaloes. My task was to instruct them how to function as a community, how to negotiate and so on. They were living far apart, one here, one there. Just to assemble them, I had to walk eight hours up and down the hills, barely managing to get an attendance of 15 families. These people were far poorer than what I had seen in Banaskantha. One fine day, together with a friend I was staying in a room that before had only been occupied by an old man. We wanted to rent the room, as we often stayed in the village. The tribal man laughed. To him, asking for rent was an urban concept, and completely foreign to him. We could stay in his house for free. One day, when the man was away, we were very hungry. There was a big basket of mangoes in one corner, so we each took two of them. The old man returned, so we offered him one rupee each. When he saw the money, he started crying. 'You are the first person in my life who wants to pay for the food that I have collected,' he said when he calmed down. He used to walk 14 kilometers to the nearby town, and local traders would offer him only one rupee for 100 mangoes. The old man takes that one rupee and goes to the shop. The shopkeeper has swept all the grain, rice and wheat to one side with a broom. And as the old man is a poor tribal man, and unaware of his rights, he holds up his shirt, gets all the swept grain and rice, and walks back home. That's his meal for the day.

After those six months, I wanted to work in the community where I was born. This was in Cambay Taluka, on the shore of the Arabian Sea where BSC was working with Dalits. Here in the plains, poverty is entirely caste based, and people work all day on the farms of the landlords. At that time, around 1980, the law said that if you worked on the farm for eight hours, you had to be paid a minimum wage of seven rupees. But the laborers were only paid one rupee. Also, there were restrictions. If you are an Untouchable, you are not allowed to ride on your bicycle as you come into the village, not allowed to tuck your shirt in your pants, not allowed to play music at weddings, not allowed to put on glasses – nothing that would dilute the distinction between Touchables and Untouchables. If the landlord visits your house, you offer a seat, while you sit on the ground in a submissive position. There was also a lot of sexual exploitation of the women. They were sexually brutalized, while nobody would say a word. If the husband returned from work and found the door closed, he would understand that a high-caste man had entered, doing whatever he wanted with the women. There's a different world that exists in this so-called democratic India.

We held workshops to raise people's awareness. 'We know our rights,' people said. 'But if I want to work, I have to go to their farms. If I want to marry my son, I have to borrow money from a landlord. If my mother dies, I have to do the same for her funeral. If I want buttermilk, if I want to graze my animals...' Their dependency was so great, the only option was to create economic programs. There were thousands of acres of wasteland, but the land is alkaline and very salty, so that not even a blade of grass grows there. But there is an acacia-like bush called Prosopis Juliflora, locally known as Ganda Bawal that is very salt-tolerant. We decided to build a cooperative around this bush to produce charcoal. 'Nonsense', people said. 'That weed has no value whatsoever!' But the roots of this plant go very deep, and the rainwater follows down the roots, which is how the salinity actually decreases. We created forests of these shrubs, and sold the seeds to nurseries.

This cooperative triggered a revolution. We had decided to pay the minimum wages of seven rupees. Nobody could believe that overnight their daily wages had jumped by 700 per cent. The area however had a lot of feudal landlords with hundreds of acres of land. They came to ask the laborers to work on their farms. 'Sure, we'll come to work,' they said. 'But what wages will you pay?' It was their first protest ever and really upset the landlords. It was also the first year ever that there was no agriculture in the village, because nobody went to work. One year later, the landlords realized that nobody would work unless they paid seven rupees. So they did. And then they paid nine. The cooperative kept on gradually increasing the wages so that the landlords too were forced to follow. Due to the absence of irrigation in the area, and the dependency of agriculture on the monsoon, the Dalits normally worked for only two months. After that, they migrated all across the state in search of labor. Now that they had some income, their children could attend school again. After four years one cooperative had grown to seven, so the effects of our work became very visible.

Prologue to a drama
The events in Golana, in 1986, were a different story. A young upper-caste Kshatriya man entered the house of a young girl to have sex with her. Three boys of around 20 who had been to one of the BSC training programs saw this, banged on the door, and challenged the man to come out. The boy inside got scared, jumped out of the window and ran away, leaving behind his shoes, a torch and a towel.

The three boys were jubilant. 'Who the hell gave you the authority to act like this?' the village elders exclaimed. 'We're up against landlords!' The Durbar landlord soon appeared. 'Show me the ones that challenged my son!' he said. 'Like my son, I can do with every woman in this village whatever I want!' Everybody folded their hands, apologizing for the three boys. 'They're young, Bapu (father),' they said, as the feudal rulers always insist on being addressed that way. 'Please forgive them for what they have done.' They addressed this Bapu with bowed heads, terrified of the possible consequences. The landlord left. As a last act of penance, the village Dalit leaders put their hands behind their backs, picked up the shoes, the torch, and the towel with their teeth, taking them all the way to the house of the landlord and dropped it there. Very pervasive, the caste system.

'Pocha, you need to run away, otherwise the landlord will kill you,' said the elder brother of one of the three boys who had challenged the upper-caste man. Next day, Pocha and his brother were going to the farm to till the land and ran into the landlord. 'You must be the culprits, right!' he communicated without saying a word. In the Dalit community, under the influence of the caste system, there are always a few that will hideously slip away and inform the landlord. That's how the Bapus rule. The elder brother lost his balance: 'Pocha, they will kill you. Run away!' Everyone in the community then said that he had lost his mind and that he had to go to a mental hospital in Ahmedabad. Ready to leave the following morning, the three boys slept next to each other. Suddenly, one of them woke up, perhaps to answer nature's call, and found that the elder brother was missing. For hours, they looked everywhere, before looking in the adjacent room. There they saw him hanging. Pocha had committed suicide.

I was still in college, but a senior colleague of mine, Gagan Sethi, and one of the professors worked immensely hard during the time with the community. One of the laws in India says that you cannot own more than a certain amount of land. If you have more, it falls to the Government, which will redistribute it to the landless people with priority to Dalits and tribals. In Golana, the Dalit cooperative had some very fertile land that the Government had taken away from the landlords years ago. But nobody had dared to claim it. 'Let's take possession of those 33 acres,' said the leader of the cooperative. 'But first negotiate.' We sent four emissaries to the panchayat, and called on the Durbar landlords. But they clung to the idea that they were the kings of the region. 'Get lost, all of you!'

I drafted a letter: 'If the Government says tomorrow that we should give back the land, we have no problem. But as the land has been given to us, we will take possession of it. On this day, at eight o'clock, we will come to till the land. If you do anything illegal, you will be held responsible.' Copies were sent to the superintendent of the police, the collector, and the panchayat. When the day came, we started out early to till the land with the tractor. Of the 500 Dalits in the village, everybody had found an excuse, apparently expecting a bloody battle. 'Look,' I said, 'if we don't go today, our story is finished and I cannot stay in the village anymore.' I decided to go no matter what. Our driver took the tractor and I asked the accountant to put his books down and come along. Nearby the land, there was a group of 20 Durbars with sticks. 'Start tilling the land!' I told the driver on the tractor. In total disbelief, the Durbars kept watching us. After some time they all left. In the evening, we celebrated our success. From then on, we planted various crops and tilled the land as our own. The news then spread to many villages.

As their houses were very crowded, the Government gave the Dalits a piece of housing land that was illegally occupied by the landlords. One night, before the Durbars were able to get an injunction order from the court, we took the position that it was ours, and Dalit villagers put small huts all over that piece of land. It was completely legal, but the landlords said: 'For generations we have ruled this area. If this continues, that'll be the end of us!' This time, they did something different. Among the Dalits, there are divisions of sub-castes. We were working with the Vankars. They were the highest sub-caste, the most numerous in the area, and traditionally those who were weavers by trade. There were also leather workers and scavengers, but the only members of the cooperative were Vankars, even though I had argued that we should build an alliance and include all of them. 'No,' said the Vankar leaders. 'The scavengers are

lower than us!' The landlords were clever. They called all the scavengers together at their house, and gave them tea, of course in separate cups and plates from their own caste.
'Has the Government given you anything?'
'No, they haven't.'
'They have only given land to the Vankars.'
'Yes, Bapu.'
'The Government gave them housing. Did they give anything to you?'
'No, Bapu.'
' Look at this cooperative. They only employ Vankars. You're not getting anything out of it.'
'That is true, Bapu.'
'Now, go and break up their huts!'

The Golana massacre
When the Vankars got up on 25 January 1986, and saw that their huts had been damaged, they had a tussle with the scavengers. But the scavengers left all their weapons and sticks behind, and instead of addressing the Vankars, they went to the houses of the landlords. 'Why there?' the Vankars wondered. They then realized that a deeper conspiracy was at play, and decided to go to police station 25 kilometers away. Just as they were boarding a truck to go, around a hundred landlords came into the village, all carrying sticks. Young people seated at the back of the truck escaped, but older people were beaten black and blue, many ending up with broken hands or limbs.

The landlords were mainly looking for the four leaders, my best friends who were the most active in the campaign, one of whom had negotiated with the panchayat on the land issue. My best friend Pocha tried to run away, but he was cornered by the mob, and they gunned him down. The postmortem revealed that he had 99 pieces of shrapnel in his body. 'Your death will not be in vain,' I said when I lifted his body into the hospital. It had so much damage that my hand went inside him. It still haunts me today. Another friend was shot as well. They first humiliated him by making him eat grass. In the end, these 14 so-called upper-caste men killed our friends: Pocha Punja, Prabhudas, Khoda Mitha and Mohan Mitha. Eighteen others were badly wounded, and many houses were set on fire. Later, the event became known as the Golana massacre.

That Sunday evening I was visiting my wife and my son of five weeks at the house of my wife's parents. After dinner, I was sitting holding him in my lap. At 9.30pm the door opened, and some of my friends entered. 'Anything wrong in Golana?' They kept quiet, so I knew something was wrong. I got up, and walked towards them. Later, my wife came in and saw that my son was lying on the floor crying. He had probably fallen to the ground, but I hadn't even noticed it. Golana was the turning point in my life: I saw the reality of caste life close-up. It's one thing to understand it in theory. But when you fight the system, this is what happens. My friends paid for it with their lives. The caste system is not a conflict between two individuals or two groups. It is a systemic phenomenon that you cannot tackle by fighting it in just a few villages. You have to organize the masses. That's the only way. Are we fighting people? Or are we fighting the belief systems and values they share with many others?

One week later, 2,000 Dalit youths from all over Gujarat came, intent on revenge. When I met them in the street, I was completely on my own. 'Come, show us,' they said. 'We will shoot all the upper-caste perpetrators, and cut them to pieces.' In the village, there were no men, for they were all in jail. I raised my hands: 'No, nobody will go any further. We cannot fight their women and children, and the elderly. I won't have anything to do with this.' Still fired up, they insisted: 'No, you are a coward! Let's go!' 'You can only do this over my dead body,' I said. 'If you go into the village and hurt these people, there is no difference between them and us.' To my relief, everyone quieted down. 'If you really want to fight, you should aim to win the case against the men that are now in jail, and set an example. Let's start an organization in every village to see to it that there won't be any fighting. Educate the children not to call the upper-caste people Bapus. That is fighting!'

Next, we called a large meeting with representatives from all 25 villages. 'We're all boarding a train to take a journey from here to Mumbai,' I said. 'The train runs smoothly across the plains. But when the mountain ranges begin, it has difficulty pulling all the carriages, and they put an extra engine at the back to push. Now, we have come to that point where the train needs that extra push. We can go back to the Durbars and tell them: 'Bapu, forgive us for what we did. We will never do it again.' That is one option. The second is this: as a mark of respect to the four people that gave up their lives for this cause, we will fight and carry the journey forward, no matter what happens. But not with violent means.' The people said: 'Yes!' Many contributed to a fund that grew to half a million rupees to fight the legal case.

There had been 147 witnesses to the events. But they had never seen a police station or a courthouse in their lives. So with the help of a new colleague, Vijay Parmar, in my office I set up a mock court, with different people filling the roles of the jury, prosecution, witnesses, defendant and so on. We ran this mock court for almost four months. The effect was so great, that out of the 147 witnesses not a single one dropped out. We won the case. Fourteen people were sentenced to life imprisonment. Nobody could believe it, as they had heard about so many murder cases where people had bribed the court officials or witnesses to turn hostile. It was the largest case in the state of Gujarat, and every village came to know about Golana. During those eight years at BSC we had first worked with 25 villages. After resigning from BSC in 1988, I set up Navsarjan which currently is working in 3,000 villages. I learnt that the leadership has to be local, broadly organized and able to handle the question of fear.

'This is my fight'
'Our approach is constitutional.' That's the stance we took. We should be able to stand in the middle of the village and say in public: 'This is my fight.' If you run away, nobody is going to listen to you. To address the many issues of violence, land rights, women's rights, minimum wages and poverty, I started Navsarjan Trust in 1989. Among the many cases we deal with are those of cruelty and atrocity committed against Dalits. These run in the thousands every year – and that is just in one State. The rate of conviction for criminal offences in India is just four per cent; for cases fought by Navsarjan

Trust it is almost 30. The first issue we undertook focused on the sub-district of Dholka, also known as Taluka that has a 17.5 per cent Dalit population. There was drinking water available, but Dalits were not allowed access to it. In one village, they were only allowed to fill their containers after the buffaloes had been allowed to drink!

Three men on a bench, Palitana, Gujara, 2006 (photo Peter de Ruiter)

We did a quick survey in 50 villages, and found that the problem existed in 42 of them. We mobilized people in committees headed by women, because they mostly take care of providing the drinking water. Next, we marched to the government office. Five women walked in front, with large water jugs on their heads containing the kind of water Dalit people in the village drank: black, muddy, and with things floating around in it. It was a silent march, nobody said a word. Hundreds of other women across different castes joined. 'We all face the same problem,' they said. The women offered the water in the jugs to the deputy collector of the city office: 'If you can drink this water, we have no problems.' Within a month the Government started spending millions of rupees to upgrade the whole water system ensuring that everyone had access to clean drinking water. Out of 42 villages, it was solved in 38.

One day, I learned the role that religion plays. There was a village called Bhetawada, which had about 28 Dalit families that grow roses. The women used to walk a long way to a private tube well owned by Patels, the local dominant caste. 'Listen,' one of the Dalit women said, 'if we buy a hand pump, the cost will only be 8,000 rupees, and we can get water in our own village. If all families put forward 100 rupees, we can raise half the money, and ask the Government to pay the rest.' Navsarjan had offered to contribute 4,000 rupees to the local community, half the cost of the hand pump. But many objected. The idea was dropped as the community didn't agree to match their contribution, insisting that Navsarjan must pay the full amount. With a heavy heart I listened to them and said: 'Look, it can be done!' A year later I returned, and saw a beautiful new temple in the middle of the Dalit locality that had been constructed at the cost of 64,000 rupees, all paid for by the Dalit villagers. But they didn't have 4,000 rupees to save the honor of the women and secure the drinking water. Religion can block your consciousness. It can numb you, and take away your power to be rational. People think the caste system was created by God, and therefore that you can't fight it.

At one point I decided that I wouldn't mind being a volunteer for Navsarjan, as I believe that even good organizations die, if the leadership doesn't want to change. Manjula was elected to become its new director. That has set me free to write children's books, as I realized that the caste system is handed down from one generation to the other through education and socialization. Look at the curriculum! It perpetuates discrimination in the name of values, tradition, religion or culture. This is why caste-based discrimination hasn't been eliminated for 3,000 years – it's a way of life. 'Tell me one thing: are we high or are we low?' I asked a group of schoolchildren without using the word caste. 'We're low,' they said. 'Who told you?' They all turned towards the back where their parents were sitting. This led to another foot march: 'We are neither low nor high, we're all equals.' Throughout the 100-day march, the children in almost 472 villages were asked this question. If you look at the movements of Martin Luther King or Nelson Mandela, they mobilized people's social awareness.

In two years, I have completed 14 books. The central theme focuses on equality, and the books raise questions to stimulate the awareness of young readers. 'How would you (re)design your village?' For critics, that is enough to say: 'Your books are political.' But the caste system needs to be addressed! Look, there are even separate barbers for Dalits, for if they touch a Dalit, they'll be defiled! All the manure is dumped near Dalit houses, because that is where the dirt should be. There are even separate graveyards for Dalits, for upper-caste people fear being polluted even after death. This year, we distributed books to 30,000 children, and set up more than 600 village libraries. Tens of thousands of children are now members of reading clubs. By focusing on primary education and vocational training, I believe that when Dalit children become adults, they will be out of the caste system. In Dalit Shakti Kendra, the Dalit Empowerment Center, in Nani Devti near Ahmedabad, more than 3,000 students have completed a course. They receive vocational training blended with personal development and social skills. Most of them are landless school dropouts. But the Center mobilizes them to escape the cycle of caste-based occupations, and fosters grassroots leadership.

March for a cup of tea
In 2002, we organized a big march called Rampatra: 'Abandon Rampatra, Adopt Bhimpatra.' When I was only 17, I had seen that in every village there is a hole on the outside of the houses in which there is a cup or rampatra. Literally, it means Lord Ram's Vessel. 'Why do they put it there?' I asked. The local people laughed. 'It's Lord Ram's vessel.' 'But if it is a holy thing, what is it doing on the outside of the house?' They explained: 'When you go to the house of the landlord, they'll ask you whether you would like a cup of tea. The cup is outside of the house, and after it is used, it is washed and put back in the hole for somebody else. This is how we too, as Vankars, the higher sub-caste, offer tea to scavengers, the lowest of all.' It got stuck in my mind in 1977, and kept me awake for a whole night. Twenty-five years later I found the answer: the caste system exists, because we cooperate with it. It is maintained by multiple acts of complicity.

I put a map of Gujarat in front of all the Dalits working in our organization. 'Can anybody take a pencil, and circle any of the 3,000 villages we are working for, where there is no Untouchability?' Nobody got up. 'What are we doing then? Why do we exist?' I proposed a foot march, calling everyone to abandon the practice of rampatra. We started in Golana on 25 January 2002, the date of the massacre. A hundred days later, we had passed through 472 villages, covering more than 4,000 kilometers. I think I lost 17 kilograms on the way. Leather workers, scavengers, and even Brahmins found they could drink from the same cup. Shortly before we started the foot march, I redefined the word 'Dalit': 'Dalits are those people who believe in equality, who practice equality, and protest inequality wherever he or she sees it.' Martin Luther King said: 'I am black. I am proud of it, because black is beautiful.' If I say that I am Dalit, and that Dalits practice equality, I can take pride in it. During a conference in Poona with 4,000 attendants, after explaining what 'Dalits' are, I asked anyone that is a non-Dalit to stand up. No one did.

We took five pledges: '(1) I shall not drink tea in rampatra while I live. I shall not offer it. I shall treat everybody as equals. (2) I shall not treat women as inferior to men. (3) I believe in equality, I practice equality, and I protest inequality. (4) I shall teach my children lessons of equality and (5) I shall not practice any faith that tells me that all human beings are not equal.' And also: 'I shall wash my own plate' – to demonstrate that I do not treat women inferior to men. Everybody clapped. But after lunch, 50 men blocked my path.
'No, you cannot wash your own plate. You are a leader, and it would be a shame on our village. What will people say?'
'Well, who would wash the plate if I left it unwashed?'
'There are women to do that.'
'Look,' I said. 'We just clapped for that pledge! I don't mind if the men wash my plate if they wish to show me respect.'
'In that case, we do allow you to wash your own plate.'

When I was finally washing my plate, a hundred women jumped in from nowhere, shouting at the men: 'What are you looking at? Pick up your plates, and follow him!' The children joined in, clapping and encouraging their dads. A very silent revolution. Here at Navsarjan everyone washes their own plate. Some students left, leaving us a note: 'We are men. One day we will die, but we will never do a woman's work.' These are the kinds of poison we carry of the caste system and gender bias. The enemy is something inside, not outside, and it runs from the poorest villages right up to the higher echelons of politics. In my view, you have to take up issues that relate to people's lives like drinking water and land ownership, because that is where their motivation comes from. The land issue had a very tangible result in the form of a new law that stipulates that 3.75 million acres of land will be redistributed to poor people and Dalits. But after 50 years, only one third of that land has been distributed to people, and even that is mostly on paper only.

Civil disobedience and class actions
'We won't fight single cases,' we say, 'only collective ones.' We did a survey in 250 villages, taking us more than a year. In 211 villages, a total land surface of up to 6,000 acres had been legally given to the Dalits, but they had not been able to take possession of it. First we wrote a memo to the Government with 8,000 signatures. This happened in 1997, when we presented to the State what the Dalit agenda should be. We tried to organize a public march, but only two people came. Fear had spread that there might be an attack by feudal landlords. But our second attempt mobilized a mass protest and a public march with 1,500 supporters. The upper-caste people in the villages began to realize that it would be hard to fight back. So we combine mobilizing the people with class actions in the High Court. The ruling was swift: the land should be given to the Dalits immediately. By now, we've already taken possession of more than 4,500 of the 6,000 acres that the fight started for, which are worth billions of rupees. Government representatives were totally taken aback when they saw our beautifully detailed and computerized documentation. It made them realize we are serious. But so are the issues. A man called Gordhanbhai of the village Thoriyali in Surendranagar had been very vocal about the land issues, and had participated with Navsarjan at the World Social Forum in Mumbai. He was murdered. A landlord ran a jeep into him when he was on his motorcycle, killing him on the spot.

While fighting a case in the session court of Surendranagar, somebody wrote a letter to the State High Court saying: 'I predict that tomorrow the accused will be acquitted, because the judge has taken a bribe of 2.5 million rupees.' The judgment was as predicted. We organized a protest march against that judge. In the history of India however, there has never been a single protest march against a judge, because you can be locked up for 'contempt of court'. I have a lot of friends who are High Court lawyers, and two of them said: 'You can't do this, Macwan, for it is contempt of court.' 'It isn't,' I said. 'When that judge delivered his judgment, he was not a judge. He was a corrupt man. I am not taking action against a judge, but against a corrupt official.' The judge got so afraid that he locked his house and ran away. Later, he issued a notice against me and three other colleagues accusing us of contempt of court. But we wouldn't bend to this, even while our act of defiance was laughed at by the present lawyers. As far as I know, the High Court ordered a departmental inquiry against the judge. But the advantage was that when people see you're not afraid when you know you're right, it empowers them.

We're now handling a major case on manual scavenging that arose in a village called Ranpur. When Navsarjan workers went there, they witnessed women head loading night soil in bamboo baskets. Terrible! When it rains, the dirt dribbles down their faces. Scavengers said to us: 'Our brooms are broken, but we don't have money to buy new ones.' A broom costs only two rupees. The local panchayat office gave it in writing that they don't have provisions to buy the brooms. Unheard of, because the scavengers were doing service for the panchayat! The Government simply denied the existence of manual scavenging, as they had 'abolished' it three times. They also accused Navsarjan Trust of paying women to pose for photographs of head loading. 'My Lord,' I asked our lawyer to say on our behalf, 'we offer 100,000 rupees to any person in this court who is willing to pose for a photograph with a basket of human excrement on his head!' The High Court appointed a special commission of inquiry that reported that manual scavenging wasn't only happening in Ranpur, but in every village they had investigated. As a consequence, the Ranpur panchayat was accused of misleading the court, and ordered to pay 5,000 rupees in compensation to Navsarjan. The Government was ordered to immediately bring about a change, and allocate 1,500 million rupees for the rehabilitation of manual scavengers.

Gandhi versus Ambedkar
One of the greatest advocates for Dalit rights was Babasaheb Ambedkar. I always wanted his photo, especially one taken at the time he visited Gujarat. That's his photo there, taken in 1939. For a while, he was working alongside Mahatma Gandhi, to represent the rights of the Dalits. But they didn't get along very well. Ambedkar rejected the special name given by Gandhi to the Dalits, Harijan or 'Children of God', as condescending. Before Independence, there was a system of separate electorates for Muslims, Sikhs, Anglo-Indians, and minority communities in India, to ensure that those elected would represent the masses and their grievances. Ambedkar demanded a separate electorate for the Untouchables. The British agreed, but Gandhi said: 'I cannot accept this, because this is against the Hindus.'

'Repairing the Faults of Society'

Bhimrao Ramji Ambedkar (1891-1956), the man primarily responsible for the Indian Constitution, was born into a Dalit family in Madhya Pradesh. Partly raised by his aunt, who read him the Mahabharata and Ramayana, along with reformist poetry, 'Bhim' was to receive a good education, but humiliation was ever-present. Walking to the front of the class to do a sum at Elphinstone High School, all the other boys jumped up fearing that Bhim would pollute their lunch boxes that were stacked behind the blackboard. As he was an outstanding student, the Maharaja of Baroda allowed him to study at Columbia University in New York. For Bhim it was a short period free of caste prejudices. After his PhD he studied in London, and back in India he worked in the Baroda Civil Service.

Bhimrao Ramji Ambedkar

While lecturing at Sydenham College in Bombay, he founded the newspaper Leader of the Dumb to champion the cause of the Untouchables. He qualified in London as a barrister-at-law, and back in India founded an association to improve the lives of Dalits by setting up hostels, schools and free libraries. 'It is time we rooted out of our minds the ideas of high and low. We can attain self-elevation only if we learn self-help and regain our self-respect.' When seeing that Untouchables were not allowed to drink or draw water from the local water tank, he led a procession and knelt and drank water from it, committed to only agitate peacefully.

At the 1930 Round Table Conference in London, Ambedkar represented the Untouchables. 'Our wrongs have remained as open sores and have not been righted, although 150 years of British rule have rolled away.' Gandhi and Ambedkar disagreed on a separate electorate for

Untouchables. 'I hope that Mr. Gandhi will not drive me to the necessity of making a choice between his life and the rights of my people,' said Ambedkar. Gandhi's fast however forced him into signing a compromise, the Poona Pact (1932). In 1947, Ambedkar became the first Law Minister of India. In the complex changes following India's Independence, he struggled with upper-caste leaders – including Gandhi and Nehru – to end a social system that is still in place today. 'The true function of law consists in repairing the faults of society'.

Having studied law, economics, sociology and politics, he was one of the best qualified persons to write the Draft Constitution, adopted in 1949. 'I appeal to all Indians to be a nation by discarding castes, which have brought separation in social life, and created jealousy and hatred.' Until his death, he relentlessly fought for social reform, embracing Buddhism, and rejecting the caste system as a disease of the mind. 'The sovereignty of scriptures of all religions must come to an end if we want to have a united integrated modern India.'

In the first and last caste-based census of India in 1931, the figures were: 20 per cent Untouchables; 8 per cent tribals; 20 per cent Muslims; 52 per cent Hindus. Ambedkar said: 'You call us Hindus, but we're not allowed to enter any temple. Your Brahmins can only read the scriptures to us, and only worship in our houses. We, the Untouchables, are not Hindus.' A big fight. In Gandhi's view, 52 per cent of Hindus, plus the 8 per cent of tribals and 20 per cent of Untouchables, the balance becomes 80 per cent Hindu, 20 per cent Muslim. This was at the time when Jinnah wanted a separate Pakistan. 'I will die, but never accept the division of Hindus,' Gandhi said. I respect Gandhi very much. He fought against the British for our Independence, and he influenced me a lot. But he made a terrible blunder over the heads of the Dalit population. He went on a fast, leaving Ambedkar no option but to compromise. Suppose Gandhi had died! There would have been mass violence against Dalits all over the country. On 21 September 1932 they agreed in

Poona that all the temples and public places should be open to Dalits, there should be no caste practices, and this should be enshrined in law immediately. Ambedkar signed, Gandhi didn't.

Since our last election in 2009, there are 84 Dalit Members of Parliament. But to be elected, you depend on the votes of the upper castes. There is not a single constituency in the whole of India, where Dalits can win by their own votes. These 84 MPs only represent the interests of political parties. Nothing beyond it. This is exactly what Ambedkar sought to prevent. It is telling enough, that there has never been a single debate in Parliament about manual scavenging. I mean, 84 members is a huge number. You can rock the army or the whole Parliament. I always say: 'There are 16.5 per cent Untouchables in India. But their votes are not Untouchable.

Everybody wants their vote.' And how do you connect between your votes and your rights? By mobilizing people's consciousness. I will never join a political party, because then you can only do one thing: politics. My role is to educate people about their rights. 'What have you ever done on caste, on manual scavenging?' people now ask their MPs. Mobilizing social movement requires that other people's lives take up more space in your life than your own. 'Just have 51 per cent of other people's interest in your life,' I tell my colleagues. 'Leave yourself the remaining 49.'

In the Dalit Empowerment Center, every evening we have a prayer. Five minutes of meditation, for example about the Buddha's wisdom that all the problems you see in the world are inside you, followed by a reading about a current issue, say domestic violence or Barack Obama. I offer my reflections on how these things connect with our lives here and now. Ultimately, every human being has a sense of spirituality that is more to do with values, ethics, understanding and vision. Can we explore that to develop rational thinking and a value-based lifestyle? Upon completion of their training, students make a pledge: 'I will strive to ensure that Dalit Empowerment becomes the way of life in India.' They return to their hometowns with a different consciousness.

Khassan Baiev, Chechnya
Operating on friends and enemies while under fire

'We have no choice but to save the nation,' says surgeon Khassan
Baiev of his native Chechnya. 'Medicine, not politics, is my passion.'
Two wars in the 1990s turned parts of the country into a 'zone of
ecological disaster'. The symbol of a coiled snake representing
renewal and healing became his professional compass. 'You have
golden hands' a clairvoyant once told him, and no doubt many of his
patients would echo these words. Accused by both parties of
operating on the enemy, he stayed true to the Hippocratic Oath, to
the point of having to flee the country. Suffering shell-shock and
trauma, he persisted, one time even saving the life of a family by
operating on their cow. Resisting a rebel commander, he said: 'In this
hospital I give the orders! Whether you like it or not, you will obey!'

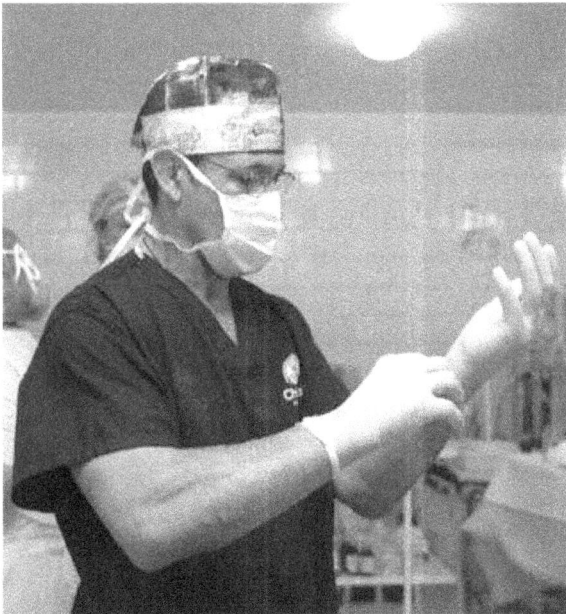

Khassan Baiev in 2008

'In war, there are no winners. It's a hellish thing that victimizes the innocent,' says Dr. Khassan Baiev (born in 1963). During two recent wars with Russia, Chechnya suffered devastation in every way imaginable. Today's relative peace allows him to return and provide help, especially to children. 'Medicine, not politics, is my passion.'

Context

'Little Switzerland' some call the Caucasian mountains of Chechnya with their snow-capped peaks, lakes, and waterfalls. But for most of its history, the country hasn't known the tranquility this nickname suggests. The region that divides Russia from the Middle East, and Christianity from Islam, became prominent in the 1990s, when Chechnya fought a war of independence with Russia. And again in our century.

Chechnya's struggle for independence goes back hundreds of years. In the sixteenth century, the Chechens rebuffed the Russian forces of Ivan the Terrible. In the next century, attempts were made to dominate the region, when Peter the Great sought a route over the Caspian Sea to Persia and India. In the 19th century, General Alexey Yermolov built a series of fortresses in Chechnya and unleashed a policy of annihilation that was so ferocious, even Nicholas I recalled him for excessive cruelty.

Following the Russian Revolution, a new surge of resistance erupted when the North Caucasus declared itself independent in 1918. During the civil war that followed the revolution, the Red Army moved in and imposed Soviet rule. In 1929, Stalin began the brutal collectivization of agriculture throughout Russia, redrawing the boundaries of the mini-states in the Caucasus according to the principle of 'divide and conquer'. Worse still, toward the end of the Second World War, he accused the Chechens of collaborating with the Nazis in the hope of gaining post-war independence. Consequently, the NKVD rounded them up, and deported them to Kazakhstan, Kyrgyzstan and Siberia. Six hundred thousand were shipped off in cattle cars, while about 200,000 died en route. Parts of this tragedy have been described in Alexander Solzhenitsyn's Gulag Archipelago.

When, after glasnost (openness) and perestroika (reform or restructuring), Mikhail Gorbachev stepped down in 1991, and Boris Yeltsin emerged as the new leader of the Russian Federation, Chechen President Jokhar Dudayev was one of the first to declare his support for him. But relations with Moscow soon deteriorated. Surrounded by self-seeking advisers, Dudayev turned Chechnya into a free-trade zone where adventurers, carpetbaggers, mafia operatives, and criminals flourished.

In 1992, a Federation Treaty was signed by 87 of 88 federal subjects. One declined: Chechnya. The following year, it declared full independence as the Chechen Republic of Ichkeria. Yeltsin and Dudayev negotiated, but never arrived at a solution. At the end of 1994, Yeltsin ordered the Russian army to invade, setting off the First Chechen War (1994-1996). Russian Minister of Defense Pavel Grachev expected 'a bloodless blitzkrieg', but the Battle of Grozny alone cost the lives of thousands of civilians. Senior Russian commanders even stepped down saying it was criminal to fight their own people, and more than 800 soldiers resigned in protest.

Chechen guerilla warfare resulted in widespread demoralization of Russian troops. During an assault by the 131st Maikop Motor Rifle Brigade, more than a thousand Russian soldiers lost their lives within 60 hours. The Russian military then resorted to carpet bombing and indiscriminate rocket artillery to pulverize the Chechens into submission, leading former Soviet leader Mikhail Gorbachev to call the war 'a disgraceful, bloody adventure'. The General Staff of the Russian Armed Forces said 3,826 troops were killed, 17,892 wounded, and 1,906 missing in action. Basing itself on information from wounded troops and soldiers' relatives, the Committee of Soldiers' Mothers of Russia put the number of Russian military dead at 14,000. This still excludes the casualties of the kontraktniki, Russia's Special Forces.

Chechen-elected president Aslan Maskhadov traveled to Moscow and signed a treaty with Yeltsin 'on peace and the principles of Russian-Chechen relations'. Maskhadov was optimistic, but unrest continued. The Second Chechen War (1999-2005) was started by Russian forces in response to the invasion of Dagestan, and apartment bombings in Russia blamed on Chechen separatists. After the siege of Grozny, the United Nations called the Chechen capital the most destroyed city on earth. Terrible events took place. One time, Russian forces bombed the village of Katyr-Yurt. Next, they aimed at a convoy under white flags, killing 170 civilians. Writer Emma Gilligan, basing herself on interviews with eyewitnesses and key political and humanitarian figures, believes the key objective of the Russian leadership was to subjugate and punish the Chechen populace.

Vladimir Putin established direct rule of Chechnya in May 2000, appointing Ramzan Kadyrov interim head of the pro-Moscow Government. A new Chechen Constitution was passed in 2003 in a referendum generally considered as deeply flawed. It granted the Chechens a considerable amount of autonomy, but still tied firmly to Russia. For some, the war ended there. For others, notably those that boycotted the ballot, peace is still elusive, especially as brutalities, arbitrary arrests, extortions, torture and murders continue. Basic social services and education are difficult to maintain. Chechen field commander Shamil Basayev launched a campaign of terrorism inside Russia by bombing a Stravropol train, the Moscow metro, and an aircraft. The siege of a school in Beslan alone cost the lives of 386 civilians.

Many areas of the country are now an environmental wasteland with oil spills, damaged sewers, as well as chemical and radioactive pollution. In 2004, the Russian Government designated a third of Chechnya as a 'zone of ecological disaster'. Today, to escape the 'peace', many Chechens seek asylum in Russia. Infant mortality in Chechnya remains high, and there are reports of a growing number of genetic disorders in babies and among schoolchildren. One Chechen child in 10 is born with some kind of anomaly. According to UNICEF, between 1994 and 2008 about 25,000 children lost one or both of their parents. A whole generation shows symptoms of psychological trauma.

Adults suffer too. The prospect of running in to burly men wearing face masks still haunts many citizens. In early 2015, such men forced their way into the office of Memorial Human Rights Center in Gudermes, Chechnya's second largest city. They pelted the staff, two women, with eggs. Meanwhile, these women feared a fate similar to that of their former colleague Natalia Estemirova, who was killed in 2005. The men screamed: 'This is for supporting Kalyapin.' Igor Kalyapin, head of the Joint Mobile Group of Russian human rights organizations in Chechnya, had filed a complaint regarding the public threat by Kadyrov to expel relatives of insurgents and burn their homes to the ground. A dozen homes were torched.

'I can deal with eggs,' said Kalyapin, 'but what if my colleagues in Chechnya will be pelted with grenades tomorrow?' Two days later, their Grozny office was set ablaze. While attending a rally against enforced disappearances, the Mobile Group's activists were pressed to go to the city hall for a 'detailed conversation.' This proved to be a meeting with Kadyrov and prominent officials, filmed by a television crew. Thus, the situation remains very risky, reinforced by public threats of Kadyrov himself. The journey towards a safe public space may be a long one.

The last of the two wars finished a decade ago. Working during both wars to help the wounded, Dr. Khassan Baiev wrote a diary whenever there was a lull in the bombings, often hour by hour. Sometimes he used code words and abbreviations, for fear his notes might fall into the wrong hands. The images of the wars still haunt him. But Dr. Baiev decided to join forces with the International Committee for the Children of Chechnya (ICCC). Today, as its chairman, he frequently returns to Chechnya for months, to help children in every way he can. Due to the language barrier, next to the interview Dr. Baiev's book The Oath: A Surgeon under Fire (Walker Books, 2003) has served as the main source for this chapter. With special thanks to Nicholas Daniloff of the Northeastern School of Journalism and the translations provided by Dr. Baiev's daughter Maryam. Dr. Baiev tells his story at his home near Boston: 'We have no choice, but to save the nation.'

Personal narrative — Khassan Baiev

We are a very small nation, but with very strong traditions. Without them, we would not have survived. The czars labeled us 'savages' and 'cutthroats'. The Soviets called us 'traitors' and 'Nazi sympathizers'. During the recent wars we were 'bandits', and after 9/11 'international terrorists'. But I want people to know the truth about Chechnya, the good and the bad.

'I was making bread one day, and rolled you out of the dough,' my mother said when I asked where I came from. I was born in Alkhan Kala in 1963, four years after my family returned from exile in Kazakhstan, and 30 minutes before my twin brother Hussein. Despite that, Hussein was taller and more robust, while I suffered a caved-in chest and bowed legs.

My parents, Dada and Nana, had lived through the repressions of 1937, and the Deportation of 1944. Stalin's police threw the unwilling and the infirm over the edge of a ravine. 'Including our cousins Karim and Uzum,' Dada said. Others were forced to walk to Vedeno to be shipped like cattle to Kazakhstan across 'the Road to Death'. Returning from exile, they found themselves third-class citizens in their own country. Their houses had been taken over by Cossacks, Russians, Ukrainians, Armenians and others who accused them of being 'traitors'. And this while my father was a war veteran, the sole survivor of his unit in Finland and he had also served in Murmansk. During Soviet times you only talked about the Deportation behind closed doors and in hushed voices. Chechens, Georgians, Ukrainians, Armenians – the history of Russia, is very bloody. As I grew older, I came to understand what my parents had endured, and vowed to do everything in my power to make their lives easier.

Until 1991, when the economy collapsed, Alkhan Kala had a large poultry farm, a grain elevator, and a large wood-processing plant that exported furniture and wood products all over the Soviet Union. Nana baked our bread, we milked the cows and grew our own food. Waking in the morning, I watched the peaks of Mount Kazbek and Elbrus emerge out of the mist. Mount Ebrus is the mountain where legend says the Greek gods chained Prometheus for stealing their fire. During the wars with Russia, when I felt my sanity slipping, looking at those peaks gave me a sense of calm.

I remember the fast-paced notes of father's accordion. He would wake up Hussein and me in the middle of the night for the lezghinka. 'Time to dance!' We jumped up almost simultaneously, and my mother and sisters also came out. 'You shouldn't bother with sports,' my father said. 'Leave it to Hussein.' But being a weakling filled me with shame. How could I defend the fatherland, women, children, and the elderly – all the things that the family elders said were important? So, one summer when I was 13, my life began to turn around with the help of a judo coach named Vakha Chapaev. After a game of soccer, he taught a group of boys judo and sambo, a self-defense sport invented in Russia in the 1930s. One day, when looking after the grazing of the cows, I swam across the Sunzha River. Vakha looked me up and down as I stood there dripping in my knee-length black 'family underpants'. We called them that, because in a good Soviet family, one size was supposed to fit all.

When the weather turned cold, we took a bus to Grozny to get trained there, and sometimes we rode freight trains. Hussein and I became more familiar with the train schedule than our arithmetic tables. A few weeks before my fourteenth birthday, I won first prize at the Grozny All-Russian Junior Championship. I felt as though I had won the Olympics. 'What's this?' Dada said. 'You snuck off when you were supposed to be in the pastures with the cows!' He unbuckled his belt, and thrashed me in the kitchen. Like most Chechen fathers, he never displayed affection or paid me compliments. Strange as that may seem to westerners, we believe that praise weakens you and education is designed to make you resilient to hardship. We believe love is demonstrated by action, not words. So to my mind, love is loyalty and support of family and friends; love is education of children; love is helping the elderly.

Middle School No. 1 was one of the best Russian-language schools. One of my schoolmates was Shamil Basayev, who grew up to become Chechnya's notorious field commander. I learned about the czars, studied Russian grammar, and recited the poems of Pushkin and Lermontov. But if you spoke Chechen at school, the teachers punished you. In the end many children in urban areas didn't know their native tongue. I fantasized about becoming a doctor, but never talked about it because of my poor school grades. One morning Dada whipped us out of bed. He forced us through the streets and into the classroom dressed in our underpants. 'Here they are! Two slackers!'

Every summer, Dada moved the family to his ancestral village of Makazhoi, located 75 miles southeast of Alkhan Kala. The winding mountain roads made me feel as though I was traveling back in time. We planted potatoes, wheat, sunflowers and corn, and all summer we mowed hay. I loved to hear the stories of the elders, especially about the heroes of the Chechen resistance against the Russians, like Sheikh Mansur and Imam Shamil. An old man with a long white beard once showed me the sword of the great Shamil. A man who had fought along with Shamil, Baysangur, was caught in 1859, and the Russians tried to hang him. 'A reward for anyone who will kick the stool out from under him,' they said. But Baysangur kicked the stool from under himself. 'Chechens don't surrender,' the old man said, replacing the sword in its sheath. 'It's not in our nature.'

Symbol of healing
Thanks to my reputation in judo, 18 cities around the Soviet Union invited me to attend. The Soviet system placed a huge emphasis on sports as a way to demonstrate the superiority of communism. In 1980 I traveled to Krasnoyarsk in Siberia with my school friend Musa Salekhov to apply to the Institute of Law. I liked the city, and strolling along the Yenisei River. One day we came across a building with a symbol. Not the usual head of Lenin or the Soviet hammer and sickle, but a coiled snake. The symbol related to medicine: as the snake sheds its skin every year, it represents renewal and healing. I said to Musa: 'Let's forget about law school, and apply to the Medical Institute tomorrow!' As I ascended the stone staircase of the Medical

Institute to submit our applications, halfway up I stopped to read a text in Cyrillic letters: 'I will use my power to help the sick to the best of my ability and judgment; I will abstain from harming or wronging any man by it.' It was the Hippocratic Oath.

As there were no rooms available, Musa and I slept in the airport lounge. After studying and training, we curled up in our blue wool sweat suits with the homeless until a female voice announced the first flights of the next day. I was accepted, and took dentistry as my specialty, hoping to develop later as a plastic surgeon. But gynecology and obstetrics were also required. 'Who knows,' the professor said, 'you might end up on some state farm far away from anywhere, and be the only one around who can deliver a baby.' The first time in a delivery room, I was very apprehensive. But after I eased the little wet body of a baby, a boy, out of the birth canal and cut the umbilical cord, and three more babies, I lost my fear.

Whenever I went to an athletic competition, I carried two bags: one for clothes, one for books. At the Medical Institute I met Russians of my age for the first time, and was shocked. The boys sometimes drank beer during lectures, smoked, cursed, and told dirty jokes. They started teasing me: 'Khassik, we want to tell a good one – please leave the room.' I did have a relationship with a Russian girl called Marina. But by then I had become so focused on a career in medicine, I no longer had time for emotional entanglements. Looking back, I don't think I would have survived the recent Russian-Chechen wars without my dual training as an athlete and as a doctor. Krasnoyarsk had prepared me for this future ordeal.

In 1983 there were the World Youth Championships in Spain. Before I left, an official of the Krasnoyarsk KGB summoned me telling me to report on other team members. 'An informer? My father would shoot me if he found out I had done such a thing!' I refused. We were scheduled to fly from Moscow's Sheremetyevo airport. Once seated in the plane, I heaved a sigh of relief. At long last, my dream was coming true. But then I felt a tap on my shoulder. 'Follow us. We will explain,' two men said. When they left, I flopped down in the waiting room, deflated.

In May 1988, I returned to Grozny. With its shade trees, parks, fountains, and alleys lined with flowers, Grozny was the most attractive city in the North Caucasus. But the atmosphere had changed. Glasnost and perestroika had created chaos after Mikhail Gorbachev came to power in 1985. I accepted a job in the trauma department of the 700-bed First City Emergency Hospital, treating victims of car accidents, burns, tumors and congenital defects. I felt much satisfaction after treating patients, and returning them whole to the world. 'You have golden hands,' a Moscow clairvoyant called Juna once told me. 'You were meant to be a jeweler.' Instead of gold and precious stones, I worked with slivers of bone, muscle, and skin.

One Sunday morning, I was urgently summoned to the hospital. Zura, a 22-year-old bride, had been rushed to the emergency room with multiple skull fractures due to a head-on collision with a truck. The chief surgeon however said: 'You're only a dentist! We'll send her to Dagestan.' Zura's relatives were even less enthusiastic. 'He looks more like a prizefighter than a surgeon,' her sister said. But the chief surgeon relented, and had a team of experienced doctors observe and assist me. After a six-hour operation, Zura began to recover. Her family invited me to their home to thank me. A strict Muslim may question the practice of cosmetic surgery, because the Koran says you shouldn't alter what Allah gave you. That may be true, but I saw myself as a sculptor who could repair birth defects, and restore people's well-being.

Medicine, not politics
Storm clouds gathered on the horizon, and talk of independence was everywhere. But no one really believed that a war would happen. General Jokhar Dudayev believed our country's oil and mineral water could bring about an enormous change. 'We will live in mansions with golden faucets like they have in Kuwait,' he promised. I didn't know what to make of his vision. 'Medicine, not politics, is my passion,' I told my friends. How could Chechnya possibly survive economically if not on friendly terms with Russia? On 1 November 1991, Chechnya declared its independence, and secession from the Russian Federation.

While stirring the borscht, my sister Malika said: 'The elders are beginning to ask if you have a family in Krasnoyarsk, and secretly married a Russian woman there.' I made several awkward efforts to find a wife, until I met Zara, whom I remembered as a small girl on the bus. She had turned into an attractive woman with dark curly hair, a mischievous smile, and she worked in a jewelry store. The wedding date was set for 19 September 1992.

For a short while I was away in Moscow for an internship on plastic and reconstructive surgery, together with Musa. 'Russian propaganda depicts us all as Mafiosi,' Musa said angrily. They called us chornie zhopy (black asses) behind our backs.

Trouble flared up in Ingushetia that summer. I flew back with Chechen and Ingush businessmen in a chartered plane carrying medical supplies. Next, I worked in Ingushetia for several weeks – my introduction to war. I wasn't prepared for what I saw, like the corpse of a young girl who had been raped and burned with cigarettes all over her body. I returned home troubled, feeling that if this could happen in Ingushetia, it could happen in Chechnya. After the birth of my daughter Maryam in 1997, I went back to Moscow to work at the Medical Institute. My sideline activity was selling truckloads of cigarettes imported from England, simply by making phone calls to line up buyers. Before long, it allowed Zara, Maryam and myself to move out of our apartment into a fancy house off the highway, not far from government dachas. For a while, Zara and I wore designer clothing. I even had a Lincoln car, but it embarrassed me. One night, when it was stolen, I actually felt as if a burden had fallen from my shoulders. I didn't even bother telling the police. Not that it mattered. Auto theft was one of their sidelines.

When I stepped from the plane at Grozny airport again, I was startled to see how militarized the city had become. On my way to the First City Emergency Hospital, I saw people lining up for food. At the hospital, plastic bags, cigarette packets, and newspapers were scattered all over the courtyard. Inside, you couldn't tell staff from patients or relatives. Doctors now asked patients to supply everything: medicine, bandages, food, nursing care, even fuel for the emergency generators and heating. Near the Presidential Palace stood a burnt-out tank with three incinerated corpses of young Russian soldiers. No longer could I in good conscience be in Moscow doing facelifts for wealthy patients. I decided to take a job at the hospital. 'War is a terrible thing,' my father said. 'Doctors are always in the line of fire.' The poor couldn't buy supplies, so I devised a scheme: well-off patients received a list of hospital supplies for their treatment, followed by a request to triple the amount for those who couldn't afford it.

At the end of August, sporadic bombing began over Grozny. As Malika and I were driving home after work one day, an explosion rocked the car, and almost overturned it. The bomb had left a hole of about 15 feet across and six feet deep. I saw three burnt-out cars with drivers and passengers cremated in their seats. A decapitated man, somebody's arm, wounded people, corpses, and bloody items of clothing littered the street. The stomach of an elderly woman was split open, her colon and small intestines splattered in the dirt. The evening was chilly, so a steamy vapor rose from her entrails. Many rescuers were returning from the market, and they emptied their shopping bags for the gruesome task of gathering body parts.

Under Soviet rule for more than 70 years, we were supposed to be living in harmony and many of us had good Russian friends. How could Russia bomb its own citizens? Grozny, where half the inhabitants were Russians? The Soviet system may have collapsed, but the mentality of the people hasn't changed. We piled sandbags in the hospital windows. In the end, the thud of bombs became like the buzz of an annoying fly in the background. In the midst of gunfire, my wife delivered my son Islam through a cesarean. After we dropped the doctors off at their apartments, we started for Alkhan Kala, driving slowly without lights over the potholed streets, fearing the slightest bump would burst Zara's stitches.

Sometimes there were as many as 25 air raids a day. People fled the city, some to refugee camps in Ingushetia, some to their mountain villages, leaving mostly ethnic Russians. I felt sorry for them, because they too considered Grozny as their home. Women throughout the republic called for a peace march. Eventually, they created a column that stretched 40 miles from Grozny to the border of Ingushetia where the Russian tanks waited. When I passed them, some of them formed a circle, and performed the zikr, an ancient ritual that stems from Sufism. But the Russians advanced anyway. On 31 December 1994, a bomb hit the Kavkaz Hotel. Our elder, Khamzat Elmurzayev, a 55-year-old surgeon said: 'We can't stay here any longer. We all need to go home to our villages and set up medical centers.' I packed my operating table and instruments into the car and headed home. Just in time. In the first minutes of New Year's Day 1995, the Russian army launched a massive tank assault on Grozny.

Hospital under siege
I told my friend Ruslan Ezirkhanov that I wanted to open a hospital, and the elders of Alkhan Kala consented. Volunteers poured in, and before long I had a workforce of more than 100 people. We called upon the mosque for beds and bedding. I had some supplies from my own, and the rest came from Grozny: glucose packets, antibiotics, anesthetics, and suture kits donated by the Red Cross, Doctors Without Borders, and Doctors of the World. I told Zulai, a seamstress to sew a red cross onto a large white sheet. We flew the flag from the 10-foot pole above the hospital. Then the wounded began coming in from Grozny, along with a flood of refugees, including many Russians. Locals took them in, sometimes as many as 20 people to a room. Each morning, I climbed to the attic of our house and looked over the valley through the old military binoculars given to my father by a Russian soldier during the Second World War. On the horizon, I saw the tanks, sitting like predatory animals, their barrels pointed in our direction. Helicopter gunships terrified the population. They flew so close, you could see the gunners feeding in the ammunition belts. At the hospital, blood was always in short supply, so the nurses, the security guards, and myself gave blood regularly. Nana refused to leave. 'Someone has to milk the cows and feed the chickens,' she said.

On 17 January 1995, a missile struck the roof of the hospital. I staggered to my feet, and felt my way along the corridor, stepping over piles of plaster and broken glass. Near the entrance lay seven or eight wounded men, their blood trickling onto the floor. Fear gripped me. The flag with the red cross lay in tatters under the rubble. So much for the protection of the Geneva Convention! I managed to convince my parents to join the rest of the family in Urus-Martan. A mass of cars, carts, tractors, buses and trucks choked the road out of town. Women and children screamed in panic as long-range Russian artillery shelled them. Dead and wounded lay at the side of the road.

Chechen fighters continued to penetrate the Russian lines. But 100,000 citizens still remained in the city, trapped in bunkers or dying in the rubble of their apartments. The Russians used fragmentation bombs. These are slowed by parachutes, and explode before hitting the ground, splitting into dozens of smaller bomblets designed to cause maximum human casualties. At one time a young Russian soldier and a young Chechen fighter were on the same ward discussing their wounds. 'These boys shouldn't be away from their mothers,' our women said. Our elders said it was all right to feed them so long as they are not kontraktniki. For them, Chechnya was just an opportunity to loot and rape. The presence of Russian soldiers put the hospital at risk, so I would discharge them as soon as possible. Nine days later, when I was working at the hospital of Atagi, the hospital was hit. 'You're injured,' someone shouted. I looked down, and saw the blood dripping out of the bottom of my sweatpants. In a hospital in Dagestan, I lay in coma for four days. Eight of the hospital staff had died in that attack. As soon as I was able to walk, I left. It takes time to recover from a concussion, but I had to get back to work!

Going from village to village, I treated patients on kitchen tables, on beds, in basements, and on the street, often without heat, without water, without anesthesia, only lighted by candles or kerosene lamps. Driving back into Grozny I passed through a number of checkpoints, but at the fifth a spetsnaz of the Russian Special Forces, a huge man of about 40 approached me. 'Get out!' he barked. 'So you have been up in the mountains operating on dukhi,' he said. He meant Chechen fighters. During the Russian-Afghan war, the Russian soldiers called the mujahedeen dukhi – spirits or phantoms – because they crept in, attacked and disappeared.

'I operate on the wounded,' I said.

'So... on cheki?'

Three men grabbed my arm and propelled me in the direction of a large house surrounded by an eight-foot brick fence. One look at the house, and I knew there was a good chance that if I went in, I would never come out. Inside, one wall was pockmarked with bullet holes, and stained with blood and dried hair.

'We'll teach you to operate on dukhi,' a kontraktnik with a vodka-flushed face shouted, shoving me against the wall. They shouted obscenities.

'Cover the bandit's eyes, so we can shoot him!'

'You can shoot me, but I will not close my eyes!'

'Cover his eyes, or he will come back to haunt us.'

Suddenly, a door burst open, and a Russian major emerged. 'What the hell is going on here?'

'I'm a doctor!' I seized the moment. 'Where's the law that says you have the right to shoot me for being a surgeon and treating the wounded?'

The major looked me up and down, and snapped at the others. 'Leave him alone!'

He turned to me and got straight to the point. 'My wife is a surgeon, and out of respect for the profession, I will let you go. You escaped this time, but next time you'll be executed.'

When I got back to my car, I was like a zombie. Returning home, I saw so many corpses that soldiers wore handkerchiefs over their faces to block the smell. An old woman dragged a cart filled with plastic bags and boxes. A rat scuttled across her path. Scores of burnt-out Russian tanks, army personnel carriers, and jeeps littered the streets. One body had been picked clean by dogs. All that remained was the back of the head protected by a helmet, and a foot covered in a boot. A military truck rumbled by piled with human bones. As it hit a rut, a spinal column and collarbone fell onto the street, to be crushed into the mud by an armored personnel carrier. A dog leapt into the air, yelping in pain as a soldier emptied his rifle into it. But my fears evaporated. On this day Allah was with me, and I was not going to die.

In early April enormous explosions could be heard near Samaskhi. When the Russians finally allowed medical personnel to enter, they saw it was a bloodbath. The Russians had just lobbed grenades in the basements, torched the houses and rained down bombs. From the remaining houses, they then loaded their trucks with video recorders, television sets, carpets and furniture. The first thing I saw when going in with the Red Cross, was the burned body of a baby in fetal position. While treating the wounded, I heard stories of young men that had been dragged with chains behind personnel carriers, Russian aviators that had thrown Chechen prisoners out of their helicopters, and a girl raped in front of her father. One soldier had even thrown a newborn baby into the air, and then shot it dead in the air. More than 200 people had died. Painted on the side of a troop carrier were the words 'General Yermolov', a reminder of the cruelty that this 19th-century Russian general visited on the North Caucasus.

By now, the Russians had set up a puppet government in Grozny. One month later, 14 June 1995, Shamil Basayev and his men crossed from Chechnya into Russia. Motivated by the massacre in Samaskhi, Bamut, and other villages, they wanted to take action to bring the war to an end. But Russian troops forced them to withdraw, so they took over a hospital in the town of Budyonnovsk, holding more than 1,500 people hostage. After lengthy negotiations, something unusual happened. Prime Minister Viktor Chernomyrdin had a telephone conversation with Basayev that was broadcast live over national radio. Basayev agreed to leave if the Russian Government would guarantee safe passage for himself and his men back to Chechnya. But the bombing and fighting continued.

Fighters and civilians
'Soldiers are asking for you,' said the 10-year-old son of our neighbor. Outside, against the fence were young recruits from Krasnoyarsk: Seriozha, Kostya, and Ivan. 'We can't take it any longer. We want out!' they said. 'The kontraktniki beat us up all the time. We have nothing against you Chechens. We don't know why we're here,' Seriozha said. 'Please help us. If you contact our parents, our mothers will come for us.' Our tradition of hospitality required us to

treat them as guests. They ate and slept with our family and did odd chores such as chopping wood or mending broken machinery. 'You must observe our rules,' I said to them. 'No smoking inside the house, no drinking, no bad language, no dirty jokes and no going around without a shirt in front of the women.' Zara cooked up a huge frying pan of potatoes, and Malika laid out homemade bread, salted tomatoes, and cucumbers. 'If this goes on, you'll all turn into Chechens,' I joked one day when they stood waiting at the kitchen table for Dada to sit down first. 'The Russian authorities never told us that we were coming to Chechnya, and we didn't even have basic training,' the boys said. 'They lied to us, to our parents, and to the Russian people!' One by one the Russian mothers started arriving. But Mother Russia would see these boys as traitors. She was unlikely to forgive.

One day, as I opened the front gate of my parents' house, there were heavily armed Chechen fighters. One of them introduced himself as Vakha Dzhafarev. 'Please come with us,' he said. The driver negotiated narrow mountain roads until we arrived at an underground chamber camouflaged with heavy branches. On one of the cots lay a heavily bearded figure, his face swathed in bloody bandages, his breathing heavy and labored. A bullet had penetrated the right cheekbone, shattering both sinuses and the nasal bones, and exited beneath the left eye. 'You'll have to shave his beard,' I said, pointing to the scraggly mass of long hair, matted with blood and bits of tissue.
'We can't,' Vakha said. 'Don't you know who this is?!' I shook my head.
'This is Salman Raduyev, our leader. We can't remove his beard.' Now I understood. Raduyev was the most famous Chechen field commander, known for his intemperate outbursts.
'I don't care if this man is Allah himself,' I said to the men. 'If you don't shave him, I can't work on him, and if I can't work on him he'll die. And, by the way, I'm going to need an assistant.' Tufts of hair fell, and minutes later a tall Russian man appeared. 'My name is Sasha,' he said. 'I'm a doctor.' I didn't have time to find out what a Russian doctor was doing in a rebel hideout. I inserted into a vein a drip of Polyglukin, and injected the commander with a local anesthetic. The

men kept asking: 'What are his chances? You know your life will be in danger if he dies.' 'Only Allah can guarantee someone's survival,' I said.

Sasha was a captain in the Russian Medical Corps and had been captured a few months earlier. The Chechen rebels planned to use him as a bargaining chip. I hatched my own plan, and convinced the field commander to let Sasha help me in the hospital in Urus-Martan, until it was time for the exchange of prisoners. To Sasha I joked: 'You are our 'Prisoner of the Caucasus,' referring to a Pushkin poem of the same name. He grabbed my arm. 'The brother of the field commander was murdered in a filtration camp. His family demands I be shot in revenge.' In filtration camps the Russians weeded out fighters from peaceful civilians.

A couple of days later, Sasha was operating on the broken nose and jaw of a refugee woman from Grozny. I watched him give her a shot of lidocaine, and thought: what has he done that he has to die? Suddenly, I made the decision. I knew I couldn't live with my conscience if I didn't do what I could to save Sasha. 'Tomorrow morning at 10 o'clock, my car will be at the back of the hospital,' I whispered. 'Get in and wait for me.' Sasha didn't say anything; he just reached over and shook my hand. The next morning, I was flagged down at several checkpoints. But I handed them the usual pack of cigarettes. Looking straight ahead I said to Sasha: 'Never, never tell them how you escaped.' 'I will never betray you,' he responded.

A few days later, bearded men in camouflage asked me: 'Is the number of your car M 0009 NM? You helped the Russian doctor escape. We have witnesses.' They shoved me into a jeep, blindfolded me, and after some dirt roads the jeep came to a stop. 'Maybe you'll remember helping the Russian doctor after a few nights down there.' The man pointed the barrel of his rifle down into a deep hole, and ordered me down a ladder. I counted 17 rungs before I reached the bottom. The ladder was then hauled up, and they dropped planks over the hole. Escape was impossible. 'Tell us where Sasha is!' someone shouted down to me. I felt a sense of anger mixed with shame. After all, these were Chechen men who were holding me in a pit! My own people! I started to lose hope. After about a week, a guard lowered the ladder and ordered me to the surface. When I reached the top, I was blinded by the light. 'If you didn't help him escape, then why did you make an appeal for his life?' a rebel asked. 'Because I needed help in the hospital,' I said. 'Say your prayers, and get ready to die.' I knelt and prayed for my family, my parents and sisters, for Zara and our children. But suddenly I heard an automobile horn sounding, and everyone turned to the cloud of dust caused by an approaching car. A man leaned out of the window waving his arm wildly. 'Stop!' he yelled. 'Don't kill him! He's not the one!' Inexplicably, I had been spared.

Word of honor
Whenever I heard a noise at night, my heart raced. I broke out into a sweat and had difficulty breathing. In April 1996 we noticed an increase in troops and military equipment in Alkhan Kala, watching, waiting, ready to strike. The people verged on hysteria. One evening, Ruslan, the chairman of the local council, came to my house. 'The Federals demand 50 rifles from each of the surrounding villages. If we don't produce them, we'll get the same treatment as Samashki.' The next morning I put on a clean shirt and tie, and with two elders walked to the Russian military camp with a white flag on a long stick. A photographer accompanied us to document the meeting in case the Russians wanted to deny that it ever happened. The Russians also assembled a delegation: a general, two colonels, two majors, and a lieutenant.
'This is Khassan, our doctor,' Ruslan said.
'Not the Khassan who saved Sasha?' The general scrutinized me.
'I don't know any Sasha,' I said.
'You worked in Urus-Martan? And you live in Alkhan Kala?'
'Yes.'
'So it was you that saved Sasha.' I kept denying it.
'Alright, alright. It will remain between us. What you did for Sasha I will not forget, and I will do everything I can to save Alkhan Kala.'
'You're a general,' I said. 'Everything depends on you. Not much depends on me.'

To our surprise, we found that 300 resistance fighters had gathered in an abandoned warehouse, wanting to defend us. Allah preserve us! If the Russians had any inkling of this, they would pulverize us. 'How can you trust them,' the commander said. 'The Russian general promised me it won't happen.' I felt stupid saying this, especially as many of these men had become resistance fighters because sisters, brothers, wives or children had been killed by the Russians. The next morning I went back alone. 'You have my word of honor,' said the Russian general. 'That is, if there are no incidents from your side. We will check passports, and then we will leave the village.' At 11am, the Russian troops moved in, going from house to house. The women offered them food and water. One came out of her house holding her passport. 'Hey synok (sonny), don't you want to see this?' This lightened the mood of the soldiers. After the Russians withdrew, Ruslan and I slaughtered a sheep for them, scrounged up 12 rifles and 20 bottles of vodka. Finding the vodka was almost as difficult as finding the rifles. The fighters had remained in the warehouse undetected.

Despite warnings, people continued to tread on mines, especially when they went out to collect firewood. Also, new family concerns troubled me. My 15-year-old nephew Ali began slipping away to help the fighters. In August that year, the Chechen fighters finally drove the Russian army out of Grozny. 'Operation Jihad' they called it. Explosions followed mortar fire sounding like muzikanty (musicians), as we called the syncopated gunfire that erupted almost every night. From the window I watched helplessly as helicopter gunships launched rockets at the Fourth City Hospital, killing doctors and nurses who were my friends. There were times in which I could hardly control my anger, and in which I was tempted to exchange my scalpel for a gun. 'You're dead!' shouted a small boy when I walked onto the street one day. 'No, I killed you first. Fall down!' Fifteen kids of all ages, including girls, were playing 'war', oblivious to the war all around them. Refugees fled, fear and exhaustion on their faces, just like Soviet wartime films of 1942 and 1943 I had seen in my childhood.

On my way back to Alkhan Kala, suddenly I heard the sound of helicopters. People screamed, dropped their bundles, grabbed their children and ran in all directions. Rockets exploded near a stalled bus with women and children, setting it on fire. Two small boys had been thrown out of the bus, and were screaming in shock. I grabbed them, pressed them to my chest, ran into the woods, and dove into an old bomb crater covering the two boys with my body. The helicopters continued firing. 'Help me! Help me!' screamed a woman with a torn leg, and a man blinded by a shell. I finally emerged from the woods again, and stood dazed amid discarded belongings, a child's jacket, a single sneaker, a stuffed animal, and bullet casings everywhere. A neighbor from Alkhan Kala spotted me. 'Get in. I'll take you home.'

Russian Prime Minister Viktor Chernomyrdin signed an agreement full of lofty ideals about preserving human rights, the rights of ethnic minorities, and the right of Chechen self-determination. The Russian checkpoints disappeared, public transport resumed services and people believed that it was safe to rebuild. But crimes by unruly warlords increased, and kidnapping became a principal source of income countrywide. 'The 400-year-old conflict has been brought to an end,' said Colonel Aslan Maskhadov. But the stamina of the people that had held up so well during the fighting, now collapsed during the 'peace'. A French physician from Doctors Without Borders said: 'The Russians don't need to bomb you anymore. In the future your people will die off like flies from the ecological devastation caused by the war.'

I solved some of my financial problems by taking private patients for cosmetic surgery after-hours at the hospital. Occasionally, I was called upon to operate on Salman Raduyev, the controversial field commander I had helped in the mountain hideout. The media in Moscow called him 'Titanik' because of the titanium plates and wires holding his skull together. Operating on him put me in considerable danger. One time someone slipped a note under my door: 'If you continue to keep Raduyev alive, the next time you'll be killed.' Raduyev was an exasperating patient who never followed my instructions. One time, after an operation, he harangued a crowd, setting off the bleeding. We needed blood urgently. 'No problem!'

Raduyev said. 'My people will donate. Take 50 of them, 100, as many as you need.' He was a cat with nine lives, and it seemed I was called upon to preserve him – a role I didn't enjoy.

The only thing that will help
In the summer of 1998 I went to Moscow again to spend a few months learning the latest skin-grafting techniques. Everything there was westernized as Russia embarked on capitalism. Instead of cheering me up, Moscow reminded me of how far Chechnya had fallen behind. We were in the Stone Age. One day, I was asked to operate on a Russian soldier. An old Russian friend pulled me aside. 'It's best not to say you're Chechen.' But the patient was already anesthetized. After I performed a successful operation I turned to the surgical team. 'When the patient comes to, tell him it was a Chechen who operated on him. Let the medical staff in the hospital know. For now, my thanks. It was a pleasure working with you.'

Often without warning, I was overwhelmed by feelings of sadness and a terrible darkness enveloped me. Several times I contemplated jumping out of the window to end it all. I stayed in a clinic for 45 days, dosed with tranquilizers, and attended sessions with the psychiatrist and hypnotist. I was suffering from post-traumatic stress disorder. Periodically I went out to a kiosk to buy snacks and some tomato juice. Invariably, a police car would drive up to me. 'You don't have a Moscow propiska (residence registration). We need to check your fingerprints to see if you're on the computer.' That was my cue, the lead-up to the bribe. I gave him 100 rubles. 'All right, then. Go get your treatment!' An old Chechen man sitting on a bench beside me said: 'The only thing that will help people like you is the hajj, a pilgrimage to Mecca.' I was ready to try anything. Someone put me in touch with a family in the United Arab Emirates. I didn't know what to expect.

On 28 October I boarded the flight to Jeddah, the Saudi city on the Red Sea nearest to Mecca. Salakh Mutabbakani, the son of my host family, and I prayed before setting off. We entered the Great Mosque through the Gate of Peace and proceeded to the inner courtyard. As I heard the Azan – the call to prayer – fill the air, my spirits began to lift. In the center of the inner courtyard stood Islam's most sacred spot, the Kaaba, which holds a black stone, the Stone of Paradise, which is believed to be the only surviving piece of Abraham's original shrine. With each rotation I moved closer to the center, chanting the Shahada – the Islamic creed – in Arabic. Convinced that my sanity depended on kissing the sacred stone, I managed to do so, and then touched it with my hand. It was smooth as polished crystal. I felt changed almost immediately. The blackness lifted, and I felt relaxed for the first time in many months. I can't really explain it. Before leaving Mecca, I spent several hours in prayer, begging Allah for help for Chechnya, our people, my family.

In June 1999, my old friend Ruslan was murdered. His mutilated body was first buried by his captors, then dug up again and dumped beside the road. 'The socks!' shrieked his wife Malizha, when she recognized him. For Ruslan's burial, people came from all over, and cars blocked the road for half a mile. President Maskhadov was a decent enough man, but he seemed powerless against the criminal gangs or the field commanders with their private armies. I came to regret that my old classmate Basayev hadn't become president. He was clearheaded and possessed the toughness required to impose order. We needed a strong hand to end the cycle of violence and avenging by opportunistic thugs whose only purpose was power and wealth. Admittedly, some Chechens were pressured by the Russians and had no way out. 'Collaborate with us, or we'll put you in a filtration camp or kill your family.'

Russian troops were gathering along our borders again, and their planes dropped bombs on 'bandit-formation camps'. Kidnapping had reached epidemic proportions. How better to prevent humanitarian workers or journalists coming to our country than to kidnap a few. Kill a few? Little by little we became isolated from the international community. I built up stocks of food from the wholesale market, and also stocks of medical supplies. As I couldn't find a surgical saw and drill, I would have to perform amputations and trepanations with ordinary carpenter's tools, which were hard to keep clean and sterile. At one stage I performed 67 amputations and seven brain surgeries in two days. The longer I had avoided death, the more fatalistic I became. As with most things, Allah decides.

All we wanted was to get on with our lives. But war became inevitable when bomb explosions in Moscow and other cities killed hundreds of people. Chechens were blamed. But to us, these horrendous crimes didn't make any sense. Why commit such crimes at a time when the international community was beginning to show sympathy for our cause? Some 200,000 Chechens lived in Russia, half of them in the Moscow metropolitan area. Amid hysterical voices from other booths, I called my friend Abek in Moscow. He said: 'This place is teeming with uniforms. It's a pogrom! They're rounding us up. Police are blocking railroad stations, airports and roads in and out of Moscow.' The line went dead. Russian police and armed forces worked 12-hour days checking thousands of apartments. The crackdown was good business for the local police, inflating the prices of bribes from $50 to $100. Chechen males sewed up their pockets to prevent the police from planting narcotics on them.

The fragility of life
In the courtyard of our mosque, I mounted a platform. 'We'll restore the old bombed-out hospital. But we need volunteers to mend the roof, reconstruct, paint walls and rebuild the toilets. We need everything!' Again, the townspeople rallied. They delivered sheets, blankets, pillows, items saved over a lifetime for their children's marriages. With so many refugee women flooding into Alkhan Kala, there were more women having babies, so I sectioned off a small space as a maternity ward under the care of our volunteer gynecologist Zina Aduyeva. At the end of the day, blood soaked my undershirt, and the floors sloshed in it. I dreamed of hot showers and steam baths. Meanwhile, newly appointed Prime Minister Vladimir Putin vowed: 'We will pursue the terrorists everywhere. If, pardon the expression, we find them in the toilet, we'll drown them there!' Russian public opinion had turned against us. When the Moscow-Baku highway was backed up, Russians fired random shots at the columns of refugees. One time, when getting supplies in Ingushetia, I watched how Russian soldiers turned back refugees unless they produced a bribe. In the refugee camps, there was no way to keep

clean, no privacy, no way to escape from the smell of human excrement. There were many shell-shocked children. A woman doctor told me: 'Their parents were killed in front of them. Sometimes they play with others; then suddenly they stop and burst into tears.'

I invited the 10 doctors and 20 nurses. 'In the first war, doctors and nurses were killed, and I can assure you that the coming war is going to be much worse. I want you all to know that if you decide at any point to leave, I will not hold it against you. You don't even have to inform me.' On Mira (Peace) Street, people gathered following the funeral of a young boy. But a crowd on the streets was always an invitation to the Russians to fire. An enormous explosion followed. Razyat Almatova, one of our volunteer nurses who was eating soup with us, couldn't lift the spoon to her mouth because her hand shook so much. Five minutes later, the wounded started arriving. Seventy of them. Some of the nurses panicked. 'Forget the stands!' I shouted. 'Stop the bleeding! First of all, stop the bleeding!' The next morning, on my way to meet the staff, one of them met me at the door, his face downcast. 'Everyone left in the night,' he said. 'All the doctors and almost all of the nurses are gone.'

The Russians also used vacuum bombs. The shock waves these caused were so powerful, it collapsed buildings and sucked bodies out, smashing them against stationary objects. You would find people dead with no evident markings, though their organs were atomized inside their bodies. Sometimes I felt that the whole population was verging on nervous collapse. One day, I saw a nine-year-old boy with half a head of white hair. 'It happened overnight,' his mother said to me. Sometimes I screamed at the nurses for no reason. I fought against these outbursts, knowing I had to find some other way to relieve tension. Doing push-ups between operations helped. I only slept two or three hours a night. The murders and rapes by Russian kontraktniki made my blood boil. When one of them was brought in, he screamed: 'I don't want to be treated by bandits!' as nurse Rumani gave him a shot to relieve his pain. 'Son of a bitch! Bastard!' he shouted at me. A Chechen fighter shouted from the corridor: 'Let him die!' For a moment I was tempted. The world would be a better place without this monster. He wouldn't rape any more women or children. But then I remembered the Hippocratic Oath. 'I am a doctor. It is my job to treat whoever needs help. Allah will punish him.'

As our medical supplies dwindled, I started cleaning wounds with sour milk and applied honey to help close them. On burns I used egg yolk and sour cream. In November, the Russians started shelling our town quadrant by quadrant. A missile smashed into the house with a deafening explosion. My house was partially destroyed and my parents' house was leveled. Fortunately they were now in Ingushetia. We build. The Russians destroy. We build again. The Russians destroy again. Some people can't take it. They have heart attacks and die. In these extreme circumstances you realize the fragility of life. You recognize what is important and what is superficial. What is true and what are lies.

As I came out one day, I saw a woman in a floral head scarf with downcast eyes. 'Please doctor, I need to talk to you in private.' It was Umazhova, who had quite a reputation for organizing protests and for talking back to the Russians about breaking their promises.
'One of our family members has been wounded. She's our breadwinner.'
'We'll treat her. No problem.'
'I don't think you understand, Doctor. It's Zoyka.'
'Zoyka? Bring her in.' My patience was running out.
'I can't. You see, Zoyka is a cow. A piece of shrapnel has lodged in her neck.'
'I don't operate on animals,' I said. 'I simply don't have the time.' Her eyes filled with tears. 'Please understand, Doctor, without Zoyka my five children will go hungry.'
The mention of her children broke me down. Zoyka the cow lay on her side in a makeshift barn. Her coat was groomed to a silky softness, and I think that the red ribbons hanging over her forehead were intended to ward off 'the Evil Eye'. Umazhova squatted and stroked the cow's head. 'There, there. Doctor has come to help you. You be a good girl.' The cow's large brown eyes stared up at me, imploring, full of trust. With some difficulty, I removed a large piece

of razor-sharp metal. Upon leaving, Umazhova's five children stood near the gate watching me in silence. For a moment, my fatigue lifted and I felt at peace. A few weeks later, Umazhova was outside my operating room again. 'Zoyka wants to thank you,' she said handing me a big can of milk, a crock of sour cream and a packet of cottage cheese.

Countering propaganda
Russian propaganda kept producing lies, so I started videotaping and interviewing patients with the help of my nephew Adam Tepsurkaev. Adam dreamed of being a journalist and his exclusive video reports found their way to Reuters news agency. He was also fearless, so I worried about him all the time. In addition to the videos I started writing a journal, for I wanted people to know what we had gone through. I wrote a few lines after work or by candlelight in the cellar, partly in a private code in case the journal fell into the wrong hands. Our conditions worsened steadily. How could Chechnya, a country of less than a million people, hold out against Russia?

At the stroke of midnight on New Year's Eve 1999, flares rose all over Chechnya, followed by bombardments. On the second day of 2000, Arbi Barayev, another Chechen field commander, entered the village with all his 300 men, claiming Operation Jihad had started again and that towns all over Chechnya were falling. Barayev was nothing but trouble. We all wished the Russians would eliminate him, but he always seemed to escape their net. 'We have to move the patients,' I said. 'About half are fighters, and they will be massacred by the Federals or sent to the filtration camps.' We moved 70 patients across a suspension bridge. An old woman flagged me down. 'Barayev is looking for you. You have to escape. The people will understand.' But near the hospital I was stopped by Barayev's men who forced me inside. 'Turn him around and tie him up,' they said. Barayev himself stepped forward, pointed his rifle at my feet, and fired a round of bullets into the wooden floor. 'You opened a hospital for Russian soldiers.'

Barayev placed his six senior lieutenants, bearded men in black woolen ski caps, opposite me to make up a sharia court. 'We are

here to judge this man,' Barayev began. Another said: 'He's treating Russian pigs. Execute him!' The list of my sins was punctuated by rounds of mortar fire outside. 'I opened a hospital for my fellow townspeople and refugees and people who needed my help,' I said above the gunfire. 'Even today, I brought Chechen fighters to safety across the bridge. The townspeople know very well I'm not a traitor. And one more thing. Have you forgotten that I operated on you in 1995 and removed a bullet from your neck? Saved your life? You're about to order me to be put to death – strange way to express your gratitude!' Surprisingly, Barayev was more concerned with his 'sharia court' than with the fighting outside. More explosions followed. 'We need a doctor!' someone shouted. I noticed then that Barayev's guard had put one of his men next to a Russian soldier.
'What are you going to do with him?' one of them asked.
'I'm going to operate on him.'
'Don't touch those pigs!'
'They're injured. It's no difference to me who they are.'
'What do you mean? Are you telling me I'm a pig too?'
I rushed over and grabbed hold of his rifle yelling: 'In this hospital I give the orders! Whether you like it or not, you will obey!' In the commotion of the next 36 hours Barayev and his men disappeared. Shortly after, I was saved by women when kontraktniki were about to shoot me. Twice in two days I escaped death. I had to make plans to leave.

Some 4,000 people had escaped from Grozny during the night, including 2,000 fighters under Barayev's command. Disoriented because of the snow, his men had wandered into a minefield. Barayev was among the hundreds of severely wounded. 'Is that you Khassan,' he asked as I bent over. 'Don't operate on me first. Deal with the younger guys before me.' Western journalists stormed the operating room, but I ordered them out, and only allowed Adam to record the operation. As soon as I was finished, Barayev's men rushed him from the building, knowing the Russians had put a reward of $1 million on his head. For 24 hours I didn't leave the operating room. Every minute was a human life. But then I sensed myself falling, only revived again when Rumani and Razyat rubbed my face outside with snow. Two days later, I could no longer control my hands, and my arms developed spasms.

Escape and return
One day, I saw a strange car parked outside our house, a red Zhiguli. A man introduced himself: 'I have come from Nazran to help you get out of Chechnya. I'm a colonel in the FSB. My name is Ruslan. We have to leave for Ingushetia right away.' I rushed inside, changed my clothes, and grabbed my passport. I hated to leave my medical bag, but to carry it would give me away immediately. Guards at checkpoints were talking about me over their radios. A mile farther we were flagged down at a checkpoint. 'Get out, one by one. Hands up! Flat on the ground!' After checking our papers, they said: 'We have an FSB colonel and two civilians, not fighters.' Next, we drove all the way to Ingushetia at breakneck speed to avoid heavy shelling. I feared for my mental state. If it got any worse, I would end up incapacitated. But friends brought me to Peter Bouckaert of Human Rights Watch. 'I need rehabilitation,' I said, 'but it is impossible to get it here.' Word came from Washington that I was welcome. Later, the American embassy in Moscow provided me with an entry visa in my Russian passport.

It was difficult for me to readjust to normal conditions, and I overreacted to everything. In my first weeks in Washington, I had frequent talks with people from Amnesty International, Human Rights Watch, but also with John McCain and Zbigniew Brzezinski. Several people suggested I should become Chechnya's representative in Washington. But I didn't want to become involved in any political maneuvering. I still wanted to return. What finally convinced me to ask for political asylum was a telephone call from Malika. 'Your photograph is posted at all the military checkpoints. The Russians are hunting you down. You shouldn't return.' Besides battling depression, my mind kept circling back to my family in Chechnya. But I realized that America is full of people who have started over, and that Chechnya isn't the only country that has struggled for independence. By today's standards however, the English would surely have called George Washington a terrorist. The Immigration and Naturalization Service approved my petition to bring my family here. On 5 February 2001, first Adam, then Khava, Maryam and Islam emerged out of customs at Kennedy airport in Boston. Then came Zara with Markha in her arms. I could hardly believe it.

The war took an ominous turn in 2002 when Chechen fighters took more than 800 people hostage in Moscow's North-East theatre. I watched the tragedy unfold on television in horror. These young men and women with dynamite strapped to their waists were desperate to draw the world's attention to a forgotten war. They had seen nothing but death at the hands of Russia. What a contrast with America! Here, Zara gave birth to our little daughter Satsita. I still struggle with English, but work as a volunteer in the radiology department at Newton-Wellesley Hospital.

The Kremlin called me a terrorist doctor because I treated Chechen freedom fighters. The extremists called me a traitor because I treated Russian soldiers. In truth, it was the civilians I treated most, and they still need my help. Whenever I pass through Moscow's Sheremetyevo airport, I'm not treated as a citizen of Russia. The secret service keeps asking me questions. In the United States they just say: 'Welcome back.' For years, I have been a persona non grata, and it's still dangerous. A good friend of mine, Natalia Estemirowa of the Russian human rights group Memorial, was abducted and found dead hours later. It shocked everybody. Just months before, she had won the Sakharov Prize for her work. Overall, the situation has improved, and during the summer my wife and I, and our children stayed in Chechnya. But I still have to watch my back.

Recently, I've become the chairman of the International Committee for the Children of Chechnya that supports relief workers and physicians. Two large air-conditioning units now cool the operating room at the Children's Hospital in Grozny, and Operation Smile dispatches surgeons to repair cleft palates and hare lips. In 2008, our international team of 26 medical personnel operated on more than a hundred children. In 2009 and 2010, I was back again. It's a time of hope.

AFRICA

'For my part, I had now become altogether too big for my chains.'

Frederick Douglass in *My Bondage and My Freedom* (1855)

Frederick Douglass (photo Wikimedia Commons)

Aminatou Haidar - Western Sahara
Fighting superpowers for independence and recognition

'I am not Moroccan. I am Sahrawi,' says Aminatou Haidar, Western Sahara's foremost human rights defender, well known for speaking truth to power. Her parents had instilled in her the value of coexistence, but when colonial power Spain withdrew, Morocco took over, without any foundation in international law. Other countries use the impasse to catch fish, mine phosphates, and explore the territory for oil, thus violating the rights of the Sahrawi. Despite UN presence, its mandate does not include human rights monitoring. Aminatou remains determined: 'When I decide to do something, I will do it no matter what. I am very stubborn, very solid and very tough.' Having worked underground and experienced Moroccan jails, she feels certain: 'We will never surrender.'

Aminatou Haidar (photo by Sofia Moro)

Most world citizens may not know Western Sahara to be a country, but it certainly is to 400,000 Sahrawis in Africa's northwest. Human rights defender Aminatou Haidar (born in 1967) was awarded numerous times for her activism, for which she endured a lot. 'When I decide to do something, I will do it no matter what. I am very stubborn, very solid, very tough.'

Context

Some of the Canary Islands' pristine beaches are replenished with sand originating 80 miles away from the coast of North Africa. But it didn't blow over by the wind. It was imported from Western Sahara, from which more than just sand is disappearing.

The country's rich phosphate deposits are mined by international joint ventures. Its Atlantic fishing grounds are frequented by EU vessels, making the occupying nation, Morocco, Africa's top exporter of fish. Oil companies such as TotalFinaElf of France and Kerr-McGee of the United States search the same waters for a new Mexican Gulf. These economic activities however are illegal and the people of Western Sahara, the Sahrawis, do not profit from them. Crushed between powerful nations and leading lives of either oppression or exile, they have never been consulted about the use of their land and territorial waters. While still on the UN list of non-decolonized countries, other nations take advantage of the legal limbo.

Once a Spanish colony, Western Sahara has been under strict military control by the Kingdom of Morocco since its invasion in 1975. At the end of that year, King Hassan II of Morocco decided to lay claim to the territory by launching a 'Green March': 350,000 Moroccan civilians walked into a strip of land that the Spanish had already vacated. 'As if calling an invasion in the name of a color respected in Islam somehow justified it,' said former US ambassador Frank Ruddy. Photos in the Parador Hotel and murals in Moroccan primary schools in Laayoune however show an abundance of red flags, the true color of the march. It was the 'Red March' of the Moroccan state and for Sahrawis the 'Black March'.

An extended conflict ensued with the Popular Front for the Liberation of Saguia el-Hamra and Rio de Oro (Polisario), which had sprung up in 1973 in opposition to Spanish colonial rule. Seeking a hasty way out, in 1975 Spain signed the so-called Madrid Accords with Morocco and Mauritania, even though the treaty contradicts the Law on decolonization of Sahara of the Spanish Government itself. Nonetheless, Morocco and Mauritania used it to lay claim to part of Western Sahara. When the International Court of Justice (ICJ) unequivocally rejected Morocco's claims of sovereignty in 1976, Polisario proclaimed the Sahrawi Arab Democratic Republic (SADR) as Western Sahara's legitimate government, engaged in a struggle for freedom and independence against the new occupying powers.

Although considered a full member state of the African Union since 1984, Morocco refers to SADR as the 'phony republic'. The ICJ ruling however insists on 'the principle of self-determination through the free and genuine expression of the will of the peoples of the Territory.' Ignoring this, on 31 October 1975, the Moroccan army started invading the northern part of the territory while, from the south, the Mauritanian army did the same in December. Fifty thousand Sahrawi refugees fled east, ending up in refugee camps near Tindouf in the Algerian desert. More arrived over the following years, terrorized by direct attacks, arbitrary arrests, torture and disappearances.

Today, based on the last count of the UNHRC in 2004, the Tindouf refugee camps have a collective population of more than 165,000 Saharawis. Their camps have all been named after the cities and towns left behind in Western Sahara. Most of these people live in tents or huts without running water and are heavily dependent on international humanitarian aid. Under international law, their host country Algeria is accountable for protecting them, but the Algerian Government, which recognizes the Saharawi Republic, has handed over responsibility to Polisario and SADR. Only one Sahrawi NGO operates in the camps, the Association for the Families of Sahrawi Prisoners and the Disappeared (AFAPREDESA).

But there are many, mainly Spanish, NGOs as well as the UNHCR and a MINURSO office in charge of daily contacts with Polisario officials and with the refugees, mainly for the implementation of the UNHCR family visits program. In the rhetoric of the Moroccan Government however, the refugees are séquestrés, captives of Polisario. But this Moroccan claim has been disqualified by many eyewitnesses. The Sahrawi refugees simply don't want to return to their country while it is under Moroccan occupation. One visitor was prominent journalist and member of the Moroccan Association of Human Rights, Ali Mrabet. After writing about his firsthand experience, he was sentenced to a 10-year ban on practicing his profession in Morocco in 2005. He now writes for El Mundo in Spain.

Near to the Tindouf camps, Polisario controls the sparsely populated 37 per cent of Western Sahara east of the 'Berm', a series of Moroccan military fortifications running for 1,600 kilometers from the northeast to the southwest. Morocco controls the other two thirds of the territory. The fortifications are patrolled by the 'sand army', an estimated 100,000 Moroccan troops, costing Morocco almost half of its military budget. For more than 30 years it has separated Sahrawi parents from their children. UN mediation has facilitated family visits. 'When you see how people meet and embrace each other after so many years, it's unbelievable,' said one Sahrawi. 'You feel the intense emotion that spans decades of separation. For many, it's like a volcano inside.' Some find, after having waited for a reunion for decades, that their distant loved ones have died, having lived lives they knew nothing about.

Morocco does not recognize the major Sahrawi human rights organizations CODESA (Collective of Sahrawi Human Rights Defenders) and ASVDH (Sahrawi Association of Victims of Grave Human Rights Violations Perpetrated by the Moroccan State), because their statutes do not 'respect the territorial integrity of Morocco.' It is impossible to meet with Ali Salem Tamek, the vice president of CODESA, or Brahim Dahan, the chairman of ASVDH. Both are in jail. Even the Laayoune branch of the Moroccan Association for Human Rights is often harassed, and activists have reported on incidents of travel restrictions, arbitrary arrest, beatings and imprisonment on trumped-up charges. Morocco formed various councils to address human rights violations, but only after great outside pressure. The Equity and Reconciliation Commission established by King Mohamed VI in 2004 recognized responsibility for many human rights violations and disappearances. But no institutional reforms have been made and the Commission has never named or brought the perpetrators to justice.

Ali Salem Tamek, vice president of CODESA, in jail (Ait Meloul Prison, Agadir, Morocco, 2005), Wikimedia Commons.

In 1988, the Kingdom of Morocco and Polisario agreed to settle the dispute through a UN-administered referendum. Starting in 1991, the UN Mission for the Referendum in Western Sahara known as MINURSO was to monitor the ceasefire and organize a referendum that would allow eligible Sahrawis to choose between independence and integration with Morocco. For a while, a just and lasting resolution seemed within reach. However, Morocco then insisted that thousands of its settlers be granted the right to vote. In the eyes of Polisario, this would nullify the referendum as the Plan of 1991 had stipulated clearly that 'all the Sahrawi whose names are in the latest Spanish census of 1974 will have the right to vote in the referendum.'

Special envoys like former Italian Premier Giulio Andreotti and US Secretary of State James Baker have not been able to break the impasse. UN mediator Baker, appointed in 1997, managed to bring the two parties to the negotiating table in Houston. Five years later, upon formal request of the UNSC Resolution 1429 of July 2002, he presented his 'Peace Plan for the self-determination of the people of Western Sahara'. Against all odds, Polisario accepted, but Morocco rejected the Plan saying that the 'Baker Plan put into question Morocco sovereignty over Western Sahara'. Morocco's argument however cannot be sustained since its claims of sovereignty have not been recognized by the UN or any nation in the world.

So 20 years after the ceasefire, the referendum still hasn't taken place and MINURSO remains the only contemporary UN mission without a mandate to monitor human rights. Although favored by Polisario, the Moroccan Government opposes giving MINURSO such a mandate. Considering its manifold human rights violations, it is clear why. Interestingly, it was the UN High Commissioner for Human Rights who recommended the monitoring in 2006, but the underlying report was 'shared exclusively' with Morocco, Algeria and Polisario. Only photo-copied or bootlegged versions could be found.

In 2007, Morocco presented to the UN a proposal for autonomy for Western Sahara. This may sound promising, but any path leading to independence is still considered as an attack on Morocco's 'territorial integrity', one of three red lines in Moroccan law that touches the limits of free expression. The other two are undermining the Islamic religion and the monarchial regime. Conveniently, just about any claim regarding the recognition of human rights can be seen as crossing one or all of these red lines. In the same year, Polisario responded with a counterproposal based on the need to hold the agreed referendum, while offering to Morocco privileged relations in the future. But autonomy as a Moroccan province ignores the right to self-determination as defined by the UN Resolution 1514 (XV) that paved the way for the end of colonialism. It would not satisfy the Sahrawi people, especially now that massive Moroccan immigration has drastically shifted the population balance in such a way that the Saharawi are now a minority in their own territory.

France, Spain, the United States and the EU also contribute to making lasting peace and justice impossible. Morocco's main ally and leading trade partner, Security Council member France, opposes expanding the UN mission in Western Sahara with a human rights mandate. Fourteen members backed it; France blocked it. Spain has left behind an incorrectly conducted decolonization process of its last colony. The United States have created an alliance with Morocco to fight its international 'War on Terror', putting the Sahrawi people in a category in which they do not belong. They hope that the Obama Administration will revise its policy which works against the right of self-determination and against a more beneficial relationship with Algeria, the major ally of the Saharawi cause. The EU as a whole is implicated too, by having given Morocco 'advanced status' as the biggest beneficiary of the European Neighborhood and Partnership Instrument and by signing fisheries agreements with Morocco that include Sahrawi waters over which Morocco has no legitimate sovereignty.

The presence of 200 UN observers might give visitors reason for hope. Their 'observing' however mostly appears to be done while cruising in their Toyota Landcruisers between fancy hotels. They are however in a good position to see that the ceasefire is undermined by systematic human rights violations and that organizing a referendum is long overdue. Most disgraceful of all is the sight of the MINURSO facilities in Laayoune: Moroccan flags from one end to the other, leaving not even the pretense of impartiality. In May 2010, Polisario restricted contacts with MINURSO, because of its failure on implementing the self-determination referendum. Around the world, referenda take six months to organize, not two decades. 'United

Nothing. That's what the UN means to us,' said a Sahrawi spokesman. In the view of Polisario's UN representative Ahmed Boukhari, MINURSO is 'turning into a protector shield of a colonial fact, the occupation of Western Sahara by Morocco.'

Demonstration at Gdeim Izik

In October 2010, a group of Sahrawi protesters started an exodus from Laayoune setting up an encampment in Gdeim Izik, a few kilometers southeast of the capital. At its height, the number of protesters grew to 15,000. It was a massive demonstration of discontent with their present situation.

MINURSO was not able to monitor the situation. Moroccan security forces shot a 14-year-old Sahrawi boy and launched a 'security operation'. They dispersed the protesters and destroyed the camp using teargas, water cannons, batons and loudspeakers mounted on vehicles and helicopters. Hundreds of people were wounded and more than a hundred went missing. Although the events unfolded on Europe's doorstep, the response was minimal.

No one characterized the situation more succinctly than former US ambassador Frank Ruddy, who served as MINURSO's deputy chairman in 1994. In his view, the referendum in Western Sahara was sabotaged by the Moroccans. Writing notes to then Secretary General Kofi Annan, testifying under oath before a House Committee and backing up his statements in interviews and at international conferences, Ruddy said: 'There is a Common Law doctrine called Res Ipsa Loquitur. That is Latin for 'the thing speaks for itself '. It means that where the accused's fault is obvious merely by reciting the facts, no proof is necessary. A recitation of Morocco's crimes, its invasion of Western Sahara, its occupation and colonization for 30 years and its cynical destruction of the referendum set up by the UN to settle the question, speak for themselves and for Morocco's guilt. Morocco has acted lawlessly and notoriously. The question is whether the UN is willing or able to restrain Morocco's lawlessness. Shamefully, the answer so far has been an unequivocal no.'

One person for whom 'the thing speaks for itself' is the president of CODESA, Aminatou Haidar, sometimes referred to as the 'Sahrawi Gandhi'. She champions non-violent resistance and campaigns for the self-determination of Western Sahara, for which she has traveled to many countries. She has exposed the Moroccan military's heavy-handed approach, its aggression and brutality. Like most other Sahrawis, she has endured the machinations of the Moroccan security services: 'The truth of my experience and the wounds of the torture are still part of me, a feeling that is amplified by the fact that I often pass my former torturers in the street. Today, our situation is still deplorable.'

As per 2015, there is no sign of progress, though there is much window dressing. There are debates and discussions, Morocco adopted a rights-friendly constitution in 2011, and cooperates with UN mechanisms. The Working Group on Arbitrary Detentions visited in 2013 and the High Commissioner for Human Rights Navi Pillay in 2014. However, meetings of human rights activists are repressed and in Western Sahara police blocks all gatherings by opponents of the occupation and of Moroccan rule. Many civilians have been sentenced by military courts, including 22 who took part in the Gdeim Izik protests. They are serving long prison terms.

Despite this grim reality, life goes on in Laayoune. Steeped three times, served three times, Sahrawi hospitality is symbolized by the plentiful cups of tea poured by our host Elarbi Masaoud. 'The first glass is as bitter as life. The second is as sweet as love. The third is as gentle as death.' In between the talks that mix Arabic, French and English with some Spanish, televised soccer matches offer a welcome relief. In the occupied capital of Western Sahara, it makes one forget temporarily the dreaded presence of a swarm of security officers and snitches that follow every move.

Personal narrative — Aminatou Haidar

My childhood in Laayoune, like that of most Sahrawi children, was unlike any other. Playing with dolls was hardly part of it. We weren't able to do things that you would expect children to be doing when they are little. This was all due to the political environment we grew up in.

One of the values that my parents instilled in me as a young girl is coexistence. I had many Moroccan friends and in my cahier de souvenirs, my book of memories, they all wrote something personal to me. I still have it today. Up till now I still have Moroccan friends and I stay in touch with them, despite all the bad things that other Moroccans have done to us. We, the Sahrawis, however have never treated the Moroccans in a discriminatory way. So then and now, we coexist with them and continue to have relations with them wherever possible. I often used to accompany my father and he always insisted: 'Whatever happens, never lie!' Among my family members they say that I am a picture of my father, like a shadow. The hospitality that we offer you is not only from my parents and my friends. It is in the nature of all the Sahrawi people. I think that my father also passed on to me a great sense of determination. When I decide to do something, I will do it no matter what. I am very stubborn, very solid and very tough.

During the 1970s, for a while my parents moved to Tan Tan in Morocco where I went to my first primary school. One of the things that is etched in my memory is the moment I was standing in the streets of Tan Tan when military vans were driving through full of Moroccan soldiers holding flags. My classmates and I were just coming out of school. The Moroccan soldiers made obscene gestures, gave us the finger and shouted foul language at us like 'sons of bitches' and 'stinking Sahrawis'. I will never forget it. These things really hurt us in our identity as Sahrawis.

Shortly after the arrival of these military vans, my father had an 'accident'. He was hit by a car that was driven by a Moroccan and he died soon after. It was very strange and suspect and we didn't really understand what had happened. Two months before however, two of my father's friends had died in exactly the same manner. Hit by a car driven by a Moroccan. One day his first friend, then his second friend, and then my father. In those days, the atmosphere in Laayoune was very tense. To this day, these 'accidents' remain a big question mark and they were never properly investigated. And it wasn't only those three men that were killed, 526 of the Sahrawis who were taken from their houses have all disappeared. People are still calling for an investigation. Things have changed since the 1970s, but 'accidents' and disappearances have become part of our life.

We moved back to Laayoune again. Both the parents of my mother and of my father were still living there, so we joined them. We were living in a neighborhood in which Sahrawi and Spanish people were living together. I remember my Spanish childhood friend Maite. In 1976, we were nine years old. I used to play with her often and we had lots of fun together. One day however, after having enjoyed each other's company for more than a year, Maite said: 'We're going to move to Spain.' I started to cry and so did Maite. We didn't understand why we had to be separated from each other.

The next year, just after the Spanish had retreated as colonizers, the Moroccan army began to wage war on the Sahrawis. One night we were preparing to go to a concert of Mauritanian singers, very late in the evening, at 11pm in Cinema Las Dunas, 'the Dunes'. When we were on our way there, suddenly we heard bombs exploding in the suburbs. We were in the middle of the armed conflict between Polisario and the Moroccan army and it was so loud that it seemed as if it was happening in our own house. All the people fled to their homes and quickly closed their doors. 'Why can't we go to the concert?' Like other children, I was sad and didn't understand that because of the explosions people would be risking their lives and might die.

Two years later, I began to notice that there were many children without parents. 'His mother is in the east,' I would hear them say. 'Mohamed is in the east.' 'The east' was the word we used to refer to the camps in Tindouf, Algeria. They still exist today. All these families had become separated, because many had fled to unknown destinations. Sometimes I saw my grandmother weeping, because one of her sons was in the east. Four of my mother's uncles were also in the east. Whenever the subject came up, my family members used to cry.

In 1981, my mother's uncle was kidnapped. At that time, he had five daughters. From time to time I heard that his wife Taslem wouldn't put on her makeup or make herself look nice with new clothes. In Western Sahara there is a custom that when a woman's husband has just died or is in bad circumstances, out of loyalty the woman doesn't put on her makeup. From time to time, I saw Taslem's daughters weeping. 'Where is daddy?' they kept asking. I also saw my mother weeping. I was only 11, but I started paying more attention to their conversations, for now I really wanted to understand. Meanwhile, other men and women were disappeared.

Joining the other side
One of my cousins, Laroussi Haidar, was raised in the same house as if he was my brother. In fact, in Hassaniya we don't say 'cousin', but 'brother'. We were nursed by the same mother, so Laroussi and I treated each others' relatives as if we were brother and sister. As a young man, he went to Spain to study and went on to become a professor at Granada University. But when he was still young, he decided one day to 'join' the camps near Tindouf as we call it. 'Do you know where my brother Laroussi is?' I asked around. Nobody knew. At that time, communication was almost non-existent. There was no telephone and no internet. Where are they? Will they ever come back? We were living with questions all the time. But we did know that when someone had 'joined the other side', they were going to fight against Morocco in the army of Polisario.

Two of Laroussi's brothers had joined before him, and in 1985 his third brother, so from one family four brothers joined. My uncle Massaoud also joined via the route of Tangier. This group of 1985 consisted of 26 Sahrawis who joined the camps. At that time, Massaoud was studying at a military school in Kenitra to become a pilot. During a training session in Spain, he had met with a number of Sahrawis from the camps and of course the Moroccan intelligence services got to know about it. They sent him a letter under the heading 'urgent' to come back before he was able to finish his training. 'We have to ask you some questions,' they said. After three months in prison, they released him. Right away, he decided to join the camps. As far as we know, Massaoud was the first and the last Sahrawi to be permitted to be trained to become a pilot.

The first real start of coming to grips with the situation was in 1982, when the armed conflict was at its peak. The Sahrawis caused a lot of damage to the Moroccan army. King Hassan II declared the acceptance of a referendum. But due to the pressure exerted by Polisario, he did this when visiting the Kenian capital Nairobi. During those days, one of my relatives observed that I was asking a lot of questions. He was a member of a Polisario cell. But talking about the conflict was taboo. Anybody who did, automatically got kidnapped, abducted, disappeared. So, as I was only a young girl, he tried to explain things to me little by little. Then, he got a radio. He took me to a room, closed the door and said: 'This is the voice of the Sahrawis.' Listening to the news got me very excited. He also brought papers with a lot of information about our situation. He only allowed me to read them behind closed doors, but never to keep them.

Despite the fact that Laroussi's brothers had joined Polisario, to tell you the truth, the majority of my family members and friends were pro-Moroccan, because they held very good positions. Some were governors, others were colonels in the Moroccan army or officials in the Moroccan state. This made it impossible to talk to them about underground activities or independence. So, whenever I listened to the news of Polisario on the radio, I made sure to use headphones and to isolate myself. Just doing that was very difficult. By then, I was attending junior high school. I was brought to school in a luxurious car, because my family was quite wealthy at the time. The Sahrawi children however always kept their distance, because they thought that I was pro-Moroccan. The fact that most of my Moroccan friends were the sons and daughters of colonizers made things very delicate for me. In one way, I was lucky. But I really suffered from that, because of course inside I was completely opposite. I couldn't possibly tell them the truth.

The suffering of the Sahrawis really pushed me to think. I felt a strong calling to do something for my people. This is how I came to meet with my relative and asked him: 'What can I do? I want to do something for my people!' In the end he agreed. 'Okay, I'm going to test you to see whether you can or cannot do this.' He gave me some Sahrawi flags and some proindependence leaflets to make the Sahrawis aware of the conflict and motivate them to act. 'Defend yourself!' the leaflets said. 'I will see whether you're able to distribute them or not. I'm not going to introduce you to the people I'm working with. Nobody will know you.' That was in the summer of 1984. The places where I distributed the leaflets were very dangerous, because they were controlled by the Moroccan police and military forces. They would not allow anyone there, unless they were 100 per cent sure that they were pro-Moroccan. The chief of police was living in the same building in which part of my extended family lived. So one day, I climbed to the top of the building which was near the Bank of Morocco. The top of the building is very open and everyone can see you. I let go of a lot of leaflets, and the wind took them throughout the area.

The Governor of Laayoune at that time, Saleh Zemrag, was very unpopular and responsible for the torture of many Sahrawis. You can still find many people who will attest to that. Anyway, I came to his house in the afternoon of the same day, which was close to the place where I used to gather with the children of some colonels and of the Governor of Boujdour, whose wife was my aunt. That made the son of the Governor of Boujdour my cousin. We used to sit together in the stairway of a building called La Casa España, a big house for cultural events, to talk and play with each other. This time, I came before the usual time we gathered there and I put the leaflets there and fastened the Sahrawi flag. Then, I hurried home. Later, I returned to sit with my friends, pretending I didn't know anything. All of us were surprised to find there was a lot of movement in the area and we were told: 'Go away from here. Go home. Just go home!' Nobody knew about me, not even my cousins.

Now, my relative knew that I had done it. But still he wanted me to pass another test, so he gave me leaflets again. On one side was the Sahrawi flag. On the other was a picture of El-Ouali Mustapha Sayed, the father figure of the Sahrawi cause. He was the man who started it all, the co-founder and second Secretary-General of Polisario and the first president of SADR. He became very famous among us, but he was killed by the French army in Mauritania. I accepted the leaflets and went to school. During a basketball match, I went to the changing rooms before the students arrived and distributed them there. Next, I went to the school's reading room. Nobody was there. I spent a little time studying my lessons, and distributed more leaflets there too. During the match, I distributed some more. I got rid of all of them.

Working underground
It never occurred to the Moroccan authorities that it was me who distributed the leaflets, simply because they believed I was pro-Moroccan. This was at the end of 1985. Instead of me, the school administration accused four boys and one girl, including a brother and sister, and arrested them. The main reason for arresting them was the fact that they had family members in the Tindouf camps and their behavior at school gave a clue that they might have done it. They never talked to Moroccans, they didn't like them and didn't even sit at the same table with them. Perhaps they had said things openly before, I don't know. But children say what they think, even today. The leaflets that I had distributed were marked. This told my elder that I could do it. So I started working with them in one of Polisario's secret cells. It was completely underground. You are the first one to whom I have talked about my secret work as a young girl. I have never told this to anyone before.

In July 1987, I went with my family to Las Palmas on the Canary Islands. There, I had the opportunity to meet with some of my family members, who had travelled all the way there from the Tindouf camps. Some of them held responsibilities in Polisario and in the refugee camps. We talked a lot and I came to understand many things. I kept asking. They kept giving me news and advice. The meetings were in secret and would last an entire month. We also watched some videos together. These were documentaries about the suffering of the Sahrawis in the camps. As I was watching, I was crying continuously. The misery of the Sahrawi people was so great, it was unbearable to watch. Unimaginable.

Some of them gave me certain voice recordings. We wrapped them in a kind of sticky tape and hid them in bottles of bathroom gel and shampoo. My family didn't know anything about this. On the tapes were the voices of Polisario officials with directions for the secret cells. We knew that my family was not going to be checked, because they included the sons and daughters of the Governor of Dakhla. The mission was successful. I brought the tapes back in August, but I had to wait until September to pass them on, because the contacts of the secret cells in Laayoune had been out of town. Shortly after, in November, we started preparing things for the arrival of a UN fact-finding commission from the UN African Committee.

At the age of 20, I was studying for my baccalaureate in experimental science. At the same time, together with other high school students, I was preparing to organize a peaceful rally in support of a referendum. Next to a very mixed group of students, there were lots of others: workers, women and representatives of other groups. I was still a member of the secret cell, so I was preparing for two things at the same time. Hopefully, none of the students and none of the members of the secret cell would get caught or arrested. Three days before the arrival of the Commission, the Moroccan intelligence services started to kidnap Sahrawi people who were suspected of being involved in any movement or preparing the demonstration. More than 400 people were arrested.

On Friday at 2pm I attended a mathematics class. A letter in English was attached to my right arm with sticky tape under my clothes. Attached to my left arm was a bundle of leaflets. The reason why I was prepared in this way is that the plane of the Commission was expected to arrive that afternoon and there was a chance that the Commission members would visit our school. I prepared for both scenarios. If they didn't visit our school, I would go to the airport. The authorities then announced that the plane would not come due to bad weather conditions. To mislead us? Whatever the reason, the plane arrived on Saturday, but as it turned out, we were kidnapped before. A few days after the plane arrived, the Moroccan police started releasing people against whom they didn't have any proof of illegal activities. In the end, they only detained 64 people.

After school I went to Elghalia Djimi to have a meeting with her at 7pm. I waited, but she didn't come. When she was still not there at 9pm I was sure that she had been arrested. I moved quickly and told my fellow students and their relatives: 'If you have anything that might incriminate you, get rid of it as quickly as possible.' Still suspicious, I went home. A friend was visiting us from Spain and she brought very well-packaged leaflets. But later on, she was arrested too. Her name was: El Alame Yegga. I said to her: 'Look, Yegga, I'm 90 per cent sure that we will be arrested tonight.' I tried what I could to get rid of anything that might put us in danger, especially as I had in my possession documents that could lead to other people.

Journey to the end of hell
During the night, police cars with sirens were driving up and down the district. I was sure by then I would be kidnapped. My uncle is a kaid. It means he is a person responsible for a region under the supervision of the Governor. The police went up to him and said: 'In the area under your control lives a woman called Aminatou Haidar. We're going to arrest her and investigate her briefly. After that, she can go home again.' I hadn't slept all night. On Saturday 21 November 1987, plainclothes police officers knocked at the door and asked for me. My uncle opened the door and left again. I was in my pajamas. A relative of mine was lying on the bed asleep. 'Go and put something on,' the police said to me. 'And don't worry. We will only investigate you for 10 to 15 minutes.' Now I couldn't carry on with my studies, achieve my dreams and ensure my future! At first I thought I was having a nightmare, but the days and years that followed turned into a long journey to the end of hell.

A Renault 4 with three men was waiting. I recognized two of them. Next to the driver was Brahim Ben Sami who used to be the Wali, the Senior Governor and head of security in Laayoune before 2005. Later on he moved to Morocco, probably to Agadir. In the back seat was Hariz Elarbi, who would later become the Wali and head of security in Dakhla. In the 1980s he was responsible for a lot of torture of Sahrawis in and around Laayoune. In front of my uncle, they talked to me very politely. 'Okay, take it easy, don't worry.' But as I left, my aunt was crying, which made me very sad and emotional. As soon as we were out of view of my family and others, the men stopped the car. Brahim Ben Sami stepped out and sat in the back as well, so that I was squeezed in between the two men. One of them blindfolded me with part of my own clothes. The other pushed my head between his knees. Meanwhile, they kept driving around in the city. I lost all sense of orientation.

Only years later, I would know exactly where I had ended up. The place was just 500 meters away from my house, where I used to play with the other children from the neighborhood. As I entered the building, I heard a lot of crying, beating and police officers shouting insults. The atmosphere was one of horror. I was taken into a big room, where they took off the blindfold that was made of my own clothes and changed it to one from them. They bound it around my head really tight and handcuffed and shackled me. I could barely move. Next, they dragged me to a kind of low wooden bench. Two men pushed me on my back and fastened my legs and my hands with ropes really tight. My head was pushed back completely, so I couldn't do anything. Another man's responsibility was only one thing: clapping. The other kept beating me. At one point this caused a sudden movement, which hurt my shoulder. I still have pains in my shoulder today, 23 years later.

While insulting me and threatening me with rape, they pressed pieces of cloth with chemical substances and detergents on my nose and mouth in order to suffocate me. It also got into my eyes. It's unbearable and feels like fire in your head. They also put me under cold showers, only to revive me when I had become unconscious. Their torture methods and ways of degrading me were very systematic and it seemed they enjoyed doing it. The more I resisted, the more they varied their methods. In the end, my body was only a heap of flesh and bones. This is why I didn't want to confess. But my friend Elghalia Djimi did. Her torture had already started before my appointment with her, when she didn't show up. She still works as a human rights activist with ASVDH.

After the interrogation and the torture, they took me to my friend and removed my blindfold.

'Do you know this person?'

'No, I don't.'

That was really true, because I didn't recognize my friend. Her face was completely swollen and bruised with blood running down her cheeks, her clothes were torn and disheveled. She looked so different, I really couldn't tell who she was. It was a catastrophe. One of the police officers then slapped me.

'You don't know this woman?!'

'No!'

'Do you know Elghalia Djimi?'

'Yes.'

'And this woman? Who is this?'

'I have no idea.'

'This is Elghalia Djimi.'

'No, this is not Elghalia Djimi.' I still didn't see it.

'Talk to your friend,' one of the police officers said to Elghalia Djimi. 'Say your name!'

'Aminatou, yes,' she then said. 'I'm sorry to tell you that I am Elghalia Djimi.'

I was utterly shocked. Elghalia was in a bad way and had been tortured psychologically. They then took me back to their office and started interrogating me again. This time they asked me about the letter that had been attached to my arm. I had taken it off before they arrested me, while still hoping that I might meet with the people of the fact-finding Commission that day. But the police officers had found it in my room.

'Who gave you this?'

'I brought it with me from Spain.'

'No, Elghalia Djimi and others have told us different stories.'

They dragged me away again and forced me back in the same position on the wooden bench, while interrogating me. When I didn't confess, they attached thick electricity cables to my toes. Before they did so, they had first poured cold water over me. I was already shivering, because it was very cold. For us in Laayoune, November is winter and I was only wearing very thin clothes that offered no comfort. It was terrible.

After a long time, they released me from the bench and took off my blindfold. They took me to a room where I saw a middle-aged man in a dark-colored jellaba. 'Do you know me?' he asked. 'No, I don't.' 'I am Hafid Ben Hachem, the friend of your family.' This same man is now the director of all Moroccan prisons. But at that time he was the left-hand of Driss Basri, the Minister of the Interior during the rule of King Hassan II and the most powerful man in Western Sahara. 'Look, Aminatou, you have to confess and tell everything you know. Then I will order my men to release you.' He had been supervising the interrogation from 3.30pm to 10.30am, and had personally asked me a number of questions to get me to confess.

Terror and torture
The physical and psychological torture continued all Sunday. Late in the evening they took us somewhere in a car. As we later found out, the place was the PC-CMI, the Poste de Commandement – Compagnie Mobile d'Intervention. In Laayoune it is well-known as a place of terror and torture, a secret jail. In the car I was in the company of Elghalia Djimi, Yegga El Alem, the one who had been in my room sleeping with me, and two men. One of the men was Sidati Salami, a well-known Sahrawi poet from a family of marabouts on his mother's side. He was blind. The other man's name is Lassiad. He is in his old age now, but still alive and well in Laayoune, and we sometimes come across him in the street.

Next, they took us to a place where we felt sand under our feet. We heard the sound of waves and felt a breeze. We realized it must be a coastal area, as Laayoune is only 25 kilometers away from the sea. My blindfold had loosened a little bit. Through the opening I could see the moon and it was night. When we talked about this later among those that were there we had all thought the same: 'They're going to kill us here.' In the first week, 17 women were put into a single room of two by two and a half meters. We could only stand and were crammed like sardines. Next to the blindfolds, we were gagged and starved of food and water.

Sometimes they forced us to stand up on one leg throughout the night. Anyone that was leaning against the wall, they would slap or kick. Each time I woke up, I was facing the wall. Most of the time was spent in half sleep. Much later, in 2006, by chance I encountered a Spanish man who had been responsible for military training. He is now the President of the Association of Friendship with the Sahrawi People in Sevilla. Between 1974 and 1976 he had spent his two years of obligatory training, la Mili, in Western Sahara. When I described to him where I had spent my time in prison, he exclaimed: 'But that's El Bir Barracks!' After they had occupied Western Sahara, the Moroccans turned the barracks into a secret jail to torture Sahrawis.

Three of the women were very old and couldn't bear the situation in the prison. One of them was middle-aged, but she had nine children and she was in a lot of stress. Who would take care of her children after they had abducted her? Another woman was a young mother who had given birth just 20 days ago. Who would take care of her newborn baby? Her breasts were still full of milk and hurt as she couldn't nurse her baby. Her pain and tears affected all of us. Whenever there was a moment in which the police officers lowered their guard, we sucked the milk from her breasts and spat it out just to relieve her pain.

The first four days, we received no food and nothing to drink. When they did bring a bottle, they gave us only a few drops of water. 'Just enough to wet your mouths,' the police officer said. It wasn't enough to quench our thirst and only intended to further humiliate us. We attempted a hunger strike, but it lasted only one day, because the guards brought in dogs to intimidate us into eating again. The beating and insults continued. 'We're going to kill you!' We really believed they would, as there was nothing to stop them from doing so and we were aware of many others who had been disappeared and killed before us. We endured a lot of abuse from these Moroccan police officers. The men as well. We could hear the sounds of beating, their cries and weeping. One of them was only a young boy: Mohamed El Khalil Ayach.
'Say: Western Sahara is Moroccan!'
'No!'

'Say: Long live the King!'
'No,' we heard him answer every time.
They tortured him mercilessly, until nobody heard his voice anymore.

Accompanied by a police officer, Elghalia Djimi and I went to the toilet blindfolded. As I got in, I stepped on somebody's arm who was lying in the feces and the dirt. To find someone in such terrible conditions was too much to bear. It shocked me deeply. Still blindfolded, I got into the toilet and closed the door behind me. I was afraid, but from an opening under my blindfold I had seen the man on the floor. Later I described him to the others: 'He had long black hair and a mole on his face.' And the others said: 'That's Mohamed!' Mohamed's mother was among those who were detained with me. She knew then that her son had died.

During that week, the officials who had come to my house to kidnap me, Brahim Ben Sami and Hariz Elarbi, and the chief of police Bel Arabi from time to time interrogated us, the women and the blind man. They also interrogated others, among whom was the future father of my children, Mohamed Ali Belghassem. But first, after that week, our group was taken back to the PC-CMI again. They left me on my own in the corridor. Here, I'll show you on a drawing. The corridor was only about one meter wide and I spent nine months alone there. The others were in the nearby cells with iron gates. Five armed police officers kept watch at ground level, another five on the roof and outside another five. Fifteen altogether.

The door was left open and I only had a very thin blanket to protect myself, so when it got cold, it was really cold. For three weeks I was subjected to questioning, enduring an endless stream of torture and insults. Because of the blindfold, I lost all notion of time and space. I spent nine months there, while they left the light on day and night. The blindfold would remain in place for three years and seven months. We never washed our faces and never had a shower. During the entire period, there was only one time in which we were officially permitted to have a shower. In the presence of police officers.

As time passed, we got lice and other insects in our hair and most of us got skin problems and rashes because of the dirt. It irritated all the time. Whenever we went to the toilet, one of the police officers accompanied us. Some of the friendlier ones allowed us to close the door, but there were quite a few sadistic ones who wanted to humiliate us. 'We'll watch you until you finish.' In serious cases of guards that didn't allow us to close the door, we simply asked to return to our cell and wait for another opportunity. Often, we relieved ourselves in the cut-off bottoms of plastic bottles. It smelled awful, but the choice was between humiliation and this.

At the beginning of that period of three years and seven months, there were 17 women, but at the end there were only 10, because seven of us were gradually released. Two months in, the Moroccan authorities accepted our demand that our families could bring us some clothes. But the remaining time in prison we wore the same clothes until they had turned into rags. During moments of little surveillance, we sewed our clothes using needles made of scrap iron torn off tins of sardines. By the time there were only 10 of us, only two pairs of sandals remained. Not because they had worn out, but because police officers had stolen them from us. They brought us a few plastic ones, but they fell apart. Some were held together by pieces of rope. Tea or water was also brought in cut-off plastic bottles. The food as well. But if you'd seen it, you wouldn't have eaten it. It was so disgusting! When the police officers lowered their guard, we peeked through the corners of our blindfolds. That enabled us to see that insects were crawling all over our food. But when you're hungry and thirsty, you have to eat. You have no choice. I began to suffer a skin allergy and conjunctivitis. This was followed by gastric complaints and hemorrhoids, which caused a lot of pain.

Click-clack, click-clack
Staying on the floor of the corridor caused me to become half-paralyzed. When they found out about that, they asked my friend Elghalia Djimi to join me and help me with changing my clothes and other things. Still the torture continued. They came with very bad-smelling detergents. This time, instead of holding it in front of our faces, they just poured it around the place where we were sleeping.

The smell is so strong, you can hardly sleep. At night, the guards kept moving around, banging the iron gates. In order to terrorize us even further, they reloaded their guns, as if getting ready to shoot. Click-clack, click-clack. When we were finally sleeping, they used their batons and beat the doors. Another way to disturb our peace of mind was when soldiers snuck up quietly and loudly snapped the heels of their boots or start clapping in a hysterical way. Some of these men were real sadists. 'Sit in front of the wall,' they would say. We were extremely tired and found it hard to keep our balance. But they didn't allow us to lean against the wall for comfort. If that did happen, they slapped or kicked you again. This gives you an idea of how the Moroccans treated us in the PC-CMI here in Laayoune.

Outside, our family really had no clue about what was happening to us. Likewise, we had no idea how they were doing. There was a complete disconnection from the outside world. Except, there was a small number of sympathizing police officers who were humane in character. Sometimes, they would leave their radio on, allowing us to listen to the news or they brought newspapers. When lifting the blindfold a little, we could read it. On a few occasions, they allowed one of us to go to the toilet secretly and to wash with cold water. But they were very afraid, because nobody should get to know about it. Some of them even took information from us to our families and returned with news from the outside world. But it was hard to believe their news and our families found it hard to believe news about us. There was such a great risk in believing anything in that situation. The names of these three Moroccan police officers I won't tell, but may history one day give them equity and justice.

Four of the Sahrawis died. One of them was called Boumehdi Andalla. Police officers pulled out the nails of his hands and feet. It was incredibly painful and afterwards he suffered lots of infections. There was no medication and no help for him, so he got weaker and weaker and eventually died. The other three died because of the bad quality of the food and we think it was poisoned. Salama ould Hniya, Karoum Mohamed Ali died of extreme diarrhea and exhaustion. A fifth person, Laasri Mohamed, died four days after our release. Khatri Bella is the sixth one. He died a few months later because of intestinal cancer. I told you their names, because they were in the group nicknamed the Committee Group as we had been abducted on the day before the visit of the UN Technical Committee.

Sahrawi with flag (photo by Michele Benericetti, Wikimedia Commons)

During the whole period at PC-CMI, I was denied any medical treatment until my release on 24 May 1991. I was urgently taken to the El-Hassan Ben El-Mehdi Hospital in Laayoune, because I couldn't move. They started treating me immediately for three weeks. In the hospital, the Moroccan authorities registered me under a nickname. But some Sahrawi nurses there knew me. They sent me their salutations and best wishes through a Moroccan female nurse. 'X gives you his greetings. What is your name?' 'My real name is Aminatou Haidar,' I answered. I found myself in a room with Laasri Mohamed who died later on, and Elhafed Baamer who, like me, was cured. Two police officers kept an eye on us inside the room, and two outside. Gradually, our families put a lot of pressure on the Moroccan authorities, as the rumor had spread that their sons and daughters were in the hospital.

One little thing happened on a Friday, when only one of the police officers was on his post. My brother, my cousin and the new husband

163

of my mother came and begged him: 'Please let us see Aminatou!' This was dangerous and normally he wouldn't accept such a request. This time he did. When they entered, they were shocked. I was crying, they were crying, unable to utter a word. When they returned home that evening, they didn't say anything to my mother until late at night. My mother and my aunt then came to the hospital right away. Two police officers were on duty, but one must have been away for a smoke or to the toilet. As I was beginning to recover, by coincidence I stood up and then I saw my mother and my aunt. They were shocked too. 'Just let us see her for a moment,' they said to the one police officer. 'Alright, but I'll be sacked if you go any further.' He allowed us to kiss and embrace on the threshold, but then quickly said: 'Enough, enough!' He closed the door and urged my mother and my aunt to leave. He was very kind to us. That night I didn't sleep, because I was so excited by that meeting and still smelling their perfume on my hand.

Release and recovery
On 12 June 1991 however, they took me back to the PC-CMI. It was the day on which King Hassan II of Morocco announced the release of all Sahrawi prisoners. A week later, on 19 June, I was finally released. During the peace process and ceasefire established thanks to UN intervention, a large number of Sahrawis were released, including the Committee Group and the M'gouna Group. Qalaat M'gouna is a small village in the east of Morocco with an infamous secret jail. Before going from Laayoune to M'gouna, which is about 1,000 kilometers, some of them had first spent six months to a year here in the PC-CMI in Laayoune. After being abducted and disappeared, this M'gouna Group spent five to 16 years in prison.

Our release was also the result of international pressure from Amnesty International and the European Parliament. I remember the day, 19 June 1991, because it is mostly associated with the first day of summer and a music festival. But by then, I was only a shadow of my former self, a phantom out of a nameless hell! Shortly after I had to be operated on, because of the painful back trouble I had developed and again in 1994 because of stomach pains. I still feel those places in my body today. I visited doctors in Laayoune, Agadir,

Rabat for medical analysis and treatment and in November I had an operation on my spine. The next year, 1992, I went from one medical appointment to another. Fortunately I was recovering. Meanwhile, my passport was taken from me and the Moroccan authorities refused to reissue it.

I couldn't really walk normally. You can imagine: three years and seven months without walking. When I arrived home, my mother started crying. For a good reason and for a bad reason. The good reason was the fact that I was free, and of course she was very happy to see me return. But at the same time she was crying, because she didn't know anything about the fate of her brother, my uncle, who had been in M'gouna since 1981. For 10 years, nobody knew anything about him. Four days later however he was released. But of the 314 Sahrawis in M'gouna, 43 had died. Still, there are another 526 Sahrawis who did not return. Their families still don't know their whereabouts or their fates.

At the end of that same year, I got married. But in 1993 I registered to study for my baccalaureate. I wanted to study science, but it was impossible for me. When I was studying before, I was studying mathematics, physics and science in French. Now the teaching was done in Arabic and the syllabi had changed. Everything was so different that I had to change. I therefore registered to study arts and literature. Four days before the exams in the second semester, I went to hospital again. This time it was to do with hemorrhoids that I had developed while sitting on the cold prison floor and because of the awful food we had to eat.

In 1994 I tried to study again, but this time I couldn't continue because I was pregnant with my daughter Hayat. The results of my studies came out on the fourth of July. Hayat was born on 9 July 1994. The next year I couldn't study, because I had a little baby and here in Laayoune there is no university. Next, for a few years I was banned from studying, until they finally accepted me in 2000 in Rabat. On one condition: 'You have to register in the philosophy courses.' I would have preferred studying law, French or Spanish literature, but it was impossible. While at the university campus, I was also working for the so-called Fifth or Coordination Committee which focused on the rights of Sahrawis in relation to the Moroccan state. The Sahrawi university students also started holding demonstrations and I participated in a number of protests myself.

In Rabat, they kept an eye on me and they started to intimidate the female Sahrawi students. 'If we see you with Aminatou again, then...' They kept threatening and terrifying us. During the second semester I withdrew because of the pressure and because of the fact that a lot of Sahrawi girls were facing problems simply by being in touch with me. I went back to Laayoune. But a new desire was born to disclose the human rights violations in Western Sahara, for the world to see. Step by step, we contacted the American, the German and other European embassies and international organizations. We also began to meet more and more journalists, members of NGOs and so on to disclose the abuse and oppression we experience here. We also received members of the International Federation for Human Rights and Amnesty International and we got in touch with many Sahrawi victims to take their testimonies. With the help of a Moroccan friend, I established contacts with a Jordanian and Egyptian employee of MINURSO. The mandate of MINURSO may not include monitoring human rights violations, but they have certainly known about it for a long time. It's not something new.

This same period was marked by the creation of the Forum for Truth and Justice. It is a Moroccan organization, but they set up a branch here in Laayoune in 2000. It was very active in spreading a culture of awareness regarding human rights here in Western Sahara. The next year, a working committee was formed for the release of Sidi Mohammed Daddach. We refer to him as our Nelson Mandela. He is a Sahrawi who spent the longest period, about 23 years, in Moroccan prisons. Fifteen years were on death row as he was accused of treason and sentenced with the death penalty. Every night, he was expecting to be executed. But of course he was only defending our Sahrawi dignity. Despite all these years of imprisonment and suffering, he hadn't become crazy. We worked just for two months and he was released in November. It was a great success for us, thanks to our many contacts in Europe and a lot of pressure on the

Moroccan authorities. Thousands of people took to the streets in Laayoune and openly called for the self-determination of Western Sahara. It was the first time that the Moroccan authorities had to back off and they really feared that this would continue and become unstoppable.

The Forum of Truth and Justice met with a delegation of the European Parliament in Laayoune, together with lawyers, human rights activists and victims of forced disappearance. But these events made the Moroccans angrier and angrier, so they felt they had to put a stop to this, otherwise they would lose their grip. So what they did was to expel Mohamed Cheikh Elmoutaoikil and other members of the Forum of Truth and Justice to Casablanca. The Laayoune branch of the Forum of Truth and Justice itself was put on trial, dissolved and banned, which was yet another illegal act on behalf of the Moroccan authorities.

We were determined to disclose the human rights violations to the wider public. But the Moroccans remained just as determined to repress us, to shadow us and to keep our houses, our cars and our activities under surveillance around the clock. There was no internet access in Laayoune then, and no international calls. If you wanted to talk directly to someone abroad, you had to go to Agadir or another city. From Laayoune it was impossible. So, our work was very, very, very difficult. Another factor was the fact that very few people were allowed to get their passports. Two of our activists had passports. One of them traveled to Paris to promote our cause, another to Geneva. Thirteen of us, seven activists and six family members of the 526 disappeared Sahrawis, were also invited to go to Geneva. But at the airport of Casablanca, the Moroccan authorities took their passports from them and sent them back to Laayoune. Prominent human rights defenders such as Lekhfaoni Bachir and Mahmoud Elhamad and others like myself no longer had our passports. But I raised an issue against the Moroccan state in the administrative court at Agadir. According to Moroccan law, the Wali has to respond, and a US delegation that visited Laayoune served as a mediator between the court in Agadir and myself. The court's verdict was in my favor and the Wali returned the passports.

I was also a member of the working committee for the release of Ali Salem Tamek, a human rights defender, and other Sahrawi political prisoners. He was released on 7 January 2004, and we organized a very big reception in the south of Morocco. Again many Sahrawis gathered singing proindependence slogans and sending a very clear message to the Moroccan authorities. I was also a member of the Freedom Committee for the 'release' of Ali Salem's passport. He was very ill due to hunger strikes and wanted to go abroad for hospital treatment. The Freedom Committee was Ali Salem's own idea. Again, we exercised a lot of pressure on the authorities and finally succeeded. Ali's passport and those of all the others were returned. Today, Ali Salem Tamek is the vice-president of CODESA, but he is in prison again.

Uprising against oppression
On 10 December 2004, the international day of human rights, we made our demands public by protests. On 5 March 2005, we organized the celebration of the international day for women on Dignity Square in the center of Laayoune. The protests were very good, but naturally the Moroccans didn't like us voicing our demands. For the Sahrawis however these days marked the beginnings of an intifada, an uprising against oppression. People filled the streets calling for self-determination. It started in Laayoune, but spread to Boujdour, Dakhla, Smara and Goulimine. Throughout 2005, people gathered peacefully in public spaces holding Sahrawi flags and chanting proindependence slogans. But the Moroccan authorities beat and kicked the demonstrators, burst into people's homes and arrested and tortured them.

On 17 June, just as I was leaving hospital, I was arrested again together with two CODESA members, Lidri El-Hossein and Fatma Ayache. They had just received stitches in their heads, after having been beaten in the street. Earlier that day, the police had already clubbed us when we arrived at the demonstration. As a rule, the police make you sign a written statement, but they don't allow you to read it. 'Admit that you incited the youth to demonstrate! Name the one who provided the ingredients for making Molotov cocktails!'

Another human rights defender, Hmad Hamad, was taken from hospital, beaten up even more and tortured by around 30 police officers. In public, right in front of the hospital! After that, he was taken to prison again. A month later, most of the members of CODESA were in prison. Also, 15 Sahrawi boys disappeared, again under very suspicious circumstances. These boys had participated in the demonstrations. Today, their families still don't know where they are, so at every occasion they protest calling for news concerning the fate of their sons. By 2006, the conflict had gotten completely out of hand. A plainclothes police officer, poured petrol on one Sahrawi and set him on fire. Even little children began throwing stones at the police officers.

One man, Hamid Bahri, came to the rescue of the man who was on fire. But he was obstructed from doing so by Moroccan police officers. The Moroccan authorities defended themselves by saying: 'Hamid Bahri was the one who set the Sahrawi man on fire.' The problem with their statement is that Hamid Bahri was already handcuffed. The contorted Moroccan version of the event fits a pattern. They systematically deny responsibility, disregard evidence and blame the Sahrawis for everything that goes wrong. Another example of this is when there was a picture of me following the torture in the middle of the street, showing me covered in blood. It was a real embarrassment for the Moroccan state and the image they wish to uphold concerning their human rights record. When Amnesty International asked the Moroccan authorities about it, their response was: 'It just shows that somebody threw a stone at Aminatou Haidar and she is bleeding from the head.' But I faced these men and know them by name. One of them is Ichi Abou Hassan, the Moroccan police officer who ordered his men to do so and who personally took part in kicking and beating me.

They then took me to the Black Prison, which is notorious for its terrible conditions. It really is a black prison. I was put in the same cell as female common law prisoners including murderers, so I wasn't really treated as a political prisoner. Ten of us were in a very crammed little cell. From 1 August I started a hunger strike. On the same day, the four CODESA members were taken from Laayoune to an undisclosed destination. Later, we found out that they were being held in a secret detention center in the middle of Casablanca. A week later, the CODESA members started a hunger strike that lasted 52 days.

Due to the pressure of the European Union and international human rights organizations, eventually a trial was held. But it was postponed six times in order to prevent the international observers from attending. It lasted 26 hours non-stop. A day, a night and another two hours. The EU demanded my release and that of all other Sahrawi prisoners, 37 in all. Other people who had been arrested before us had been given sentences ranging from 10 to 20 years, but we were released. The day before my release, Moroccan security officers had come to my family's home. 'If any reception is held here, we will stop it and ransack the place. Do not receive Aminatou Haidar in this house.' My family members left, went 36 kilometers into the desert and during the night set up tents in Izik to receive me. When I finally arrived at the site of the celebration, I was really surprised by the number of Sahrawi people, singing, chanting and waving flags. There must have been around 3,000. It filled me with joy. But the place had been surrounded by 40 vans with police officers. Towards the end of our festivities the Moroccan police charged. They chased many of us, beat us up, registered names and threw others into the nearby dry riverbed. So soon after the joy, I was full of sorrow. But what remains strongest is the massive support of my fellow Sahrawis.

While still in prison, I had been awarded the Juan Maria Bandrés Prize by CEAR, the Spanish Commission for Aid of Refugees. I had to go to Spain to accept the award. After receiving my passport back, I seized the opportunity and turned it into a seven-month tour to disclose the human rights violations of the Moroccan state against the Sahrawis and Western Sahara. After Spain, I went to France, Belgium, the Netherlands, Austria, Italy, Sweden, South Africa, the United States and the United Nations. In Belgium, I met with the President of the European Parliament in 2006, Josep Borrell. After that, I visited the Scandinavian countries, Great Britain, Ireland and Nigeria. In Italy, I was given the recognition of honorary citizen of the city of Naples. The Moroccans always try to present a good image about their human rights record in Western Sahara. My visits presented the facts and how the Moroccan state builds that image on lies, which people in Morocco and abroad can only understand when they hear the eyewitness testimony from a Sahrawi from the occupied territories.

When I returned from that long trip, the airport in Laayoune was under complete military control and swarming with plainclothes police officers and a few in uniform. 'We would like to ask only Moroccans to disembark,' the captain of the plane said. They did this, because after those seven months the Moroccan authorities believed that there might be Europeans on the plane to observe the situation in Western Sahara. They wanted to block them right there. All the Moroccans and Sahrawis disembarked. Except me. 'Why haven't you left the plane?' said an official. 'You asked that only Moroccans disembark. I am not Moroccan. I am Sahrawi.'

It's very similar to what happened in 2009 when I was in Arecife airport on Lanzarote. When the pilots came to me they asked: 'Madam, what is the problem? Why don't you leave the plane?' 'Well, I don't have a problem with you. I have a problem with the police. They said that only Moroccans should disembark. I'm not a Moroccan. I'm a Sahrawi with a Moroccan passport. It's a Moroccan colonial document as it was under the Spanish colonial era.' Every time they give me the form on which you fill in your details, there is a box for your address. I write my address, ending with Laayoune, Western Sahara. If I end with 'Morocco', it would mean I accept Moroccan sovereignty over Western Sahara. I don't. On many previous occasions they had no choice but to swallow it. But that day in Lanzarote they changed their minds.

Laayoune, Western Sahara
Returning from a trip to the United States, where I had received the 2009 Train Foundation Civil Courage Prize for 'steadfast resistance to evil at great personal risk', I arrived at Laayoune airport on 13 November. It was one week after the speech of the King, in which he said that on the matter of Western Sahara 'one is either a patriot or a

traitor.' But I wasn't fearful and wrote: 'Western Sahara.' I wanted to show the King personally that I am not a Moroccan. As I descended from the plane, two journalists from Las Palmas, Spain, were accompanying me. I joined the queue for passport checking.

The chief of police, Mr. Fellah approached me:

'Madam Haidar, we would like to have your passport and the forms you completed in the plane.'

They looked over the papers and said:

'There is no Western Sahara. There's only Moroccan Sahara.'

'No, there is no Moroccan Sahara,' I answered. 'There is only Western Sahara. And if you believe there is no Western Sahara, you can also disregard MINURSO. Isn't MINURSO the acronym of la Mission des Nations Unies pour l'Organisation d'un Référendum au Sahara Occidental? The United Nations Mission for the Referendum of Western Sahara? It has never been Moroccan Sahara. If it's not Western Sahara, then none of MINURSO's resolutions are valid. If it's not Western Sahara, why did the King of Morocco sign all these UN documents starting and ending with the words Western Sahara? Why are you asking me to write something that doesn't reflect the truth?' As the proverb goes, you cannot hide the sun with a sieve.

This upset the officials, so they took me to the international zone and kept firing questions at me. The chief of police. Police officers from Laayoune. The general prosecutor. One of my uncles who used to work for the Moroccan Government. Finally, they even asked pro-Moroccan Sahrawis to come and change my mind. For 24 hours, police and security officers interrogated and humiliated me. They confiscated my passport and deported me from Western Sahara against my will and put me on a plane to Lanzarote on the Canary Islands, which are part of Spain. I ended up in no-man's land: the airport of Lanzarote. I longed to return to my home in Laayoune and see my daughter Hayat and my son Mohamed again, and of course my mother and my sisters. But while in the airport, I decided to take a stance. I started an unlimited hunger strike to defend my inalienable rights to liberty and dignity, part of which was my right to be immediately repatriated to my country. My demands were threefold. First, my immediate repatriation to my homeland, Western Sahara. Second, the respect of my dignity as a human being, and the return of all my confiscated documents, including my passport. And third, the condemnation without appeal of the political repression and systematic human rights violations conducted by Morocco, as well as its illegal occupation of the Western Sahara.

On the phone with a reporter from The Guardian, I said that Spain was complicit in my predicament by admitting me to Lanzarote without a passport and preventing my return. 'I'll carry on my hunger strike until the Spanish Government accepts its responsibilities and allows me to return to my homeland, where my children live… or I die.' After lengthy negotiations between the Moroccan and Spanish authorities, my passport was returned, and I was allowed to fly back to Western Sahara on a private plane and reunite with my children. It was a victory for human rights and justice. My hunger strike had lasted 32 days. Fortunately, I had been admitted to hospital, because my health had suffered a lot. One of my sisters had come to join me and, together with a doctor, we landed in Laayoune at about midnight. Around my home and other places in the city, there was a heavy security presence. All along, Moroccan officials had offered to release me, if only I would publicly acknowledge Morocco's 'sovereignty' over Western Sahara. I refused. Meanwhile, Amnesty International had written to UN Secretary-General Ban Ki-moon, again calling for the inclusion of a human rights monitoring component in the UN Mission for the Referendum in Western Sahara.

My first desire is to see one day in which peace prevails in Western Sahara. Not only in Western Sahara, but also in Morocco. I would like to see peace among the Sahrawis and among the Moroccans. My second desire is that those who are separated and in Diaspora are reunited. To see them again living happily and in harmony with their neighbors and in circumstances of their own choosing whether their choice is to be independent in their own state, to integrate with Morocco or as an autonomous region under Moroccan control. The most important thing is that they themselves decide about their future, so I will never be satisfied unless the values of human rights of the Sahrawis are respected. It is those values that I devoted all my life and work to and fight for, heart and soul.

A military solution would neither be good for the Sahrawis, nor for the Moroccans. The Moroccans may think they have won because the referendum has been skillfully placed on the backburner and thousands of them are colonizing our land attracted by tax breaks and business opportunities. But the Moroccan Government knows they never truly conquered the hearts and minds of the Sahrawis or convinced them into becoming Moroccans. The determination of the Sahrawis to be recognized as Sahrawis is non-negotiable. We may be small in number, but the Sahrawis will never give up their conviction, which is their right to independence. The Moroccan state has illegally occupied Western Sahara and has subsequently been strengthened in its control over our people and our land by France, the United States and Spain. Together, they have caused this drama without ever showing the will to say: 'The Sahrawis have the right to independence.'

Spain, France and the United States
In my view, the economic ties that Spain, France and the United States have developed with Morocco, while it occupies and oppresses Western Sahara, represent obstacles to a resolution. Spain still is the country that should assume responsibility for the decolonization of Western Sahara. Up to now, it has that control, because effectively it still colonizes Western Sahara administratively by its economic interests. We still hope that Spain will one day retrace its steps and accept responsibility for the tragedy they have left behind. It is high time that the Spanish Government compensates for the sins they have committed against the Sahrawis. It is high time that it recognizes the Sahrawi right to independence. It is high time that it acknowledges the treason they have committed towards the Sahrawi people and withdraw from the contract they entered into with Morocco and Mauritania, for it is against the wishes of the Sahrawi people. The Spanish people I salute for their commitment and solidarity. They are still loyal to the Sahrawi people and our rights. But the Spanish Government is not.

To France, the country of human rights and democracy, I would say that it opposes the improvement of human rights and democracy in

Western Sahara. France is against finding a final resolution to the Moroccan-Sahrawi conflict. They allow economic and financial interests to dominate their political decisions. The proof for this is very simple. In April 2010, France was the only country that voted against expanding the mandate of MINURSO to include the protection and monitoring of human rights in Western Sahara. It was isolated in the United Nations. That was a disgrace for France and a disgrace for the Security Council! If the Security Council doesn't help people towards their legal rights simply because there is a country with veto power, it will make us in Western Sahara lose confidence in its resolutions. It is very hard to convince the younger generations coming up to continue building on the path of peaceful ways. How can they have faith in it with such actions by Security Council member France? Have we not seen terrible examples of things in the past like East Timor? A great responsibility rests on France as a permanent member of the Security Council, which should anticipate or stop such events from happening. France has made a big mistake.

To the United States I would like to say this. If they thought in the 1970s that giving Western Sahara to the Moroccans would guarantee stability of the political system in Morocco, the following 35 years have proven that that was not true. In 1971 and 1972 there were coup attempts against the Moroccan King and Morocco today isn't really in a much better state. Occupying Western Sahara certainly isn't contributing to the stability of the Moroccan state and an independent Western Sahara wouldn't be a threat to Morocco. Also, helping Morocco in keeping Western Sahara in order to minimize the danger of terrorism doesn't make sense. No Sahrawi has ever been involved in terrorist attacks. Never. Not a single one. So terrorism is not a threat from among the Sahrawis. It may be from among the Moroccans. The United States should realize that this small number of people, even though they are Arabs and Muslims, is very different from what they fear. Therefore, they should be given the opportunity to develop, and be encouraged and protected. Even more so, as the younger generations might get the wrong idea. If peaceful ways never bring about any resolution to their problems, they might be forced to consider trying violent ones.

My message to these three countries is that the Sahrawi people have a history, culture and language that are very different from its neighbors. Yet, we have always respected our neighbors, and coexistence is close to our hearts. Among the Sahrawis there is no gender discrimination and the position of women is very good compared with other Arab countries. Perhaps this is so, because centuries of nomadic life encouraged that. The United States and other western countries criticize Afghanistan and Iraq especially for their maltreatment of women. But in Western Sahara women are held in esteem. Their potential contribution to a Sahrawi state is considerable. Tolerance and coexistence are good signs for the viability of a democratic state. We'll make sure to build a democratic state marked by peace and coexistence.

After receiving the Robert F. Kennedy Human Rights Award in 2008, I addressed the UN Special Political and Decolonization Committee. This is what I said then: 'We hold the United Nations responsible for the stalled state of affairs that characterizes the issue of Western Sahara and for your complete silence in the face of crimes against humanity being committed by the Government of Morocco against civilian Sahrawis who demonstrate peacefully for the right to self-determination. Thus, we demand your urgent intervention to end the prolonged misery of these people caused by the Moroccan Government's consistent refusal to accept international legitimacy and all proposals offered by the United Nations to reach a solution that respects the will of the Sahrawi people to determine their fate.'

International politics are based on strategic or economic interests. That is our problem in a nutshell. But neither the Moroccans nor the Americans, the Spanish nor the French can ignore an entire people that continue to stand up for their human rights and their legitimate rights to simply exist. Over the past 35 years, we have never lost hope, because the young Sahrawis are even more courageous than previous generations, whether they live in Laayoune, the south of Morocco, in Mauritania, in the camps near Tindouf or in other countries. We will never surrender.

Samuel Kofi Woods - Liberia
Building up a scarred country as an activist and reformer

'Good will eventually triumph over evil, but it cannot triumph by retreating. Good must confront evil.' In 'A War Without Purpose in a Country Without Identity', human rights advocate and later minister Samuel Kofi Woods at times escaped death by a hair's breadth. Plagued by two civil wars around the turn of the century, Liberia became such a dangerous place to live, that Woods' own daughter once denied she knew him, and his son told him not to come home. Raised in one of Liberia's slums, Woods would later become a community and student leader working under the motto 'light in darkness'. After leading several human rights organizations, he became minister in Ellen Johnson Sirleaf's government. As a reformer, Woods aims to 'demystify government' and to promote 'dignity without borders'.

Samuel Kofi Woods

'To shed light in darkness, that's what we wanted,' says Samuel Kofi Woods II (born in 1964), now serving as the Minister of Public Works in the Government of President Ellen Johnson Sirleaf. Two civil wars left Liberia traumatized, but since 2003 the country has experienced a period of relative peace. Woods sees his life as a testimony to the triumph of truth and justice.

Context

Impressions of Liberia's Civil War were once summed up by New York Times correspondent Jeffrey Goldberg as 'A War Without Purpose in a Country Without Identity'. In the 1980s and 1990s, the world was startled by the sight of children that headed off into battle, high on dope. Some of them painted their fingernails red, donned women's wigs and pantyhose and even Donald Duck Halloween masks, baby dolls and inflatable beach balls.

Many of these teenage 'warriors' smeared their faces with makeup and mud in the belief that juju, West African magic, would protect them from the enemy's bullets. Some boasted of eating human hearts or adorned themselves with human bones, taking their inspiration and 'combat techniques' from Hollywood action videos. There was even a 'Butt Naked Brigade'. These soldiers would strip off their clothes before going into battle. Believing they were now either invisible or invincible, they committed the most unspeakable atrocities. A person could be tortured by a child soldier with a teddy bear in one hand and an AK-47 in the other.

All this happened a century and a half after Liberia's independence. African- American settlers, 'free men of color' and people of mixed race from the United States, founded Monrovia on Africa's west coast in 1822 – named after American president James Monroe. Later joined by people from the West Indies and the Congo, the Americo-Liberians first established a colony supported by the philanthropic and abolitionist American Colonization Society. In 1847 Liberia, 'Land of the Free', became a republic, initially known as 'the great Negro democracy'.

Even a century later, in the 1940s, visitors noted that church sermons regularly referred to 'the hope of the race' and 'the land to which all blacks will someday return to live like the Jews in Palestine'. Many related to events in biblical terms. The 'Exodus' from the United States to the 'Promised Land' honored the words 'Get then from out of this land, And return to the land of thy kindred' (Genesis 31:13). They found, in the words of writer Charles S. Johnson, a Bitter Canaan. James Wesley Smith, writing in 1987, after having diligently worked his way through the Annual Reports of the American Colonization Society, concluded: 'If the volume has a message, it would have to be that the notion of returning black Americans to Africa to dwell happily in the land of their ancestors was one of extreme folly... When black Americans settled in Africa, their divergent cultural habits were almost diametrically opposite those of their African brethren. Conflict was thus inevitable.'

The rule of the True Whig Party that mainly consisted of the descendants of American settlers confirms this. Adamant to maintain a position of superiority, they ruled over the indigenous people that had occupied the region for centuries. Moreover, since Liberia's independence, many government officials were members of Masonic orders, which were seen as a status symbol and a precondition for playing a role in the corridors of power. However, there was also a lot of intermarriage and close ties developed between powerful indigenous leaders and the coastal elite. Beyond the coast, the Liberian state had very little effective control until the second half of the 20th century, and the indigenous people could not feel represented in the motto of the Great Seal of Liberia: 'The Love of Liberty Brought Us Here'. Moreover, the tribal custom of pawning, 'the equivalent of a native banking institution' allowed the exchange of livestock, but also a son, daughter or other person in exchange for money. Having escaped slavery in the United States, the settlers found themselves in a country where similar practices went under a different name.

In Liberian culture, indigenous religious traditions coexist with Christianity and Islam. Many Liberians were initiated into adulthood by male or female secret societies, kept in check by the motto ifa mo ('do not speak of it'). Even presidents King, Tubman, Tolbert and Doe were members of for example the Human Leopard and Crocodile societies. Many believe that invisible forces control everyday life, interacting with humans at every juncture. They consult prophets, healers and soothsayers for their talent to communicate with this invisible world. Many Liberians still believe that the burdens of Liberian society, especially significant political events such as the murder of Samuel Doe, reflect that daily life is determined by this invisible world of esoteric forces. The course of the war however was determined by arms trafficking, global flows of capital and the deliberate strategies of terror employed by leaders. As scholar Mary Moran says: 'Liberians might hold a range of beliefs, but they were well aware that what was killing them were AK-47s and rocket-fired grenades, not magic.'

Today, Liberia is home to about 3.5 million people. In 1980, the Government was overthrown in a military coup, followed by two civil wars (1989-1996 and 1999-2003). It displaced hundreds of thousands of people and devastated the economy. President Samuel Doe's rule was described as years of 'rape and plunder by armed marauders'. Charles Taylor's rule was equally disruptive, poignantly characterized by young supporters of the National Patriotic Front of Liberia who sang: 'He killed my Pa, He killed my Ma, I'll vote for him.' Taylor referred to himself as 'the most mischievous man in Liberia' – mischief being synonymous with witchcraft in Liberian English. So obsessed was he with solving political problems by wiping out opponents, that he kept lists of people to be 'erased', to be pursued 'even in their mother's womb'.

Ten years after the end of the armed conflicts, Liberia's Government has difficulty addressing the failings of its judicial system, which undermines development and human rights. President Ellen Johnson Sirleaf had to be pressured into expediting reforms and dealing with high-ranking officials accused of corruption. The police force remains undisciplined and almost routinely demands bribes. Fair and speedy trials are rare, and officials are often negligent in the dispensation of justice.

There has been some improvement in the freedom of expression, independent media establishments and the passage of a Freedom of Information Act into law. However, the imprisonment in 2013 of editor Rodney Sieh of the investigative paper, FrontPage Africa, has raised concerns. The United Nations Mission in Liberia (UNMIL), the US, and the EU have stressed the need to address these issues. Between 2013 and 2015, UNMIL decreases the number of 8,000 peacekeepers by half, but increases the number of UN police officers.

Despite the fighting and the general dissolution of society that took place up till a decade ago, there have been many Liberians that tried to stem the tide and to make it possible for their country to return to a more stable and humane society. In the process, many lost their lives. Others have survived, at times only by a slender thread of hope. For many years Samuel Kofi Woods II, now Minister of Public Works in Ellen Johnson Sirleaf's Government, was in danger of his life. On a few occasions, pursuers were on his heels. While working as a human rights activist, he was often on the run, which also affected his family. 'My daughter of eleven had to deny she knew me, and my son told me on the phone not to come home, for the police were looking for me.'

Nowadays, Woods is able to move freely. In the Netherlands he is paying a visit to the Justice and Peace Commission of Justitia et Pax for their 40th anniversary. 'The theme of the gathering is very powerful: people can change the world. I worked with them back in 1996, and have remained close ever since.' For Woods it's a week of celebrations with friends, and an opportunity to speak to Lawyers for Lawyers and former UN representative Jan Pronk, now working at the Institute of Social Studies. Finishing his 'testimony', Woods folds his collapsible reading glasses. 'They fit neatly into your pocket. I realized that I needed it.'

Personal narrative — Samuel Kofi Woods

Just before a live interview with CBS' Sunday Morning Live in 2003, I met Mike Wallace, a popular broadcaster on 60 Minutes in Martha's Vineyard.

'What is this? Everyone refers to you as the future President of Liberia.'
'No, never. I don't want to talk about that. I only want to be of service to my country.'
'No, no, no! Don't say that. Don't say 'never' and don't say 'no'. Let me warn you. I'm older than you. I interviewed many leaders around the world; I met Castro when he was very young and many others. Always tell people you leave your options open. Never say 'never', because in 10 or 20 years from now, you don't know what circumstance will drive you into certain things.'
And yes, at the end of the interview, the journalist asked me:
'Do you want to become the President of Liberia?'
'I'm leaving my options open,' I said.

When I reflect on it now, I really grew up in conditions of squalor, poverty and difficulty. But those conditions propelled me to find a way out, and the memory of that continues to motivate me to change society. I knew that people are not made to live in those conditions by fate; those conditions were forced upon us by society itself. Society compelled people to live there and did not allow them to lift themselves up from poverty.

I grew up on Bushrod Island in a community called Logan Town, one of Liberia's slums. The houses are built of wood and plastic, with zinc roofs. I lived in a little two-bedroom house with my mother, and most of the time I was alone with her. My father had several wives and about 18 kids; my own mother had five kids that were raised with me. There was no safe drinking water, and there was a lack of hygiene and lack of food.

When it rained, our homes got flooded, because it was an area of marshlands with uncountable mosquitoes that practically live off human beings. I remember rolling up my pants and holding up my shoes above my head, because we were walking through the water to get to the road that led to our school. That took 20 minutes. A lot of children used to walk through those croc-infested areas. Many people, out of desperation and poverty, got frustrated and resorted to smoking marihuana, sniffing glue and drinking alcohol as a way of dealing with their trauma. There was a whole mixture of people from different tribes and backgrounds from all over Liberia. Many of them had come from rural areas looking for jobs in the city.

I just went along with everybody else and accepted my situation as normal. I didn't understand the differences in society yet. By the time I was in seventh grade, I took the entrance exam for a catholic school in Monrovia. It was outside of our community, but on the same island. Our all-boys school was called St. Patrick's High School. It was run by brothers of the Congregation of the Holy Cross from the University of Notre Dame in Indiana. They were Irish. I had no idea about my school being one of the most prestigious in Liberia. But after my first year, I was confronted with a hard reality: the tuition fees were very high and my father and mother couldn't cope with the expense. I then approached Brother William Casey, a catholic priest, who I don't think is alive anymore. 'Well,' Brother Casey said, 'we have a work scholarship program for kids who clean up the school and work on the campus. All you have to do in return is to make the grades!' So that's what I did, until I graduated. Those of us who came from Bushrod Island were not very proud to be studying on a work scholarship. But there were also rich kids that attended this school, and some very high-class kids of the president and government ministers. It was a good school.

St. Theresa's Convent was a nearby all-girls school. Whenever the girls came around, my school mates would suddenly call me: 'Kofi Woods!' The girls would see you cleaning up or scrubbing floors and the boys would make fun of you. But one day, there was a gala program in honor of the founding day of the school. A man called Johnny McClain, the Minister of Information at the time, was our guest speaker. In his speech, he shared his personal experiences with us and his difficulties in obtaining his education while on a similar scholarship. 'Wow! This guy was on scholarship too!' I said to my friends. 'And now he is the Minister of Information!' So we realized it was possible to lift ourselves up to a different level. Interestingly, in 1980 the military coup took place, and this Minister was one of the few who were not executed. The next time I saw him was in 2006. Now he was a member of Ellen Johnson Sirleaf 's Government, again as the Minister of Information, and I was first appointed as Minister of Labor. We were colleagues for about a year, and he is now the ambassador to Senegal in Dakar. Whatever the case may be, God made it possible for us to see each other again. An interesting coincidence.

Disparity and discrimination
I felt uneasy about the hardship my family suffered and the wrongs in society. I saw the disparity. There were young rich kids my age that came to school in Jaguars, Citroëns and other expensive cars. It was such a scene of distinction. But by 1978, a wholly different political movement began to develop that was very progressive and active in articulating the inequalities in society. My friends and I were drawn to it, because we were living that inequality. It struck us even more that these conditions were created both by the people that founded our country, and by our current leaders. The disparity had been created by institutional lies, by people who had come from America as freed men and women. They had experienced discrimination in America with its plantation mentality and plantation culture (see box). But once they arrived here, they adopted the position of slave owners, seeing themselves as new masters!

Declaration of Independence

On 16 July 1847, representatives of the Commonwealth of Liberia published their Declaration of Independence. In Liberia, they had found 'an asylum from the most grinding oppression' and from 'that curse of curses, the slave trade'. The Declaration also formally severed them from the American Colonization Society. It synthesizes elements of the American Constitution, the American Declaration of Independence, the Magna Carta and other documents. Important additional sections read like a history of Liberia's beginning:

'We, the people of the Republic of Liberia, were originally inhabitants of the United States of North America.

In some parts of that country we were debarred by law from all rights and privileges of man – in other parts, public sentiment, more powerful than law, frowned us down.
We were excluded from all participation in the Government. We were taxed without our consent.
We were compelled to contribute to the resources of a country which gave us no protection.
We were made a separate and distinct class, and against us every avenue of improvement was effectively closed.
Strangers from other lands, of a color different from ours, were preferred before us.
We uttered our complaints, but they were unattended to, or only met by alleging the peculiar institutions of the country.
All hope of a favorable change in our country was thus wholly extinguished in our bosoms, and we looked with anxiety for some asylum from the deep degradation.
The western coast of Africa was the place selected by American benevolence and philanthropy for our future home. Removed beyond those influences which oppressed us in our native land, it was hoped we would be enabled to enjoy those rights and privileges and exercise and improve those faculties which the God of nature has given us in common with the rest of mankind.
Under the auspices of the American Colonization Society, we established ourselves here, on land, acquired by purchase from the lords of the soil (and so on).'

But then, this phenomenon exists all around the world. We see victims who next see themselves as victors, perpetuating abuses against other people. It's a tragic part of human nature. If you look at America, it was started by people who were fleeing persecution from Britain and next they subjected the American Indians. Look at Australia, a very similar story. It's all around the world. Somehow, human psychology tends to impose a certain kind of ideology on people. You see the trend of victims turning into victors too often to ignore it. They cannot resist the temptation of perpetuating misery and agony on other people. In Liberia, these freed men and women sought liberation, paradise. But instead of building harmony with the indigenous population, they subjected them to marginalization, inequality and discrimination. It diminished substantially, but various signs of it are still present in today's Liberia.

In 1980 there was a military coup. It was an attempt by military officers to reverse the inequalities in Liberia after more than a hundred years. But it was ill-conceived and instead it set Liberia on a path to anarchy and civil war. But it also set in motion other developments that have changed our course as a nation. There were many intermarriages and integration processes that have blurred the lines of the disparity and inequality. It is no longer as visible as before. But even those who received an education that came from an indigenous background adopt the elitist attitude and behavior of the Americo-Liberian settlers, believing that this will make them accepted and successful. The pattern still exists today.

Following the coup there were many executions and a lot of repression. In 1981, students sponsored by the Liberia National Students Union (LINSU) issued a statement: 'Recognizing the military government, but requesting a timetable for the return to civilian rule.' One year after the coup, this was a very serious demand. The military was unhappy, arrested some of my colleagues and friends. They were tried by a military tribunal and ordered to be executed. A lot of demonstrations and campaigns followed, until finally Samuel Doe pardoned them. But it had become clear that this military government was not in favor of civil rights or the kind of change in society that was necessary.

My awareness of differences in society developed into activism. I started as a youth leader in my own community and we set up the Logan Youth Development Association. It was created for volunteering to clean up the community using wheelbarrows and shovels, to bring some decency to the slums. Very hands-on. But it changed after we read about Martin Luther King, Malcolm X, Mahatma Gandhi, Nelson Mandela and Karl Marx. They inspired us and we began to realize that there was more that we could do. Shortly after I entered university in 1982, I was one of the leaders of the first bus strike. The reason was the fact that the Government of

President Doe had decided to move the university to another campus. But as there was a shortage of buses, we staged actions demanding more buses. As a result, the university was closed down. This prompted me to actively campaign for change.

'Good must confront evil'
In August 1984, some of our professors were arrested on political grounds. We immediately demanded their release. Doe responded by sending more troops to the campus. Many of us fled. On a fateful day, 22 August 1984, the University of Liberia was invaded. Some female students were raped, male students were brutalized. I don't know why I stayed in Liberia, but there was always an inner feeling in me to continue to endure. It is also my strong faith in God. Being educated in the Catholic tradition, I had learned about such values as self-esteem, the need to help and respect others. But I was not especially courageous. It was just something deep inside that kept telling me: 'People must live for something and die for something. There must be a purpose and a meaning for your life. Otherwise it's empty.' I always said to others: 'Good and evil are in a permanent universal contest. Good will eventually triumph over evil, but it cannot triumph by retreating. Good must confront evil.' When we confront evil, we offer society moral alternatives. The only way people can be 'converted' to your conviction is when they are willing to die defending it.

Following the elections of 1985, Samuel Doe was inaugurated as President, ushering in a return to civilian rule. But it was a sham election, very fraudulent. Since 1981, political and student activities had been banned by a military decree. When the civilian government was inaugurated, after years of military rule, we openly declared that we had the right to embark on democratic activities, and to reactivate a political student movement at the University of Liberia, because all the characteristics of civilian rule should be present and applied. We publicly challenged the Government and the University's administration. Our justification was deeply ingrained in the Constitution of Liberia, Article 2: 'With the coming into force of the Constitution, all statutes or laws that contradict the Constitution or that are inconsistent with it, are void ab ibnitio. Therefore we call on the university to allow students to organize themselves.' As students, we were involved in the opposition, including some underground work mobilizing students into popular action, preparing leaflets against the Government and other militant actions.

The opposition allegedly lost the elections. On 12 November 1985 there was an attempt at toppling Samuel Doe's Government by Thomas Quiwonkpa, one of the previous members of the military coup of 1980 who fell out with Doe. The coup failed and society fell into chaos and anarchy, with the Government looking for opportunities to eliminate perceived enemies. And being a student activist, I ended up on their list of 'radical troublemakers'. On 14 November, two days after the failed invasion, I was almost killed. Military personnel from the Executive Mansion went to my house, which was only a little shack. My younger sister was cooking outside, because we couldn't afford a kitchen. I heard her talk to someone. 'Where is your brother,' a man said. I almost got up to go to the door. But then I heard someone say: 'Where is your frisky brother!' The word frisky made me realize they were hostile, so I ran to the back of the house, climbed out of the window and took refuge in another house. I spent a month in hiding. Many people were killed, but I survived.

Lux in tenebris, 'light in darkness' was the university's motto. To shed light in darkness, that's what we wanted. As students we saw ourselves as the eye-opener of society. Our agenda was clear. We wanted to create awareness about freedom, political participation and freedom of association. Secondly, we wanted to pursue an agenda of academic freedom and social justice. And thirdly, we believed then and I still believe now, that student activities were actually the framework for building mature and responsible leadership for the country. That is the training ground where young people begin to understand the extent and the burden of leadership, and how to serve the well-being of society.

'The university students are treading on dangerous ground,' the Minister of Justice said. But after a long struggle and many difficulties, by October 1986 elections were held. I contested office as President of the students union of the University of Liberia, and won. The Government and University Administration summoned me many times, and I was threatened with arrest. But I was fired up by idealism and the excitement of change, in Liberia and in the world, and by what ought to be. You could easily be a martyr or a saint and die for a good cause that people would remember. We were also witnessing the effects of the ANC movement under South Africa's apartheid regime, and various other liberation struggles. We motivated each other by the words of the Mozambican freedom fighter Samora Machel, repeated by South African freedom fighter Solomon Mahlangu on his way to his death by hanging. Solomon said: 'My blood will nourish the tree that will bear the fruits of freedom.'

Their courage moved us deeply. By the example they set, and by the songs that we sung, we knew that we could sacrifice. You could be in jail, but it was the price you paid for freedom. Instead of fear, it was more a deep realization that we could make change possible, if we were willing to suffer blood, sweat and tears to achieve it. Throughout this period, political parties were either banned or in difficulty, and their leaders were always terrorized. The student movement was seen as the only viable and serious opposition to the Doe Government. We staged marches and demonstrations. Perhaps it was so strong exactly because students are young and adventurous, and still living on borrowed time. Most of us came from rural communities or from urban slums. We saw the difference, we saw the change! We lived the reality! We realized that it was the entire nation that had to be liberated.

In the 1970s and 1980s there was a lot of agitation in the world. Many countries were being liberated and we were directly influenced by the changes that were occurring. In those days we had the international union of students with contacts in the former Soviet Union and in Eastern Europe. There were so many movements fired up by communism and socialism. But in the post-Cold War era they all disappeared, and the level of student activism diminished considerably. Colonialism and neoimperialism have taken a different form and the world is moving in a new direction: multilateralism.

Imperialism is no longer being felt in the conquest of nations by other nations or the exploitation of colonial powers, but by indirect means. There are a lot of multilateral institutions that give 'aid' and 'support', and the struggle is taking on another dimension. Unless students become sophisticated enough to understand these things, the level of agitation in the age of cell phones, iPods, Blackberries and internet will not be the same.

Arrested and banned

Despite the many threats I received, I graduated in 1987. But only two days later I was arrested. It must have been a Friday, as I had left the house to buy bread. 'Kofi,' my mother said looking through the window when I returned, 'some friends are here to congratulate you on your graduation.' Inside were two men from the National Security Agency, the NSA.

'Who are you?' I asked.

'Oh, our boss sent for you.'

'I don't work for you, so I don't know who your boss is.'

'The head of the NSA sent for you. They want to see you.'

'For what?'

'We don't know, but you have to go.'

'Can I put on my sneakers?'

'No, you might escape.'

There was no one else around, so I had to tell my mother what was going on. I asked the two men for their names.

'Look,' I said to my mother, 'please give these names to anybody I know to take it to the press, so they will understand I have been arrested.' My mother was weeping profusely.

'If you are killed, please forgive me. I have betrayed you.' She had assumed that, as I was a student leader, these men were friends.

'You didn't betray me. You didn't know who they were.'

The NSA men took me.

'You are a security risk,' they said. 'And when the guest speaker, the Vice President, arrived during your graduation ceremony, you refused to stand up.'

This was true. After a lot of pressure from my fellow students, I was released again. But that started a lot of problems: I was banned from travelling and banned from working. Shortly after, my fiancée was dismissed from her secretarial job. The NSA's intent was to suffocate me by depriving me of an opportunity to earn a living. They forced me into a choice between frustration and accepting a job in the Doe Government. I refused to be cowed into submission.

The Great Seal of Liberia: 'The Love of Liberty Brought Us Here'.

Before this, I had come in contact with Mike Posner of the Lawyers Committee for Human Rights, now called Human Rights First. The Lawyers Committee had sent a team of researchers to Liberia that included a lady from Kenya by the name of Binaifer Nowrojee. Binaifer remains a very good friend today. She now works for the Open Society Initiative for East Africa in Kenya, and just a few months ago we met again in Nairobi. When I met her in 1988, she was reporting on human rights throughout the continent. But at that time we had to smuggle into a little house to meet in secret. I already knew about Amnesty International and their campaigns. But in 1987, after my arrest, I could not do anything, so I went to law school. I was still very attached to the student movement and very active. Again, there was a series of incidents at the campus, and some students were expelled. I was linked to them, so obviously the Government was on my heels. Then the war came. It started in December 1989.

Tell-tale Acronyms

Every Car Or Moving Object Gone
The Economic Community of West African States Cease-fire Monitoring Group (ECOMOG), led by Nigeria and consisting of soldiers from a range of West-African states, developed a special reputation. So notorious was the marketing of cars, consumer goods and scrap metal looted by these 'monitors', that some Liberians rephrased the presence of this peacekeeping force as meaning: Every Car Or Moving Object Gone.

People Repeating Corruption
The People's Redemption Council (PRC), the military junta chaired by Samuel Doe from 1980 to 1985, also qualified for a new interpretation: People Repeating Corruption. The late Henry Andrews, one of Liberia's few former ministers to be widely respected for his integrity, said: 'If even the Angel Gabriel became President of Liberia, he would within five years – or less – become totally and irrevocably corrupted.'

I had left Liberia in August 1990 on an ECOMOG ship headed for Ghana, where I spent some time before returning in 1991. And it was in October of that year that Mike Posner and Binaifer visited Liberia. 'We just met with Archbishop Michael Francis,' they said. 'He wants to set up a Catholic Human Rights Organization. Why don't you pick it up?' This would later become the Justice and Peace Commission. While banned from employment and travel, I was supported by the Catholic Church. But also, as the Bishop had personally assisted me to go to school and had been close to me, I was interested right away. Today, Michael Francis is paralyzed as he suffered from a stroke a few years ago. But as my mentor, he had reinforced those values of simplicity, honesty, and respect for human dignity that I had learned from my mother. 'Go and write down your ideas about how it should be,' he said. I got myself a typewriter and wrote up all kinds of ideas about human rights and what could be done to improve things. 'Impressive!' he said. 'You can start.'

Bishop of the Land of the Free

Archbishop Michael Kpakala Francis (1936), who himself lost 17 relatives in Liberia's conflicts, is seen by many Liberians as a powerful moral voice, and for a while 'the only man feared by Charles Taylor'. With schools, social services and Radio Veritas, the Catholic Church has made a big impact on Liberian society, even during times of fighting.

A church service held in 2003 mixed West African and Roman Catholic elements, and to an American reporter it felt 'as American as Alabama'. The Archbishop denounced Liberia's past leaders and pretenders to power and told the congregation: 'Those who came to kill us, want to rule us.' During periods of intense fighting the Archbishop spoke at the White House, stressing the 'historical relationship' and the 'moral imperative' of Americans to help Liberia. The 200 US marines assisting the 1,000 Nigerian-led peacekeeping forces since 2003, are largely due to his efforts.

'We have gone through hell. Yet, at the end of the tunnel I see a bright light – and we shall overcome,' said Francis, at which churchgoers started singing the well-known hymn. 'Pray for our country, that our country, so beautiful in the past, can come back, and be better. Let Liberia truly be a land of the free.'

Unprecedented progress
A table and a chair in a little office was all I had. I used to go round other offices to borrow typewriters. I had no road map and no training, but a year later I became the director of the Justice and Peace Commission, and since then it has grown into a big commission with support from Misereor (Germany), Caritas,

CORDAID, Catholic Relief Services, National Endowment for Democracy and many others, with some 15 people in various parts of the country and a lot of volunteers. It took human rights issues to an unprecedented level in our country's history. We did things that previously had been unimaginable. We took the Government to court for the first time ever. People had no idea that it was even possible to do so. We took them to court about the arrest of journalists without due process, and we went to the prisons with documented cases unveiling that incarcerated people had not had trials.

Under my administration, the Commission was the first human rights institution to enter into a memorandum of understanding with the Press Union. We offered journalists free legal services, especially when they were arrested. We started a legal aid program, we conducted a radio program called the Justice and Peace Forum, and we documented and monitored human rights abuses in Liberia. We were the foremost organization for data and fact-finding reports on massacres and human rights abuses of the regime of Charles Taylor during the Civil War. The Commission has done fabulous work.

A deeper inner spirit leads you to humanity because of the passion you feel for something that happens. And growing from that experience you find yourself duty-bound to help society, to lift society up, to make it a better place. By working hard, you can help society to change. That's the commitment I've been living all these years. At one point, it caused my life to be in such danger, that again I almost got killed. In April 1996, a combined rebel fighting took place in Monrovia. The city was closed off. During that period, I was very vocal about condemning atrocities on all sides. As a result I was targeted to be killed. I went into hiding but my hiding place was attacked twice one night by armed men. I survived because I made a last minute decision to change my location that night. This near-death escape compelled the US Government to evacuate me. I was airlifted from Liberia by the US marines.

After Charles Taylor was elected President in 1997, he offered me a job on the National Human Rights Commission set up by the

Government, and I was even offered money. But I chose to do my work without selling my soul and keeping a clear conscience. In 1998 I left for exile and spent two years in the Netherlands to study international law at the Institute of Social Studies and Leiden University. Next, I went to the United States in 2000 and Sierra Leone to work on the issues of transitional justice from there. 'I need time to fight back and make sure that Mr. Taylor will be brought to justice,' I told my Liberian friends and colleagues. From the Netherlands I also fought to make sure that sanctions were put in place for the diamond and timber industry, because we knew that Mr. Taylor was using these to fuel the war machine. We worked with the United Nations to enforce these sanctions and to establish a court in Sierra Leone to address the widespread impunity.

Diamonds, timber and death

Charles Taylor, in prison for theft in the United States and later trained as a warlord in Libya, was elected President of Liberia in 1997. During his reign unspeakable crimes and cruelties occurred and an estimated quarter of a million Liberians perished.

Next to rubber and iron ore, between 1990 and 1994 Taylor exported 300 million US dollars worth of diamonds, most of which proved to be from Sierra Leone. Throughout the 1990s the numbers grew. Belgium recorded 2.2 billion worth of diamond imports from Liberia until 1999, a staggering amount unsupported by the Liberian Government's bookkeeping. When, through weapons embargoes and sanctions, Taylor was cut off from the diamond trade, he returned to timber, produced by some 20 companies, mostly fictional. If not 'the pursuit of politics by other means', Liberia's off-budget expenditures were more likely 'crime by other means'. It was used for weapons, training camps or ties with other Libyan-trained neighboring presidents. Or simply to make money under the cover of war.

After having been in hiding in a remote town in Nigeria, Taylor tried to escape in 2006 by crossing the border into Cameroon, accompanied by his wife, his son and an aide, and wearing his customary flowing white robe. His driver and aide tried to bribe officials, but fled when this didn't work. Taylor's SUV contained two boxes filled with US dollars. Flown to Liberia on a Nigerian presidential jet, he was passed on to UN soldiers. As per 2011, he is still awaiting trial at the International Criminal Court in The Hague, the Netherlands.

Dignity beyond borders
In 1998, I came to The Hague as a guest of the Dutch Government. This was a unique privilege. I went to school. Now, 10 years later, Mr. Taylor has replaced me as a prisoner on trial for war crimes and human rights abuses. The fact that today he is only a few blocks away from me, tells you something about how people can change the world. Mr. Taylor terrorized people and I was seen as his 'Enemy Nr. 1'. I was almost killed by his men. And yet, I came to exile in this same country. Personally, I never felt like anyone's enemy. I am just a normal person in search of truth and justice. And I am the first person to insist that Mr. Taylor must be given a free and fair trial and due process. Like anybody else, he's innocent until proven guilty. This is a principle I respect and that I will not compromise for any reason, no matter who is involved.

After my studies and spending some time in the United States, I returned to Africa in 2001. Until 2005 I was based in Sierra Leone, working on transitional justice issues. It was a special UN program relating to the Special Court and the Truth and Reconciliation Commission. The program was implemented through the International Human Rights Law Group, now called Global Rights, and based in Washington DC. I served for about six months as head of the Sierra Leone program. Following that, I set up my own organization, the Foundation for International Dignity (FIND), because I felt there was so much that was not being done to deal with impunity. Nothing was being done to address the real victims, the Liberian refugees and displaced people in Liberia itself, Guinea, and Sierra Leone. In the camps, we provided them with capacity building training, legal assistance and advocacy. Most of the eight Liberian refugee camps were located in the eastern part of Sierra Leone in areas such as Bandajuma, Gondama, Gerihun and Jembe. We needed to improve their capacity and uplift them from being objects of pity. Next, FIND was established in Liberia, Sierra Leone and Guinea. It's still active today.

The backbone of FIND is the UN Universal Declaration of Human Rights, International and Regional Refugee Conventions, specifically the rights of displaced people and refugees. Our motto is: dignity beyond borders. Even beyond your borders, you can have dignity. I have been working as the head of the organization from 2002 onwards. In 2006 I was invited by President Ellen Johnson Sirleaf to join the Government to lead a reform agenda on employment issues.

Prior to that, we were part of a group that took the Firestone Rubber Plantation Company with its large rubber plantations to court in the United States about exploitative labor and child labor. We filed the case in 2005. I feel there is support from the President for the negotiations with Firestone. It was also needed. Firestone would not have been transformed prior to the time when I was the Minister of Labor. 'This is terrible,' I said when I visited. 'The poor housing, poor sanitation and poor wages are like slave-labor conditions. It is unacceptable. It must be changed.' I used my position as a vehicle to change society. Workers now have an independent workers union, better transportation and higher wages. They entered the first independent collective bargaining ever in history, honored by the President just last Saturday, and they have set up a committee to monitor, jointly with the company's management, child labor, as well as an anticorruption commission. All those issues are being addressed for the first time in our country's history. It represents a radical change in perception. It's not perfect, but we never had a transitional government before that actually creates a completely new framework of laws and policies that will take us to the next stage.

Tappers, children and rights

'Forced labor, the modern equivalent of slavery' were the words used in the case filed by the International Labor Rights Fund in California against Bridgestone, a subsidiary of Firestone. Workers at the Firestone Plantation in Harbel felt they were 'trapped by poverty and coercion on a frozen-intime Plantation', similar to the conditions that had existed when it was first opened in 1926.

Firestone rejected these allegations, but after the UN released a report in 2006 called Human Rights in Liberia's Rubber Plantations: Tapping into the Future, Firestone's president Dan Adomitis stated: 'During the 2003 fighting, we had thousands of refugees come to Harbel for the safety that it provided. When those people came, they occupied any open area of land that was available. They put up temporary housing made out of mud, out of bamboo, out of thatch, out of tarpaulin, out of corrugated steel. Anything they could do to get shelter. And those conditions are not Firestone housing, but they are on our property.'

Over the past five years Firestone has implemented more strict policies about child labor, and a union that represents the workers. Parents are being educated about why they should not bring their children with them into the field. Some policies were difficult to follow through during the Civil War; others only came into force after consultations with the Ministry of Labor.

The fact that President Ellen Johnson Sirleaf appointed me in 2006 as Minister of Labor, and in 2009 as Minister of Public Works, may seem like a personal victory. But I never see things through the perspective of victor and vanquished, heroes and villains. All I see is a normal person. On top of that, I don't think victory has been achieved yet. There still is a lot that must be done in Liberia and in the world. The world is being challenged by religious fanaticism, the scourge of deception and interpretation of what terrorism is, the war on terror, and the changing dynamics of human rights and compromises of liberty on the platter of terrorism. In Kenya and Zimbabwe, where finding common ground is too difficult and complex, leaders don't accept the victories of democratic choice and the will of the people. They insist on remaining in power, using ethnic clashes to undermine democracy. It's an aberration of the democratic gains that were made over the years on our continent. If these trends continue, it will be tragic for Africa.

Spoilers, preservers, reformers
In the past, Liberia suffered from institutionalized violence and the criminalization of the nation state. What we need now, is to reform our institutions, and to develop new laws and policies to create a strong framework against corruption. I believe that there are three types of people in Liberia. The spoiler (those who want to continue on the path of violence, crime and lawlessness), the preserver (those who believe that the old status quo must be preserved) and the reformer (those who believe that the institutions and the mentality of our people must undergo transformation). I am a reformer. We need robust institutions to prevent the deprivation of our people, to deliver justice, and to lift them up from poverty. We need to find more indigenous and local means to address the issues of debt and AIDS. 'There is AID,' I always tell people, 'and there is AIDS. The only difference is that one of them has an 's'. But I think that if we're not very careful, they almost have the same effect.'

Aid can be destructive because of the way in which it is given and because of its side-effects. Over the decades, so much aid has been given to tyrannical regimes that have used it to exploit their people and to enrich themselves. That trait has become entrenched. A lot of aid has been given not for the real needs of people, but because those governments were favored by other governments. Not because of a deep sense of humanity, but for their own political agenda. Most of the money goes unchecked and gets stolen. Unless there is a paradigm shift in the world, it will be very difficult to change this. With passion, a good heart and commitment it can happen. Those of us who call ourselves leaders must recommit ourselves to a strong sense of self-denial and resist the temptation of being corrupt.

'You are a Minister,' someone said to me in the United States. 'Don't you have an aide?' I do my work without the protocol. I think government should be simple. It should be of service. We are servants and we should have a deep sense of humility, as in that saying from Dorothy Day 'live simple, so that others may simply live'. Shortly after I took office, I went on a trip. And for such a trip you get an allowance of about 5,000 US dollars for expenses. When I came back, I returned the money from the government coffers that I hadn't used. Some 4,000 US dollars. 'What kind of Minister is that?' people said. Now, in Africa that is strange, because government officials exploit; they do not return the money. Some people really think I'm stupid, simply because I don't want to get rich.

About a year later, I returned from the United States after Christmas. 'You have some gifts!' my staff said as I walked into my office. 'For what?' I asked. 'What did I do?' By way of tradition, during the Christmas season in many parts of Africa companies send gifts. I returned the money and I returned the gifts. 'What's wrong with this guy?' Some of my staff even said: 'Give it to us! We need it!' This is the tradition. And it is precisely why we have got to break with tradition! For years and years it has kept our people backward. It's ethically wrong, because it puts the receiver in the pocket of the company that gives it – or the government that gives it. Secondly, it creates the perception of being controlled by big companies. As a cabinet minister working on labor matters, how can I advocate for poor workers who can't give me gifts? Only the rich and powerful can. No matter how fair I may want to be, if I accept gifts, the ordinary workers in the field would never see me as objective.

Historically, many Liberians have seen themselves being deprived, because the rich and powerful have always been bought government officials. So unless we want to perpetuate the same system, we have to embark on a radical transformation of society. Strangely, for this people accuse me of being extremist. Unless the awareness of this debate spreads, unless you open new frontiers, society will not change. You have to advance new attitudes. It is difficult, and you will be criticized for it. Those who know me are aware that I stand by my principles, even when everyone thinks differently. 'It is not right,' I say. To some extent, these principles were caused by having grown up poor. But most important is my own sense of conviction.

Ordinary Liberians continue to endure and to persevere. They give me hope. On their faces I see a fighting spirit. Even though many of them have been desperate, frustrated and deprived, they share a collective resilience to progress and succeed. And with that, we can surmount any challenge or difficulty. It worries me however that there still are people that violate the public good, use public funds, undermining public trust. There still is widespread corruption, greed and abuse of power and some level of injustice, private and public. It's unacceptable. These things are difficult to address, although as a government official I can do more than before. I have even criticized certain government actions. I think that the Government is also sensitive to what I say, now that I have the opportunity to publicly influence this change. And I will. I must.

Encounters and transformations
I don't see myself as a cabinet minister. I see myself as an ordinary person who must serve our society, and demystify government, especially for societies in Africa. The overwhelming authority of government and of government officials needs to be demystified and made simple. They are there to serve. But it can only be achieved by people who demonstrate this by example. Human rights are the key. We must adhere to universal conditions of respect for human rights and human dignity. Foreign governments should expect the same of Liberia as they do of themselves.

Working as a Minister is a difficult psychological condition for me. The difficulty is that when you engage in radical transformations of society, the government itself is not an easy vehicle for that. The nature of the beast is that it resists change – not because of the paperwork, but because of the kind of people governments attract. There is the arrogance of power, exploitation, corruption and enriching yourself. That's not what it is for. We're now putting in place mechanisms to restrain individual excesses. If you wish to change things, you have a big battle on your hands. It's not easy. Sometimes you're ostracized.

I'm writing a book at the moment. Its message is not just for Liberians, but for a much wider audience. I'm trying to link my personal experience to a universal principle of human transformation, a search for truth and justice. But how can one link one's trials and tribulations, one's strengths and weaknesses to these universal principles? My life, and therefore likewise the book that I'm writing, is a living testimony of the triumph of truth and justice. The search for justice is practical. It can be realized. Think of Bishop Francis who I worked with for a long time. 'I'm an incurable optimist,' he says. I am too. If you look at the course of my life, working and fighting for justice, living in exile for five years, going back, becoming a Minister, working to change Firestone, Taylor in prison... So many things have happened! It's possible. It wasn't me that triumphed. Truth and justice triumphed. Anger and hatred can be transformed into something positive. Otherwise they blur the human sensibilities and diminish the spirit. When I was in prison, banned from employment, banned from travel, I still wanted to challenge the system. Many lawyers didn't dare to challenge the Doe Government. I went to law school and became a lawyer. Ninety per cent of my time was spent on human rights cases of people who cannot afford to pay anything.

One chapter of my book is called Encounter. I see encounter as an interaction with an event, a person or a thing that changes your life and that creates a different sense of passion. It may be triggered by anything that creates an attachment to you – an experience, a person, even a dog that needs your help. In my own case, while growing up my mother was always sick. As a young kid going through elementary school I saw my mother going through difficult times. I got closer to her and developed the greatest respect for a woman who was single-handedly taking care of my brothers and sisters and me. She was one of the greatest examples in my life, because of her triumph over illness and difficulties, and she's been a great inspiration to me. She is a special person, simple, not sophisticated.

She taught me Christian principles like 'thou shalt not steal' and 'thou shalt not kill', and when I did things wrong, she would discipline me. That made a great impact on me and helped me in later life. Even in times of difficulty, she stood by me. And I learned that that passion can be transferred to other people and to society as a whole – the same depth of passion. The encounter is a turning point in a person's life that creates a passion for something.

I have met other people who were touched by the same ideals, including rich people who feel they want to assuage their sense of guilt. They too had an encounter and felt it was their duty to help, to redeem themselves for the way in which they had accumulated their wealth, and to live up to values they used to lack. I once heard a speech about lions, leopards and the many other animals that live in the forest. Nobody wants the forest to catch fire, because none of the animals would have a place to stay. It's better to keep the forest intact. We must all preserve the forest, so that the people from different cultures and backgrounds that inhabit the forest can all live together.

There are moments, encounters that people don't forget. As you interact and have a dialogue with someone, there is a mutual process that goes on that cannot be ignored. It strengthens your belief and your conviction, and it reminds you to stay on course, to be consistent. As I talk to you or any other person, I'm testifying of my conviction and my commitment to demonstrate that I believe this. What society denied me and deprived me of, is what I want to offer to others. I want to offer to others the opportunity not to grow up feeling denied or that society must be seen as the enemy. It is possible to transform, to make a contribution to society, and become a living testimony of the good arising from the human passion.

Those who are seen as nobody can become somebody. People who were sold as a slave or who became refugees, whether it's Joseph in the Bible or Albert Einstein in history, were thought of as objects of pity. But history shows that the best may come out of such people. It's a message of hope and redemption. I want a little kid in the Firestone plantation, whose father is a tapper, to believe that he or she can become a Minister or the President of Liberia tomorrow. We must remake Liberia to ensure equality for all.

Vuyiseka Dubula - South Africa
Serving health to the disadvantaged in the fight against Aids

'There is no other thing that can shake me now' said Vuyiseka Dubula after contracting Aids. With one out of every nine South Africans being infected, it is one of the world's highest infection rates. In a culture of 'sugar daddies', family sense has eroded, and due to poverty, lack of education, and unemployment, the problems are multiple. Having worked herself up from counselor and branch leader to Secretary General of Treatment Action Campaign, Vuyiseka endured all the hardships she now helps others overcome. Surviving an abusive home, she feels she was 'born to the class struggle'. She learned to challenge everything, including the healthcare system and the power of pharmaceutical companies. 'The Government sees us as enemies, because we are watchdogs.'

Vuyiseka Dubula

'HIV was the last challenge in my life, because there is no other thing that can shake me now.' Vuyiseka Dubula (born in 1978), Secretary General of the Treatment Action Campaign (TAC), is outspoken about everything. 'Come inside, so you see the reality! It's almost as if the Government and the people live in different countries.'

Context

No South African has to say 'ja, baas' ('yes, boss' in Afrikaans) anymore and 'die swart gevaar' ('the black danger') has dissolved – as has 'the white danger'. The same black people that were feared during the time of apartheid now run the country through the ANC majority Government.

During the transition of power, some felt 'an immense fear that the black hordes would rise up and kill us' as writer Steven Otter puts it, 'not only because of our terrible treatment of them, but also as a confirmation of our theory that they were savages'. But the transition went well and many television viewers around the world recall Nelson Mandela's famous 'Madiba shuffle' – dancing being central to Xhosa culture – at the occasion of his inauguration as the first black President of South Africa in 1994.

A generation later, institutionalized apartheid is over. But it still exists in poverty and lack of opportunity. A walk through a wealthy suburb and a poor township makes this abundantly clear. The gulf between rich and poor is still widening and there is a worrying influx of immigrants, notably from Zimbabwe. People from Zim escape Mugabe's regime to the more affluent South Africa. But they come in huge numbers, which is leading to tensions, fighting, riots, and deaths. Some openly discuss: are we slowly going the same way as Zimbabwe?

On top of these problems, the HIV/Aids epidemic has run rampant with a further 1,500 people infected daily in South Africa alone. One out of every nine South Africans has contracted Aids. On large billboards Mandela used to say: 'Those who do not educate themselves do not understand the gravity of the situation.' At the

Barcelona conference on Aids in 2002 he summoned people: 'One of the most difficult things in life is not just to influence others, it is to change your own character. We are required to do this today.' After the death of one of his sons, he declared: 'You must not be ashamed of speaking out and telling the community "I suffer from HIV/Aids"... When you keep quiet, you sign your own death warrant.'

The rate of infection and the habits that allow it are so worrisome that the Minister for Welfare and Population Development, Dr. Zola Skweyiya, warned: 'The effects of Aids will turn us into a minority in our own country.' Writer Mmatshilo Motsei equally worries about the fact that elders don't show a good example, but are 'entrapped in a spiral of insatiable acquisition of wives, positions, money and power by any means necessary'. 'How on earth do we envisage inculcating any values in a society led by individuals who show little regard for the fundamental principle of Botho, i.e. what it means to be humane?' In a culture of 'sugar-daddies', 'sugar-mommies' and 'teaspoons' family sense has eroded and young people have sex for social status or stylish gifts. Or even for food, paying the rent, bus fares or a pair of sneakers.

One of the most prominent moments of greater awareness about Aids came through a little boy first known as Xolani Nkosi, later called Nkosi Johnson. Despite his short life, he made an impact that many remember. But whatever amount of information or examples are available – like the ABC policy 'Abstain (or delay), Be faithful to one partner, and Condomize' – it can hardly balance the social dynamics of today's South Africa. Some think that HIV only happens to black youths, gays, migrant workers or poor black women. But if you are white, heterosexual, married and in a steady job, you can get it just as well. Aids spreads easily in a culture where people are killed on the roads because of alcohol, children are raped, women are battered by their partners and people are murdered for their cell phones.

Nkosi Johnson (1989-2001)

Born Xolani Nkosi in a township east of Johannesburg, Nkosi never knew his father. His mother, Nonthlanthla Daphne Nkosi, passed along the HIV virus to her baby. Volunteer worker Gail Johnson saw them in 1991 in a crowded Aids care centre in Johannesburg. 'It was a very personal and mutual understanding,' says Johnson. 'I wanted to do something more than just talk about it. And there was Nkosi. All I had to do was to reach out to him.' Nkosi's mother agreed for Gail to become his foster mother. As Nkosi Johnson, he had a home in a neat Johannesburg suburb and a wide circle of friends at Nkosi's Haven, the Aids care centre Johnson founded and named after him. 'Mommy Daphne' died in 1997. In the same year, Gail and Nkosi Johnson won the battle of enrolling Nkosi in a primary school, making him a national figure in the campaign to destigmatize Aids.

'Hi, my name is Nkosi Johnson,' he said at the opening ceremony of the 13th International Aids Conference in Durban in 2000. It's hard to forget this tiny figure in a dark suit and sneakers. Nervously holding a wireless microphone, he told an audience of thousands the story of his life, 'Mommy Daphne' and 'Mommy Gail'. 'Please help people with Aids. Support them, love them, care for them. I want people to understand about Aids, to be careful and respect Aids. You can't get Aids if you touch, hug, kiss, or hold hands with someone who is infected. Care for us and accept us – we are all human beings. We are normal. We have hands. We have feet. We can walk, we can talk, we have needs just like everyone else. Don't be afraid of us. We are all the same!'

Nkosi Johnson (photo source: Gail Johnson)

Part of the remedy therefore may lie in community support, and a renewed sense of the Xhosa concept of ubuntu – 'humanity'. Archbishop Desmond Tutu, himself of Xhosa descent, describes it as 'the essence of being human': 'A person with ubuntu is welcoming, hospitable, warm and generous, willing to share. Such people are open and available to others, willing to be vulnerable, affirming of others, do not feel threatened that others are able and good, for they have a proper self-assurance that comes from knowing that they belong in a greater whole. They know that they are diminished when others are humiliated, diminished when others are oppressed, diminished when others are treated as if they were less than who they are. The quality of ubuntu gives people resilience, enabling them to survive and emerge still human despite all efforts to dehumanize them.'

In recent years, South Africa's Government's has been unable to address major social issues such as corruption, unemployment, and human rights violations. In 2014, when Jacob Zuma won a second term in office, the victory was marred by reports that he misused state funds for his private residence. Serious concerns remain about the conduct of police officers, and often demonstrators are dispersed with excessive force. During the Marikana miners' strike in 2012, 34 of them were killed and 78 wounded. Observers have questioned the integrity of the investigation and court case.

The life expectancy of South Africans however is rising. In part, this may be due to the state-funded availability of antiretroviral drugs, the largest rollout program in the world. Despite this, the BBC's South Africa Profile of 2015 still mentions the number of HIV/Aids patients as the second-highest in the world. Many people and organizations work day and night to change this. The Treatment Action Campaign (TAC) is one such organization, made famous by Zackie Achmat (see box). The TAC has been working on the front lines of Aids treatment, making medication available to all and fighting governments, pharmaceutical companies or simply public opinion to change things for the better. Recently, Zackie has passed on the baton to new Secretary General Vuyiseka Dubula.

Vuyiseka, always in between meetings and busy as a bee, works either in Cape Town or in Khaya – short for Khayelitsha township. Next to her work, she takes care of her family, studies for exams in Public Administration and tries her best to keep her curious two-year old daughter away from the cleaning liquids under the kitchen sink. In fact, our talks were delayed by the hospitalization of her child, who had accidentally drunk Thinus paint liquid. Before reaching the TAC offices in Khaya, you pass iLitha Park, with neat houses in cheerful pink, yellow, blue or white. But the rest consists of shacks of corrugated iron, plastic and wood. For Vuyiseka it's no small effort to tell her story undisturbed. 'As soon as I get out of this door, everyone wants to say something to me or talk to me. Everyone wants to talk to me. Eish.'

Personal narrative — Vuyiseka Dubula

I'm not sure whether I got all the immunizations! When I was born in the Eastern Cape, access to healthcare was still very limited and I wasn't born in a hospital, but in a mud house in Ndakeni Village in Idutywa in the former Transkei. I was one of seven children, and as my father's siblings were three brothers and two sisters, I grew up in a very big extended family in one household. We grew up very poor. In the rural areas there are not many people that have the money to buy everything they want and you have to struggle to send your children to school or to sell your mealies – bread baked with sweet corn – which you grow on your own farm.

After my parents divorced when I was three, my father stayed in the Western Cape. My youngest sister was only one year old and we stayed with the wife of my father's older brother. All my life I have been used to many children around, sharing food on only one plate and not having eggs or milk while others did. And we fought over jam, which we loved to eat as a child. It was rarely available and once you did have access to it, it had to be shared by many of us.

We had to walk to school, about 20 kilometers from where we lived. And whether it was raining or not, icy or not, we had to go there on foot. My school was not made of brick; all the classrooms were mud houses. We went to this school until a big tornado swept through the village and the school collapsed. So we didn't have any rooms anymore and had to move to other schools in other villages even further away from home. High school at that time was like an extended 8th grade, which I had to finish at another school. After that I moved to Cape Town, because my father wanted me to study there. That's when all the trouble started.

Growing up in the Eastern Cape, in a big family with love, you get used to that. But for me it was difficult to adjust from the circumstances of a village to those of a town. And to staying with my father. I didn't love him that much because the apartheid system used to take our fathers away and therefore that bond in the family was broken. This resulted in the fact that I didn't have a strong relationship with him after he divorced my mother. Most of the time he was away. We didn't know him very well and were not used to his style of parenting. We felt that he was spending all his money in Cape Town and did not bother about us in the village. I didn't care very much, because I did have a loving home in the village, where my cousin brothers were looking after us, cooking, helping us with homework, teaching us gardening, making dolls and even platting our hair. We also knew that everyone had duties to do when they came back home.

So when I came to Cape Town in 1995, my other life started. My father was very abusive and violent. And I hadn't been used to anything like that with my other 'mother', my aunt, at home. My father even had other children outside the marriage. He was a taxi driver and every weekend he came home drunk and beat the hell out of my stepmother and my brothers and sisters. All the girls were chased out of the house, for if our mother was 'bad', we must all be bad. We even asked our stepmother: 'Can you please stop what you are doing? We are tired of knocking on other people's doors, reporting to the police, and everybody is tired of us looking for a place to stay the night.' We didn't understand. When I was preparing for my matric exams – the final year of high school – I couldn't do it at home. I had to go to my friends and study there. When I returned home I was beaten up again, because my father thought I went out with boys. I was very confused as a child – is this a loving father or an abusive father? Maybe where I come from things are done differently?

He used to buy us school uniforms only, but no clothes to wear at home. Sometimes we didn't feel like other children. Going to school was hard. But I passed my matric exams with flying colors. After that, my father told me that he didn't have any money for my further education. And I was his firstborn, imagine! So if he didn't have money for me, what would that mean for those that came after me? I had to look for a job. I was so determined to do so, because I came from the Eastern Cape. There, even though you may be poor, you are encouraged to go to school. And we had seen the role models in our own village, people who were nurses and doctors. It was natural for me to aspire to get a good profession. That was my dream and my goal.

'If you can't send me to school,' I said to my father, 'I'm going to go get money and do it anyway. I don't know how, but I want to go to school.' So I asked my cousin brother to ask anyone who is a friend or anyone who can send me to school and I will get part-time jobs to pay them back while studying. Luckily we got the money for registration. 'I don't care,' I said, 'as long as I can get an entry, even if it's just to get a certificate. I just want that satisfaction that I've done something.' Anyway, it got me that far. I did human resources for one and a half years and I had to work after school, doing anything from car washing to selling chips at the Philippi station, the busiest in Cape Town.

In 1997 a major breakthrough happened. I had never known my mother for almost 18 years. She started writing letters to us and when we moved to Cape Town we started corresponding with her. We agreed to meet in the train in the 3rd class carriage Nr. 3 at 7.15am on Wednesdays. Even if it was only an hour per week, my sister and I started our relationship with our mother on the train.

No way out
After matric, standard 10, I had thought I would just play it tight with my father. I didn't have to listen to him anymore and worry about what he was doing at home. I could just escape this with my sister knowing that we had an alternative parent now. I thought that at least when we don't have to spend our lives crying every day, we can stay in a safe home, not having to worry about our father barging into the room and wanting to sleep in the same bed. But disaster struck again. My mother, who was a domestic worker, had a car accident and broke her spine. From that moment she couldn't move anymore. We had to do absolutely everything for her. And she didn't have a lot of money. We asked permission from my father to stay with her and he agreed although not happily. I felt that I had to look after her and look for a job. That's when I started a part-time job at the Shoprite supermarket. It wasn't much, but it was an income and my mother and my sister depended on it. Coming from one struggle,

you go to another. There never was a time to take a break and just be a child.

Again, in 2001, I thought things were going reasonably well. I had a job and even though my mother wasn't well, she was fine and there was a chance she might walk again one day... 'You're HIV positive.' That was my diagnosis at the Greenpoint Clinic. It was a terrible shock, because for a while I had been thinking that after all these struggles, there must be a way out. By that time I was 22, still single and I didn't know anything about treatment yet. I had already struggled a lot in my life and I was very scared of having a child, because I knew a child would be an extra burden. I felt I couldn't survive on my own and I had no secure foundation. If I did have a child, who would look after it? When I heard I was HIV-positive, I didn't expect it. But I took it as another struggle. And I told my mother: 'Look, I know all of you are all looking up to me in terms of support as I am the only one working and I am the oldest child. But HIV is here and for now I don't know what to do.' For two months I was confused and I wanted to stop work, because I didn't understand things. How can all these problems come to one and the same person? I am tired of struggling!

I then realized that I was born in a struggle and that I will always struggle, because unfortunately I was born poor! I guess I am living my life as a socialist, because my mother was a domestic worker and my father was a taxi driver. I was born to the class struggle. But perhaps the major good thing in all of this is that my coping mechanisms became very well developed. Because when you're used to so many struggles, you kind of take things lightly, thinking oh, I've already overcome so many obstacles in my life, this is just another one. They come and go, and tomorrow there will be another one. And that one will also go again. So I think that somehow my body has become used to dealing with obstacles almost automatically.

A counselor in the Greenpoint Clinic advised me to go Khayelitsha Township. She referred me to the Ubuntu Community Health Centre down the road, only two minutes away from the TAC offices where we are now. 'Go there, even though there are no ARVs –

antiretroviral drugs for the treatment of infections, primarily HIV – available, but there is treatment for opportunistic infections, and MSF – Doctors Without Borders – is just piloting ARVs in poor resource settings. And you'll be able to meet with other people who are living with HIV and who can motivate you.' It takes only 15 minutes by train or 10 by taxi. But it took me two months to go, because Khayelitsha is one of the worst areas in terms of poverty, unemployment and HIV – everything is just worse. And I felt that by going there, I would become associated with all the bad things of this place!

But I did go. When I arrived at the clinic there was a TAC peer educator called Nomandla Yako, now working as a Red Cross counselor. She was also HIV-positive and just a few months younger than me. She welcomed me and explained why she joined the TAC and why it is important to come to the HIV clinic. You know, when you are told those things by a person who is healthy, who can articulate herself very well, you think to yourself: oh, she's just saying these things to make me feel good, for otherwise I feel bad anyway. But after Nomandla introduced me to TAC and to my current partner Mandla Majola, whom I have been with since late 2001, I never stopped coming.

Breaking through limitations
During the time I first went to TAC, Zackie Achmat was the chairperson. I met him in many meetings and of course once you start in TAC, you see all these dedicated people and you're scared to go to them, feeling they are too big for you and that you can't even shake their hand. I saw Zackie from a distance, because I thought: how dare I go and ask him any questions? You know, people in TAC are so empowered, they speak a special language, and if you come for the first time, it's very overwhelming. How can these people speak so fluently about science and law, while some don't even have matric? The way they speak, they must be lying. They must be lawyers, doctors or medics. But I understand now, that everyone goes through a process of empowerment in TAC and understanding their own diseases. And then you realize what your limitations are,

how you may break through them and be positive. You go through a guided process by way of a course.

'After shouting at the health minister, I gained 20 CD4* cells.'

Zackie Achmat (born in 1962) is a South African activist, most widely known as founder and former chairman of the Treatment Action Campaign (TAC) and for his work on behalf of people living with HIV and Aids in South Africa. Achmat grew up in the 'colored' community in Cape Town during apartheid. At the age of 14, he set fire to his school during the period of the Soweto Uprising to force his fellow students to boycott classes. He was arrested and tried in each of the years between 1976 and 1980.

The TAC's notoriety is in no small part due to his dynamism. A former antiapartheid and gay rights activist, Achmat was skilful in marshalling the support of existing activist networks and mobilizing a grassroots membership to work at community level, as well as employing classic anti-apartheid tactics such as civil disobedience. TAC has become the most well-known and most successful Aids activist group in South Africa with a mission to ensure that HIV/Aids is not a death sentence. Initially, it focused on access to medicine for those who could not afford private health care by taking on government policies and brand-name pharmaceutical companies. After scoring major victories against both, it broadened its outlook to improving all aspects of health care provision, particularly with the implementation of an anti-retroviral program in the public health sector.

Achmat publicly refused to take Aids medications until all who needed them had access to them, which drew former President Nelson Mandela to plead with Achmat at his home to begin drug therapy. Achmat respectfully refused Mr. Mandela, and held firm in his pledge until August 2003 when a national congress of TAC activists voted to urge him to begin taking his medicines; he announced that he would start shortly before the Government announced that it would make antiretrovirals available in the public sector. Achmat is a card-carrying member of the African National Congress and has been a supporter of the party since his days as an antiapartheid organizer. This left him in the ironic position of protesting and criticizing the party he helped to put into power, as President Thabo Mbeki, Achmat's long-time nemesis, became the leader of the ANC and head of Government, later followed by Jacob Zuma.

* CD4 or T-helper cells are white blood cells that help protect the body from infection.

I left the Shoprite supermarket and got a part-time job as a cashier at McDonalds. McDonalds was another nightmare, because you work long hours, you don't eat good food, and if you are a person like me with no other income at home, you work extra overtime to get that extra cent. Travelling regularly to Khayelitsha meant extra costs. At first I wouldn't mind if I ate bread all day. But now I was told I had to eat beetroot and garlic. I couldn't afford that, so I had to work extra hours to buy those vegetables. Many people still believe that as long as you eat beetroot, garlic and other things, you will be all right, because for many years it was portrayed to them that that was the way to beat HIV. It was just a lie. Yes, it's good nutrition. But there's no way it's going to sort out your HIV. Some people are beginning to understand and are no longer confused between nutrition and treatment.

So I continued coming to the TAC offices, until I realized that I was growing a passion for this. It was also a healing process for me to understand that HIV is not going to go away and I might as well normalize it as part of my life and use my status of being HIV-positive to help others. If it hadn't been for Nomandla, who was living healthily with HIV too, I don't think I would have been the person I am today. She guided me from the beginning. She empowered me and gave me a new sense of life and meaning.

From then on I thought: let me do this to others as well. So I opened a TAC branch in the Samora Machel Township on the Cape Flats, close to the city. While still working at McDonalds, I met Dr. Eric Goemaere who was at that time MSF head of mission there. 'You do not belong here,' he said. 'It's a waste of your time and potential. I have seen how you organized a workshop for your branch Samora.' He took me in at the MSF/TAC office as a volunteer receptionist. For the first time since I was diagnosed, I felt a sense of belonging, of being together with other people who were living with HIV in a place where I could speak freely without the fear of other people judging me.

Challenging everything
I left McDonalds in 2002. Since that time I was working in my first ever professional job as a receptionist in the MSF/TAC office in Khayelitsha. Even at the TAC branch level, you get all the books that you see here and you go through them page by page. Every weekend there was a workshop and the room would be packed with branch members, asking innumerable questions about why things were this way or that way. And still, every Saturday there is a workshop in this room. Zackie would be part of those meetings, empowering more comrades. That's how TAC created such a great foundation in communities and branches! People like me, who were diagnosed with HIV and who at first didn't know what to do, the moment they did, they were empowered to start branches in their own areas.

There is a structured program called Treatment Literacy. It presents science in language that people can understand, so that the poor can also 'own' it and better care for themselves. The program educates people starting with why they should be tested, up to the point of advocacy for accessibility of better health care for all. Once you're tested, what are the things you should know about the healthcare system? How should the healthcare system respond to you as a user of that service? And if it doesn't provide, what does the law say about it? New TAC recruits ask questions like: 'If you don't give me treatment today, what would be the implications for my health and for the general public of South Africa?' You challenge each and every thing.

We started Samora Branch with six people, mostly consisting of my family members. Naturally, it also empowered them about the meaning of HIV and it encouraged them to test as well. Now that they knew they had a family member who was HIV-positive, they realized what the threats are behind HIV, because at first we hadn't taken notice and hadn't read enough about it. Even my mother, my brother and my cousin are TAC members now. And after my family, many of my neighbors got tested, especially when we had trainings and workshops in our branch. And they knew they were going to be fine, because I was also fine!

When I say 'I'm fine' it's partly because of medication, but it's mostly because when I was tested, my CD4 count was 250. HIV destroys CD4 cells, a type of white blood cells that are critical to the immune system. But I was not yet too late, compared to other people who were very sick at that time. Some of them had CD4 counts of 1, and I knew that even with a CD4 count of only one you can still make it, but it's dangerous to wait that long. Some people do not wait by choice, but the system is too slow and access too limited. I kept myself busy, focusing on HIV and access to treatment, because I knew: now that I'm HIV-positive, if there is no HIV treatment tomorrow, what can I do to find it? I can't be told that I must wait again! When I was tested in 2001, I was told there was no treatment. But now, I'm in the struggle for access to treatment itself and I must be able to access it. I went for that goal, tirelessly.

Knowing that there are not so many people who can access antiretrovirals and that many of them will die if they can't, I wanted to make sure that at least some of them would get it. It's work in progress. Some day it will be possible for everyone to have access to treatment. I was very stuck at that point, because my dream was to go to university and my father couldn't grant me that dream, so I thought it was my responsibility. He had lost his dream somewhere, so he wanted to ruin mine. So I was a very, very determined young girl who wanted to be someone. Yet again, there was a barrier. But HIV was the last barrier in my life. I'm saying 'the last', because there is no other thing that can shake me now.

Shall I go back to school? Is it worth empowering myself, knowing that I'm going to die anyway? Is it worth getting married? Is it worth having a child while I'm going to die? For four years I had been struggling. But 2004 was a breakthrough year. 'I'm starting the treatment. I'm going back to school and I'm going to get married.' I started treatment on 14 June 2004 with AZT/3tc and Nevirapine. That was the moment in which I changed my life and for the first time I had a normal life, with HIV being part of myself. I went to school, I shaved my relaxed hair and I had dreadlocks and I got pregnant, and in 2006, within two years, I had a daughter and she is a healthy child. There was no chance she could contract HIV, because I started treatment two years before. And by then I felt very good about myself. I felt that my dignity had returned, but also that my dignity will only be fully back once I get my degree. Then I would be really me and I would be able to dream even better!

Myths and controversies
Have you ever heard of this myth that Aids and HIV were invented by western nations to suppress African people and wipe them out? There's that. But there's also a myth of hoping that there will be an African cure for HIV. In South Africa, many people believe the disease started in Europe, but the idea that the cure should also come from Europe is seen as too oppressing. Because of our history, it is felt as dependence and a new form of colonialism. Do we have to depend on Europe for the treatment of HIV? Why should it be European experts that are fighting the disease through their HIV treatment access programs? Of course, South Africa can't do everything at once. But we cannot wait for Jesus to come. We have to meet Him halfway. There must be something we can do. That's why President Mbeki used to link HIV to poverty, and because it is one of the most widespread problems of South Africa, there has to be a South African solution. Of course, poverty is a contributing factor, but it's not a direct cause of Aids. So I think Mbeki was simply caught in between. I'm not sure what books he reads. He's a very sharp and clever man on other issues, but very confused when it comes to HIV. And the Virodene Affair reflects that.

The Virodene Affair

'The African Renaissance is upon us,' proclaimed Mbeki in 2000, after helping to establish in the 1990s an intellectual movement to bring cultural, spiritual, economic, and political renewal to the continent. Likewise, many people in South Africa's Government were enthusiastic after presentations to the cabinet by Olga Visser, a medical technician at Pretoria Hospital who claimed to have found a 'medicine developed in Africa for Africa' called Virodene P058. 'There was this sense that this drug would be the thing that offset the perception of Africans as substandard and less than capable,' said Quarraisha Karim, the first director of South Africa's national Aids program. 'All eyes were upon [the ANC] and the expectations were very high and they were really trying to find their feet, but they didn't want to exercise caution.' Unlike the days of Christiaan Barnard's first successful heart transplant in 1968, this medicine was not quite what it seemed.

Virodene was rejected by the scientific community. Its research procedures, political interference and the safety and efficacy of the drug itself remained disputed. And the main active ingredient is the industrial solvent dimethylformamide (DMF), which has been shown to cause liver damage. Olga Visser and her businessman husband Zigi administered the drug to 11 patients without approval. They were rebuked by the South African Medicines Control Council (MCC), and senior toxicological expert Du Plessis acknowledged that these Virodene researchers knew 'sweet nothing' about medicine research.

But in 2000 more human trials were conducted in military hospitals in Tanzania, even after the MCC had ruled that such trials would be in contravention of the law. In the late 1990s however, the support from Mbeki, then deputy President, and Nkosazana Dlamini-Zuma, the health minister, was so great that Mbeki even criticized the MCC: 'I and many others will not rest until the efficacy or otherwise of Virodene is established scientifically.' The originators of Virodene were able to draw into their enterprise the ANC leadership, the National Intelligence Agency, businessmen with close ties to Mbeki and some prominent Western scientists. They sought to protect the 'national asset'.

For the medical establishment, it had become evident that earlier pilot studies of Virodene had broken all the ethical and scientific rules. But the Virodene researchers continued to enjoy high-level political support and in 1998, MCC chairman Peter Folb was removed from office, setting in motion a breakdown of proper medicines control, reflected by the many bogus Aids treatments that came onto the market. The prospect of 'an African cure for an African problem' had blinded many people to the scientific integrity required to ensure it. Quarraisha Karim: 'This was driven by this need to show the world: "Yes, Africans can do this. We can do this." Virodene became our redemption.'

Since the 1990s, there has been this controversy about the possible Aids cure Virodene. The Government and the Presidency have always denied having anything to do with it or having a financial stake in the Virodene Affair. Mbeki already publicly addressed the controversy in 1998. But it has never been properly investigated, so together with my colleague Lihle Dlamini, I wrote a letter to Mbeki about Virodene in October 2007. It's a formal request for a judicial commission of inquiry into the Presidency and the Health Ministry concerning their possible involvement in the promotion and testing of Virodene. Serious allegations have been made by the media and researcher James Myburgh and we want to know whether any legal steps should be taken and whether the independence of the MCC has been undermined by the fact that unlawful human experimentation has taken place. So far we have received no answer.

Mbeki has declared that the Government is fully committed to combating Aids. And obviously it would have suited an ideal scenario that the solution to the Aids epidemic would be found here in South Africa by South Africans. But any medication has to be approved and has to go through certain steps. And once it fails any of these steps, it means the medication is not good. In my view, this obsession is the problem. The MCC at that time had found that Virodene does not have any ingredients that can fight HIV and that it is actually dangerous for the liver and sensitive organs. But regardless, Virodene was funded by the President's office and people from the MCC were fired, apparently because they were supposed to just pass it, without anyone knowing. So the Virodene researchers went to Tanzania, where it was tested on another population, but with the same ingredients! The company that produces Virodene should have been the one that takes the initiative in correcting its own products, not the Presidency.

Why does this obsession for an African cure exist? I think it's because people want to try to prove that first of all we cannot depend on the West for everything and that we should solve our problems ourselves. Secondly, there is this concern that TAC and other organizations were pushing an agenda for pharmaceutical companies, and that we were funded by the West to promote ARVs. We were not seen as people who were advocating affordable treatment, so that the Government could supply more people with medicine. People used sinister words and they were suspicious of us. They felt that ARVs were not an African solution. 'Look, they said, 'the TAC leadership is white and male, so it's obvious you're pushing this agenda.'

So, as far as I can see, there was a lot of debate inside Mbeki's head and maybe other people about what they should do about HIV. They are ashamed, because the numbers of infected people are still increasing. And one day it might be too late and they will realize that they have messed up. Already during Mbeki's Presidency so many people have died, while he was still making up his mind about what he believes and what he doesn't believe. One time he declared that he doesn't think that HIV causes Aids. But he doesn't realize the impact of such statements on people on the ground. I don't have a clear answer on why this is happening. The only thing I can think of is this obsession with finding an African cure, which is why they are now looking again at traditional medicine. But traditional medicine has never treated TB, diabetes or HIV! It's just this obsession that we want to feel proud that we have done something, coupled with a fear that the West is trying to control us.

No Garden of Eden
One control the West does have is through the pricing of medicines by their pharmaceutical companies. This is why we pressure them to lower the prices and to open up the market so that more companies can manufacture the same drugs and everyone can have access. This is why South Africa now has generic manufacturers of other developing countries like India and Thailand, so that we're not dependent on the West. It doesn't matter who produces the ARV medicine, whether it's Boehringer Ingelheim or Glaxo SmithKline, as long as it is affordable. The ultimate goal is free healthcare for all. The South African Government lacks commitment, political will and leadership on HIV issues. The top leadership, especially of the current President and of the Health Ministry, is really problematic.

You know, after our own Government took power, there was this hope that we were going to create a Garden of Eden. So yes, we have achieved some of that, because now everyone has freedom, even though we may interpret 'freedom' differently. But there is a level of freedom, because everyone can express themselves without the fear of the police coming to arrest them. We have a Constitution that is very progressive on human rights. In fact, TAC would not exist if we didn't have that progressive Constitution! Otherwise, what would be our foundation to argue? So in that regard there is progress.

But at the same time, we had the illusion that once we had a black Government in power, all would be well. Unfortunately, things didn't work out that way, because the current Government inherited some of the things from the previous Government, such as a collapsed healthcare system for the poor. It was in fact the struggle to combat HIV that saved the healthcare system. And we have saved the healthcare system, because when TAC started in 1998, you would go to a clinic and be told: 'There is no treatment.' Healthcare providers were leaving South Africa in droves, because the conditions were getting worse. What we have done for HIV is to push the profile of the healthcare system by putting a lot of attention on the fact that by demanding access to treatment, you are in fact asking for many things. In a nutshell, you're asking for a pharmacist to be employed. And for a doctor, because he has to prescribe. And for a nurse. And if it's a hospital, for security guards. What are you doing in the long run? You're investing in human resources, and because of the increasing demand the focus will turn to providing a comprehensive healthcare package. It won't allow people to forget that healthcare is in a situation of crisis.

Our Government is becoming arrogant and that really troubles me. They don't want to be asked questions and they don't want to consult with people on the ground who have put them in power. Because we keep them accountable. We use the same process of mobilization that we have used for HIV to mobilize our own people against any injustice in our community, including crime or simply access to water. Are we just supposed to wait like we have waited for the last 50 years?! People are tired and frustrated and at the point where they will go to the streets and protest – that's their last resort. The Government sees us as enemies, because we are watchdogs. At the same time, they don't give recognition to what the communities and NGOs like TAC are doing. When something is successful, the Government takes the credit. 'We have done this and that.' But 80 per cent of what is being achieved is done by organizations that save the Government from embarrassment. When we remind them of taking responsibility for their own piece of the cake, they get irritated.

After so many years of apartheid and domination by whites, it will take time for other people to feel empowered as well... With nearly a million people, Khayelitsha is the second largest township in South Africa after Soweto. And then there is this growing unemployment, linked to poverty, which causes the social-economic conditions in communities to collapse. And it's a pain in the butt – if I can put it that way – for women and children. The more men get frustrated, the worse it gets for women and children. There is a crisis of sexual violence against women. Women and children are always in a wedge, because they are the ones who get violated all the time.

We have a case in court on Saturday of a guy who was engaged in a gang rape of an 18-year-old girl and who then killed her. It took us two years and a demonstration at every court hearing to put pressure on the magistrate to sentence them. These men got 10 years. Ten years only. There are many people who don't even care to go to the police station or the court, because they know that justice won't prevail. As long as this problem continues, we're going to have endless problems and we're going to march, after march, after another march... Something has to be done urgently, because women live in fear. If I drive after 7pm and it's dark, I have to drive like a madman for else I might be a target for hijacking or God knows what. We can't live in conditions like this.

One would think: why do so many people stay here? Sometimes you just don't have an option. You stay in South Africa and you stay in Khayelitsha, because where else would you go? Eastern Cape? There is no healthcare system there. Most of us came here basically for only two reasons: employment and healthcare. Yes, we're getting healthcare, but unfortunately people are not getting jobs anymore. For many years, Jo'burg was seen as the City of Gold, but it is no longer. Many people run away from Zimbabwe to Johannesburg. But now, when they reach the City of Gold, they get killed, because the people that are already here are also looking for jobs! It has come down to fighting for survival, and the more problems there are, the more vulnerable people are going to be to contracting HIV (see box).

'You are everything and you are nothing.'

'Any single child out here has a story,' say Con and Marion Cloete (born in 1951 and 1955). In 1990, they started Botshabelo, a village outside of Magaliesberg near Johannesburg to break the poverty cycle and offer Aids orphans future opportunities. Now, it is home to more than a thousand people.

Con: 'We are living in a Coca Cola culture, because everything is in cans. Kids don't speak about toothpaste, cool drinks or washing powder, but say: 'Where's my Colgate? Give me a Groovy. Hand me the Omo.' They talk in brand names. They have no points of reference, and this disconnected, unreferenced life exists all over Africa.'

'The social trends are worrying. When we started here, kids were coming in for an education. That changed from the mid-1990s onwards. Food and education became secondary. Even now, many kids come to school, because at least they get a decent meal a day. But since the beginning of 2008, I had 120 kids coming in from just one place, an informal settlement outside Rustenburg. Not for education or food, but purely for safety! Parents bring their kids saying: "Listen, our children are being raped or murdered for body parts used in tribal medicine..." So from education to food to safety, it shows you which way the graph is going.

'I am about to embark on writing a book called Poverty Economics. How do people ever support a Champagne taste on a beer income? It connects to this idea that there is a system within the system. Case in point: speak to any of the guys who've been to jail and they'll tell you that within 20 minutes of getting inside you are raped, possibly five times. Now, we also know that there are incredibly high levels of Aids in the prisons. Think of a young guy in the rural areas. There's no work out there. He is starving, so he steals a loaf of bread from a farmhouse. He gets caught and goes to jail. But by him going to jail he gets a death sentence.

'Sure, you've got to have law and order, otherwise you'll have chaos. But then, the law is made up there. By the time it gets down here, it's no longer applicable, because people simply are too poor. One night, a family stood at the door: "Please, we desperately need help. We've got nowhere to sleep, no beds, no mattresses, no blankets." Marion said: "We'd love to help, but we've got nothing!" We carried on talking and a few minutes later Marion felt something pulling her linens. She looked down and there was my three-year-old grandson, who had dragged his bedding. "Granny," he said, "they can use mine." We have never said no again.'

Marion: 'The main ingredient for the success of Botshabelo is to make someone feel they are worthwhile so that they get switched on to get on with their own life. It's for someone to look into your eyes and say: 'You are here for a purpose. You are born for this. Let's go for it! We may eat less food than we should, our nutritional diet may be bad, our education may not be what it should be, and our clothing may not be what we should have. But we have each other to say that it's OK. It is really OK. It doesn't matter what you do. We are here for you. We are going to make it and you are going to make it. And we will look after your back. You just concentrate on moving forward.' That has done it. That is the secret ingredient.'

'The thing is: we are social activists and there aren't many around, because 'working for humanity' is a very unreliable career, ha-ha. There's no swimming pool at the end of a working day. At this stage in my life I could be retiring comfortably. But then I would have to turn around and say to myself: 'In my lifetime, is this OK for me? To just accumulate and consume?' It doesn't make sense to me. The way we live as communities – I just know we can do better. That belief is so deep, nothing can shake it.

'This is what we do. We love our lives. It's really just wonderful to live in the village, because there's no veneer. Even though sometimes I miss that veneer. It's nice, it's cuddly. But life is short. Living in an environment with people that you love, but also with people that die on an ongoing basis, really keeps you on your toes about enjoying your life and seeing who you are in the bigger picture. You are everything and you are nothing. And you have to be able to hold that view without becoming depressed. You have to make it work.'

The top of the agenda
Nelson Mandela's son also died of Aids and he spoke about it openly on TV. In some respects that made a difference, but it didn't change anything in Mbeki's head. It was just one of the deaths and he was sorry it happened. But I think it was a political statement that Mandela made, because not so many political leaders or family members in South Africa talk about HIV or the fact that one of their own family members died of HIV. It was a big thing for a political leader to say his son had died of HIV, because it encouraged other people, who are still in denial about the fact that HIV exists. Suddenly it was right in their face. But it's not like in Malawi. There you find the president easily wearing a T-shirt saying: 'Go and get HIV tested. It's important!'

Yes, the Government has programs to combat HIV. But it was a struggle to even get there, because we lost many comrades. Many people died, because during that fight, they didn't have access to treatment. When we started, there was only a policy to treat opportunistic infections. ARVs were not even mentioned. As for myself, I'm alive today thanks to ARVs, although it is difficult to know how long you can live without treatment. For some people it takes one or two years, for others up to 12 years, depending on whether your infection is progressing fast or not. But I don't want to go there, because I don't want to lose my dignity by getting sick, skinny and weak. That is the worst: losing your dignity. HIV takes part of your dignity, because you feel ashamed about the fact that you could have prevented it, because it's sexually transmitted. And it's not a nice way to die. It's better to be killed by a car, because HIV makes you skinny and people feel sorry for you.

Of the 6 million HIV-positive people in South Africa there are only 450 thousand that receive treatment. It's unacceptable. Treatment doesn't reach the other 5.5 million South Africans because of three reasons. First is the lack of the Government's willingness to increase access. Second are the pharmaceutical companies, because the prices are still very high and there still are no generic drugs. And thirdly, people are testing very late. We still have to continuously encourage people to go. But the problem remains: even when people do get tested, the other two reasons come into play. The clinics tell people: 'We can't take any more people, because we cannot afford the drugs.' Our Government is responsible for 60 per cent of the inaccessibility. If it was fully aboard and didn't send out all these conflicting messages, everything would be so much easier. The major reason why people test so late is that they are confused about what to do all the time.

Another issue is that TB and malaria are still a problem in Africa. Western countries still have to commit themselves in giving us money to support us in fighting these diseases. And it's a pity that some countries don't want to commit themselves anymore for the next five years, because they don't think it's worthwhile to invest in Aids anymore. It's better to invest in the healthcare system, they say. I'm not sure whether there is any difference. Because HIV is a health issue. And so are TB and malaria. So if you invest in the healthcare system, you should also invest in Aids!

'Universal access' to treatment is spoken about at every conference, but it still doesn't exist, not even in South Africa. By 2011 we should have 1.6 million people on treatment in South Africa and about 7 million in the world, but we are very far from that. It will never be realized, unless we invest in HIV and Aids, TB and malaria as healthcare issues. Healthcare shouldn't just be the work of NGOs, but should be on the top of the Government's agenda. But it's almost as if the Government and the people live in different countries. We hear about the economic growth of South Africa and the picture of our country looks very good from the outside. Come inside, you see the reality. Go to the Camps Bay suburb. It's almost as if you're not in South Africa. Once you're there, you forget that there are poor people in Khayelitsha. That's why I didn't want to have an interview with you in town. I don't like interviews anyway. I like doing things and people follow me around and just watch and write. That's much better. Because there are so many things that TAC does, I want you to see them, rather than tell you about it.

THE AMERICAS

'If your government will not rise to the level of common decency, if it will not deal fairly, if it will not protect the land and the people, if it will not fully and openly debate the issues, then you have to get in the government's way. You have to forbid it to ignore you.'

Wendell Berry in *We All Live Downstream* (2009)

Wendell Berry

Maria Gunnoe, United States
Taking a stand against environmental destruction

'Everyone lives downstream', environmental activists will tell you.
When 'mountaintop removal moved into my backyard in 2000',
single mother Maria Gunnoe sprang to action. 'One thing about West
Virginia people is we're not the kind to give up and walk away.' A
crime of geological proportions is taking place in the five Appalachian
states, where more than 500 mountaintops have been leveled and
2,000 miles of streams have been buried. Residents suffer the greed
of corporations, reminding everyone of the fact that 'democracy
doesn't work on automatic pilot'. Like a modern-day Mother Jones,
Maria is unstoppable. 'Our environment is all we've got. Our lives
and health depend on it.' For that, she insists on the abolishment of
mountaintop removal and of the dirty politics that allow it to
continue.

Maria Gonnoe in 2009 (photo by Tom Dusenberry)

'Mountaintop removal moved into my backyard in 2000,' says Maria Gunnoe (born in 1969), a mother of two and activist awarded with the Goldman Environmental Prize in 2009. With a coalition of regional groups she advocates the passage of the federal Clean Water Protection Act. 'One thing about West Virginia people is we're not the kind to give up and walk away.'

Context

'I had no idea,' most people say when they first hear about a crime of geological proportions in the heartland of the United States. That crime is coal mining by mountaintop removal. The practice is monumentally disruptive, and some critics refer to the affected regions as 'climate ground zero'. But as it is only happening in the Appalachian hill country, nothing seems to change. In 1989, an oil tanker called the Exxon Valdez spilled an estimated 10.8 to 32 million gallons off the Alaskan coast. Strange as this may seem, it was a small spill compared to another that occurred in Appalachia. Estimates vary, but the coal slurry spill in Martin County (KY) in 2000 was at least 10 times larger (306 million gallons).

The Appalachian Mountains stretch from Canada to Alabama along eastern North America. The deciduous and hardwood forests that grow on them are among the most diverse in the world. When the last Ice Age occurred 10,000 years ago, glaciers didn't progress beyond the Ohio River, leaving these forests untouched. After the Ice Age, the only way for the rest of North America to be reseeded was from this 'mother forest' with 150 different tree species, 250 different nesting bird species. Many of these are rare, making Central Appalachia the most biologically diverse part of North America.

Residents of West Virginia, Kentucky, Virginia and Tennessee are fighting a human rights and environmental battle against huge corporations that are causing damages that no money in the world can repay. The World Wildlife Foundation calculated that our planet cannot regenerate its resources if each of us uses over 4.45 acres of arable land. The American average is 23.47 acres. Four more planets would be needed for the rest of the world to live like Americans. 'We are spending nature's capital faster than it can regenerate,' said WWF's Director General Claude Martin in 2004. On a mountaintop removal site you can witness the effects: our planet reduced to a moonscape. The United States still depends on coal for more than 50 per cent of its electricity, mainly to supply more than 600 coal-fired power plants, so the coal is mined wherever it may be found. Consequently, these mountains that are among the oldest in the world are destroyed and its communities uprooted.

To date, more than 500 mountaintops have been leveled, more than 2,000 miles of streams have been buried and 1.4 million acres have been destroyed. On average, 800 feet is blasted off the mountain to access coal seams underneath. Enormous amounts of rubble, euphemistically called 'valley fills' or 'overburden', are pushed aside, creating vast dumping sites with toxic debris. 'In the language of mine operators, everything that lies above the coal is overburden,' says Beverly May, a nurse practitioner and member of Kentuckians for the Commonwealth. 'That means I am overburden, it means my neighbors are overburden and the people of Appalachia are overburden. To a coal operator, we're simply in the way.'

The land is usually not 'reclaimed' as coal companies say, but the mountains are most definitely 'disappeared'. Cost-effective these mining methods certainly are, and with politicians and regulatory bodies bought off, coal companies can run over any opposition that stands in the way of their quest for profit. 'Campaign financing is the most popular form of bribery,' says environmental campaigner Larry Gibson. Try and insist on environmental protection with governors that proclaim to be a 'friend of coal'. Are government agencies subsidiaries owned by coal corporations?

The coal industry has long been the backbone of the region's economy. Over the years, its methods have changed from mining deep down in the 1900s to strip mining, and then to mountaintop removal – 'strip mining on steroids'. Since the 1940s however, the number of coal workers has fallen from 120,000 to fewer than 15,000, mainly due to modern technology and the practice of mountaintop removal. A century ago, coalfield residents would sell their land for mineral rights for as little as the cost of a sewing machine. By signing 'broad form deeds', residents sold their mineral rights, but they could keep their land. This was still simple underground mining. Since then, the number of coal miners has steadily gone down, but the scale of the operations has dramatically increased.

In Kentucky, a statewide campaign called 'Save the Home Place' sought a constitutional amendment to those broad form deeds. It was won by a 98 per cent vote after eight years. Now the land owners have some rights again, and surface owners have to give their permission for strip mining. But a century ago when people signed these documents, they had no idea that Appalachia would remain one of the poorest parts of the richest country in the world. Harry Caudill's appeal to the American conscience Night Comes to the Cumberlands (1963), which attributes the historical poverty of the Appalachians to coal mining policies, still applies today. In 1964, President Lyndon Johnson declared his War on Poverty and in 1968, Senator Robert Kennedy visited Appalachia. Little has changed, much has worsened.

Since 1977, there was the Clean Water Act to 'restore and maintain the chemical, physical, and biological integrity of the Nation's waters'. It allowed for the granting of permits to place 'fill material' into waters, provided its primary purpose was not waste disposal. This changed in 2002, when the Army Corps of Engineers under the Bush Administration altered that definition to include mining waste. The destruction of the ecology accelerated. The 'valley fills' leach acids and heavy metals into streams and the wells many Appalachians draw water from. The water and soil become polluted with higher than normal levels of arsenic, cadmium, lead, mercury, nickel and other contaminants. All this violates – and many mining companies violate – the Clean Water Act. 'Fill' does not equal 'waste'. This is why, in 2009, Senators Benjamin Cardin of Maryland and Lamar Alexander of Tennessee introduced the Appalachian Restoration Act into the House of Representatives. The bill should sharply reduce mountaintop removal mining, protect clean drinking water for many American cities, and protect the quality of life of

Appalachian residents. While the mountains and streams are lost forever, the additional ecological damage done will take centuries to remedy and remediate.

Returning to Bob White (WV) on Route 85, Goldman Environmental Prize (2009) winner Maria Gunnoe says: 'My schedule is nutso!' An eighth generation 'mountain holler girl', Maria lives with her teenage son and daughter where her forebears made their home. Since the late 1990s, she has been working as a community activist to stop mountaintop removal. But following death threats and the killing of her daughter's dog, her house and the barn built by her brother and grandfather are now surrounded by a chain link fence. 'The people around here are my friends. I'm not so worried about them. It's the ones who come from outside to work for mountaintop removal operations – they're the ones who are causing us all trouble.'

Coal company employees sometimes try to keep Maria from making her rounds of visiting sites and people affected by coal mining. She has switched cars to throw them off pursuit, but she is afraid of what would happen if she got caught out alone. 'Appalachia can support all sorts of economies, all kinds of industry. But it's not going to happen until the Appalachian Restoration Act is made into law.' Our talks end in Charleston's Blue Grass Kitchen. 'I like their food so much, I wear their shorts!' We run out of time, but Maria never forgets the many volunteers and 'super-volunteers' she works with and the sympathetic movements in the other affected states. Whistleblower Jack Spadaro (see box below) calls her 'our Joan of Arc.'

The assault on the mountains continues with full support of State and Federal agencies. Both residents and activists however will tell you that all Americans should perhaps be given a health warning not to live downstream or downwind from Appalachia. Many local people suffer from ill health and a high incidence of cancer and would be happy to see King Coal leave. 'Friends of coal' disagree with those referred to as 'jihadis', 'enviros', 'pagans' or 'tree huggers'. Pro-coal roadside billboards proclaim: 'Coal. Keeps the Lights on!' or 'Support coal, or sit in the dark.' But at a crossing you might read

'Yield to Alternative Energy'. When it comes to stopping mountaintop removal, Maria has only one rule: whatever it takes.
'You must see Larry Gibson,' she concludes.
'You must see Ken Hechler,' Larry says.
'You must see Jack Spadaro,' Ken and Larry agree.
Here we go.

Appalachia Rising

After a weekend conference of 'Appalachian Voices', on Monday 27 September 2010 thousands of Appalachian residents, sympathizers and activists from across the United States converged in Washington DC under the banner 'Appalachia Rising'. They were calling on President Obama to end mountaintop removal mining. As one speaker put it: 'We will not be a national sacrifice zone! We will not be collateral damage!' A high school teacher: 'Democracy doesn't work on automatic pilot.'

Judy Bonds
One of the great leading voices of the resistance to mountaintop removal mining and winner of the 2003 Goldman Environmental Award, Judy Bonds, died on 3 January 2011. 'There is nothing like being in the hollows,' she once said. 'You feel snuggled. You feel safe. It seems like God has his arms around you.'

Personal narrative — Maria Gunnoe

Just before I was born, in the 1960s President Lyndon Johnson and Senator Bobby Kennedy visited this region when it was already known to be poverty-stricken. The least they did was giving it attention and exposure. The miners may be 'faithful' and live in 'tightly-knit communities', but they stay poor. The industry won't allow them to make too much money. Money equals power. They're afraid it might go to their heads.

Even before the coal industry began here in 1792, my family has been in Appalachia since the early 1700s. They started migrating this way during the forced removal of the Cherokee in 1838, when the Government removed them from 'valued land' in northern Georgia. Later, their route came to be called the 'Trail of Tears'. Some of these Cherokee families however knew that they couldn't make it on this travel to the west. They escaped, followed the Kanawah and Coal Rivers to the headwaters, and found safety in the fertile hollers of Central Appalachia. My grandfather was a full-blooded Cherokee and shaped my life and heritage to a big extent. The porch where we're sitting right now is my favorite spot, looking out on the community and the river. It's where he used to end his day, every day.

I have a way of saying that if my grandfather had asked me to dry up the river, I would have tried it. You know, with a bath towel. I very much respected him. He raised his kids and worked in the coal mines while taking care of this place. Here in Boone County, he bought the land where my home still stands today and he taught us to love the land and to depend on it. The Native American name in my family is 'Peate'. But as they were Native Americans and did not go along on this forced removal, most of them were caught and killed. Those generations were not taught our Native tongue, and the women intentionally married into white men's families in order to breed out the Native Americans, so that their children would be safe. That's how the Gunnoes, a French name, came into it. 'A necessary tactic of survival,' that's what we called it.

So I grew up very connected to my family and we did things as a family. Every Sunday was a social day. We had dinner at our home and invited family and church group members and other folks from our community. Our house was just full of lots and lots of people. It made us feel very connected to our history here, and we were very protective of it. My family attended a Freewill Baptist Church, and I was raised to live by the Golden Rule: do unto others as you would have them do unto you.

As a little girl, I dreamed of becoming a mother and I always had a strong sense of caring for people. My parents hunted deer and bear, and we grew up knowing how to sustain ourselves by means of the wilderness. What stands out most to me was the time with the women of our family gathering the foods that we gardened or collected in the mountains – berries, roots, medicinal and edible plants – and prepared for dinner. The way I see it, it's a unique culture of survival by living off the land. My first awareness of the wider issues in Appalachia or global issues was only based on what I heard on the radio or saw on TV, until internet came along in the 1990s.

At 4 o'clock in the morning, when daylight got there, we were ready for work. We spent our day working, and when it got dark and we got tired, we went to bed. There was no need for lights at night time, because that's when people rested. And always we gathered, every season of the year, our vegetables from the earth. Sometimes, in winter, we even broke ice to dig up roots from under the ground. It's important that our children learn about the plant life in the mountains and the things they can eat, how to hunt, how to fish and how to gather. Ultimately, that's what's going to keep them alive. In short, the other strong connection I felt as a child and still today, is to nature and the land I grew up in.

Coal propaganda
In driving up here we passed my former high school. As a young girl I thought it was called a 'high school' because it was up on a hillside. The coal companies were allowed to come into our school and preach their propaganda. I knew growing up: coal companies are just mean, inhuman. There is no other way to put it. Many of the beautiful places that I knew as a child have been destroyed. Gone forever. Near Danville, I used to collect Molly Moochers, a kind of mushroom, during our family outings. But we don't do that anymore. In Pond Fork River I loved to fish. But that stopped too when I started catching fish with black holes. I witnessed the impact of mountaintop removal mining on nature and on the people. But it took me a long time to make sense of it all, because it was the coal companies and politicians who educated me as a child. I had to learn about the laws and politics of it all in order to protect myself and my children's birth rights to our native home.

I also saw what the coal companies were doing to young boys. At the age of 15, 16, they went to work in the coal mines, because the coal companies were in our schools to get their new employees. Ever since, my brothers have been working as miners 12 hours a day, six days a week. They make around $64,000 a year. But their health is wasted. I have a brother who looks like he wears eye-liner. The coal that settled in the moisture of his eyelids is permanently embedded in his skin. You can't wash it off. He has never been a smoker, but he has breathing problems, high blood pressure and signs of black lung disease. He is 46 now, and he will have to work until he's 62 to retire. All these years he has been paying into a retirement fund. But most likely he won't see any returns. He may not make it to 62 or become incapacitated before that time. So my own brother is an example of the coal companies' propaganda.

The coal companies would get to these young boys before the military could. They were asked to put in job applications and were trained for certain kinds of jobs in our schools. It's very tempting for a lot of the youth here to go to work for this industry, because it's good money. Initially. Eventually though, they mine out, and then these kids are stuck with no education and no future other than coal mining. So it's one way of the coal industry ensuring their slave labor. Employing them in coal mining creates a self-perpetuating system: it keeps them away from education, and their children will also not have any other options. Our schools don't teach about global warming, renewable energy or all the other promising things that are going on in this country, because that would pull us away from coal and our dependence on finite energy resources. It would reflect negatively on the coal industry. And the coal companies don't want the kids in the hills and hollers – their workforce – to hear about that. In later years, the coal companies got even cleverer. They gave grants to the schools, so you couldn't hand in a project that tells the truth about mining and 'reclamation'.

I love coal miners, don't get me wrong. As a teenager I used to pack my brothers' lunches before they went off to the mines and kept the house quiet when they needed a rest. They're some of the most honest, hardworking and genuinely good-hearted people you'll meet in your life. But I have to remind myself of the fact that they are a whole lot more loyal to these companies than these companies are to them. My brother never missed a day's work, not even when my father got killed. While driving his four-wheeler ATV on a mountaintop removal site, he came unexpectedly upon an erosion ditch that hadn't been there before. The four-wheeler bounced into the ditch and came back on him. He was only 51. When that happened, we even had his service on a Sunday, so that my brother didn't have to miss a day's work.

My dad left a lot for us though, more than any education system ever will. He passed on to us the knowledge to survive just about anything and used to have us build a fire to have hot water. Not because we couldn't afford a hot-water heater, but because he wanted to make sure that we knew that you can have hot water by just building a fire and having a coil on the back of your stove. Every morning after collecting the eggs, we built a fire so that we could have a hot shower. 'You're so poor!' people would say. But we weren't. We chose to live that way. I still thank my parents for raising me that way and giving me the knowledge I needed.

When there's a power outage here it's like: 'Yes!' Occasionally, I will even fake it: 'Oops, the power went off!' Like most other kids, my kids love their iPods and their laptops. But when the power goes off, they'll say: 'Mom, time to dance!' We get our wood stove out of the garage and we have 40 acres of wood. I cook on that wood stove. There have been many winters when everybody else was wondering how they were going to cook and eat. You have to grasp those opportunities. It's critical that our youth understand that we made it this far not by depending on our Government, on electricity and all these inanimate things in life, but because of our wit and having learnt how to survive. That family history is a big part of what helped me to realize what things are like, and what they will be like in the future if we don't stop mountaintop removal.

Reality check
I left for a while to go to college and worked as a waitress in Charleston, a city my grandfather called 'the cesspool' because of the

hypocrisy of the politicians there. I studied to become a medical technician. When I moved back in 1997, it was like a reality check for me. 'What's that?' All of a sudden, I heard this blasting going on around my home, and we started getting covered up by dust. The nearby mountains used to be called Twin Peaks, but one peak was blown off. All day, the dust got in our faces, and everywhere else. I started calling the regulatory agencies to try to force them to do something about what the coal companies were doing. First I raised air-quality issues, because my son has asthma and the dust from mining and coal fires got worse and worse. The air quality got so poor that many people in the community had to stay inside. 'I need a respirator just to get down the road,' one of them said.

Then there's Lindytown. Most of the people that were living there were elders and the whole community depended on each other. Massey Energy, led by CEO Don Blankenship (see box below 'Justice up for sale'), comes into that community and first of all makes the quality of life really bad by blasting off the mountaintops and using heavy equipment. As a rule, after all that they send in a man called David Trent, who is assigned to buy up people's homes. But their homes make up the entire community. Lindytown became a ghost town. In another town, Prenter, the water got polluted. The gall bladders of the people that had used that water deteriorated so quickly that most of them had to be operated on. Ninety-eight per cent of them no longer have a gall bladder. As we speak, another town called Twilight is quickly disappearing. That's why we're taking a stance there. Just to keep Twilight on the map, we're trying to increase the amount of mail that it gets through the post office. By now, Mr. Richmond and his son are the only ones left.

The Appalachian Mountains

A little further south are the four communities in Mingo County: Merrimac, Rawl, Sprigg and Lick Creek. They all depended on the same aquifer to get the well water that came into their houses. Massey Energy installed a sludge dam nearby. When it got too full, they started pumping the sludge out of this coal-waste dam into underground abandoned mine shafts. Without the people knowing, this sludge polluted the underground aquifer. Next, all these people were picking up their water from mine runoff! Not much later, everyone that had drunk that water started falling ill. After a while, the water turned black or orange. One of OHVEC's organizers, Abraham Mwaura, has led every step of the way to give the residents of those four communities access to the law.

In my view, Don Blankenship is an evil man. His wealth has come from the destruction of people's lives, though he speaks of 'the allowable cost of doing business.' If he has a heart, it's made of money. The mining industry has instilled fear into people and many Massey Energy workers fear Don Blankenship. I know this firsthand, because many of them got in touch with me about safety violations, afraid of speaking up for themselves. They despise him, because he is uncaring and cruel. He won't spend an extra dime or shut down mines to ensure his workers' safety. Production must move forward, no matter what the conditions in the mines are like. When soldiers go on a dangerous mission, they get hazard pay. These coal miners do that every day, but they get nothing. Meanwhile, Don Blankenship lives on the top of the mountain in a big mansion without any sign of remorse. I mean, women have miscarriages or can't have babies anymore because of the heavy metals in their bodies. I'm sorry, but you have to be evil to know that those are the consequences of putting profit before safety. How can anyone live with that and not do anything about it?

Co-opted in crime
Many people become co-opted in these evil practices. It's remarkable how often the coal companies employ contractors and workers from out of state. Perhaps they do so to prevent them from informing the local people. But there are also many Government and agency officials that act the same way. In many ways, Appalachia is a third-world country. You can tell by the way the laws are handled here. The coal companies even get a tax reduction when they have to clear a lot of rock to get to a small seam of coal. This industry is being protected by law enforcement and by our politicians, but the people that live here are not. We're being victimized and sacrificed. The coal industry is a criminal enterprise. It's organized crime. The politicians have no idea what the flick of their pen does. It may look like something that works on paper in Washington DC, but it looks like destruction in the coalfields down here in Appalachia. The only thing they 'regulate' is destruction. Most of the people that make decisions about mountaintop removal have never set foot in these mountains, let alone on mountaintop removal sites or in our communities. They have no idea what they are putting us through. And my work is exactly that: exposing what people in the coalfields are put through.

This area covers five different states. It's so vast, that we keep saying: Everyone lives downstream. Last time I checked, we were all living on the same planet. No doubt, if the tap water in Washington DC turned into an orange-colored toxic cocktail smelling like rotten eggs, everything would change immediately. After all, the headwaters of the Potomac start in West Virginia. But before it reaches that point, as a country we really need to start looking into what is in our water! This area here constitutes the headwaters of all of the southeastern United States drinking water, and it's all polluted. Everybody that drinks water is affected without even realizing it.

But what do they teach our kids? In ninth grade, my son Jessie brought his history book home and showed me the chapter entitled 'The Environment and the Economy'. The second paragraph read: 'Strip mining leaves the land in better-than-before condition.' But my son knows better, because he has a valley fill in his backyard! Thank God my kids grew up to be much smarter than when I was their age. I was very intentional about seeing to it that what they were taught at school down here wouldn't be the only education they would get. Each and every kid that I come in touch with finds out real quick that there is no future in coal mining. There really isn't.

Appalachian voices and voices about Appalachia

Larry Gibson (born in 1946), environmental campaigner: 'Freedom of speech? When I went to George Bush's rally in 2003, I was arrested five times. All I did was hold up a sign that said 'Stop Mountaintop Removal' when George came to town to endorse it. They enforce the law when it comes to people that protest mountaintop removal. But when it comes to the coal industry, they give them a free hand.'

Robert F. Kennedy Jr. (born in 1954), attorney and environmentalist: 'If the American people could see what I saw, there would be a revolution in this country.'

Mother Jones (1837-1930), prominent labor and community organizer: 'When I die and go to heaven, I am going to tell God Almighty about West Virginia!'

Judy Bonds (1952-2011), the 2003 winner of the Goldman Environmental Prize: 'When powerful people pursue profits at the expense of human rights and our environment, they have failed as leaders.'

Silas House (born in 1971), after completing a tour and flyover in 2005 with 14 colleagues: 'We were all writers, yet we had no words. There still are no words adequate to describe it, so I don't even try. I don't know how to articulate complete destruction, utter disrespect.'

Eric Schaeffer (born in 1955), former director of EPA's Office of Regulatory Enforcement, after resigning in 2002: 'The EPA is no longer a public health agency. It's become a country club for America's polluters.'

Ralph Nader (born in 1934): 'More coal miners have lost their lives from cave-ins, explosions and lung disease since 1900 than all the Americans who died in World War II.'

In 2000, a 1,200-acre mountaintop removal mine began on the ridge above our home. Shortly after 9/11 happened in 2001, my kids were running, because they thought that Bob White was being bombed. But it was the huge amounts of ANFO, short for 'ammonium nitrate (with) fuel oil', that the coal companies were exploding to get to the coal seams. Dynamite is cheaper than people. Over time, they created a 10-storey valley fill that contains two toxic ponds of mine waste with run-off from the mine. Since the mine became operational, my property has flooded seven times. In 2004, one of these floodings destroyed part of our home and our yard got covered in toxic coal sludge. 'An act of God,' is what the coal company called it. Rather than accepting liability. As a result, our groundwater and well water have been contaminated, and we can now only use bottled water for cooking and drinking. Up there used to be my grandfather's garden. But the soil is now contaminated with chemicals. Mercury-laden tomatoes I can grow and they might even be tasty. But I don't think I'll eat them.

Appalachia, my backyard
I was devastated. But the flooding was also an eye-opener, because I love our home place here like no other place on earth. I had already seen how the valley fills polluted the streams, and how the ponds with toxic sludge had failed and destroyed many homes and even

killed people. But now that it nearly killed us in our own home, something clicked in me. I realized that somehow, throughout my life, I've sat back and watched as the coal companies demolished community after community and ran out many, many people that I knew. I can easily think of 20 communities that have literally been erased by this industry. I realized that I had allowed all this to continue, up to the point where it is in my backyard! 'It's time to stop it!' I said. It was seeing the effects of mountaintop removal that made me an activist. When the coal sludge entered my own home, I was left with no other choice.

Then I started thinking: in the next 40 years, what is going to happen? I mean, this place literally went from heaven to hell in the 40 years that I have been living here. And in the next 40 years, either it's going to get better or worse. This place belongs to my children. As it stands right now, they're getting a fairly nice place in the middle of hell. With 'hell' I mean mountaintop removal. I support responsible underground mining. When a man goes down to do underground mining, he knows he is risking his own life. But with mountaintop removal mining, he knows he is risking other people's lives. Most of the practices of mountaintop removal, and even some of underground mining, are destroying one of the most important and bio-diverse eco-systems of this country, second only to the rainforests of China. There are things that grow and live in these hills and hollers that will never grow anywhere else. And part of the uniqueness of this region is our loving and warm-hearted people. That probably explains why the industry has been able to take advantage of us so horribly.

In 2004, I joined the Ohio Valley Environmental Coalition (OHVEC) as a volunteer, mainly to advocate for passage of the Clean Water Protection Act. Many people are lit up by what OHVEC stands for. There should be clean water in our streams and from our wells and taps and a ban on mountaintop removal. The people of Appalachia should have access to the promised prosperity through a renewable energy transition away from coal and toward wind and solar energy. The US Geological Society says we will be out of coal in 20 to 25 years. Then what? We have to make this transition to survive as a species. Water is the most valuable resource we have, not coal or any finite resources. People should care about this, because all of us use the energy that comes from these mountains. At the same time, these mountains are the filters for the drinking water of the entire eastern United States. The mountains of Appalachia belong to the people of the world, and not just to the coal companies. The 'reclamation' of this land will never be what it was, but we must do what we can. That alone will create more jobs than mountaintop removal.

As long as I can remember I have been seeing trains come through here, and now there are more than ever before. One train pulls 70 carriages of coal. To burn one ton of it only takes one and a half minutes. Multiply it across the country. I'm 41 years old now, and I've only seen trains taking out coal, but they never bring anything back. It would be nice to see them return with solar panels and wind turbines. Our work at OHVEC is done by a truly transparent and very open-minded group of people ranging from school teachers and Presbyterian ministers to law students and former union coal miners. Our agenda includes the reinstatement of the buffer zone rule that would strengthen environmental laws regulating mountaintop removal, and the promotion of viable renewable energy opportunities for the region.

I started organizing monthly Boone County meetings to provide community trainings on the environmental dangers of mountaintop removal and how to combat it. The trainings included how to read mining permits, write letters to the editor, interface with the media, and protest using nonviolent methods. Also, I created neighborhood groups to monitor coal companies for illegal behavior and to report toxic spills. The time had come to speak out, and I encouraged people to voice their concern at hearings about mountaintop removal. Working with OHVEC has changed my life and I now have a support network unlike any in the world. Had I not been doing this work, the coal company would already have put me out of my home and destroyed all that remains. We've had some successes. But the overriding feeling is that the coal companies want to erase us and pretend that we were never here. Google 'Lindytown' and you'll see what I mean. One day, I was still organizing people there. Now, except for three homes, they're all gone. In some cases the mining operations also destroy our cemeteries, some of which stem from the Civil War days. One of them has the graves of George Cook and James Gadd, the men who organized the Home Guard.

The final straw
Together with many other groups we have built a movement to stop mountaintop removal. If we don't stop that and the abuses of the coal industry as a whole, the people here won't have a future. That's my first focus. And then, our culture is probably one of the most unique on US soil, because of the fact that we are one of the only ones left that have the ability to live off the land. I feel that we have a responsibility to teach our kids the culture that we were taught as we grew up. Not only do we want to bring them into a modern world with modern technology, but we also don't want them to get so disconnected from the land that they don't know how to survive when that technology fails. Because it will. There's no way that our electricity grid can be sustained by continuing to blow up our mountains and poison our water. We're one of the most powerful and educated nations in the world. Are you telling me we don't know what coal does? Coal kills.

Part of our mission is that those responsible for the devastation of our livelihoods will be brought to justice. When anyone uses the word 'genocide', it has to be done very carefully, but I firmly believe that what is going on here amounts to a cultural genocide, because they're destroying an entire culture of people and, for the ones that remain, our ability to pass it on to other generations. Without it, we are dependent on our Government to take care of us. But it's ingrained in us to be very independent people. We take care of ourselves in Appalachia. We've survived almost 200 years of the coal industry. But now they're destroying the land and the waters that kept us alive all these years. That's very much the final straw.

In defiance of the federal judge's orders, the Army Corps of Engineers granted permits to Jupiter Holdings to construct two new valley fills above Bob White where I live. No adequate environmental measures had been taken. In March 2007, OHVEC together with a coalition of regional groups decided to challenge these permits in federal court. A hearing was scheduled for September. A few days before the hearing, I organized media training for 20 local residents, some of whom were scheduled to testify with me. Unexpectedly, more than 60 coal miners showed up at the community hall. They intimidated and harassed us to the point where we had to stop the meeting. My neighbors decided not to testify. I don't blame them. But I ended up being the sole community resident to do it. One month later, federal district court Judge Robert Chambers ruled in favor of OHVEC and ordered Jupiter Holdings to halt the construction of any new valley fills at its Boone County mine.

We have a massive amount of 'reclaimed' land here where the coal companies have blown off the mountaintops. But there is no economic development planned for these places, because they can't figure out how they can get healthy water there. Solar farms are the only thing that makes sense for it. Or switch grass. It grows fast and burns quickly and hotly, the heat of which can be used to turn turbines to generate electricity. There really are so many different ways and alternatives. The people in the coal communities need to learn about their situation from the cradle to the grave before it impacts them. Most of them do not realize the impact it has on their health. That would make a dramatic difference.

'We're all suffering the corruption of bought bosses and officials.'

Ken Hechler (born in 1914) served under five presidents and wrote the Coal Mine Health and Safety Act of 1969. Today, he participates in the Congress to Campus program and works on several books. During a protest at Marsh Fork in 2009, actress Daryl Hannah handed him an autographed picture. Hechler thanked her by saying: 'I'd love to be arrested with you any time!' In 2010 he received the Martin Luther King Achievement Award.

'One of the real problems of this world is that you can pass a good law, but the people in charge of enforcement can weaken it. That was particularly true when George W. Bush was President. He would even make statements specifying the parts of the law he agreed with and those he disagreed with, which gave a signal to the bureaucracy that it should not try to enforce those. Our current Congressional delegation has five cheerleaders for mountaintop removal. They were in the forefront of the election of President Obama. Now they're saying: 'We supported you. Now you support us.' The governor of West Virginia, Joe Manchin, is another cheerleader.'

'As long as you have big bucks in the coffers of the coal industry that invest in the campaigns of every member of the legislature, the governors and even the court officials, then it's pretty obvious what will happen: He who feeds the piper calls the tune. Gold can buy anything. And you know what the Golden Rule is? Those that have the gold, rule. In 2010, the US Supreme Court decided that it is a violation of the freedom of speech to deny corporations the right to buy elections. This scares me, because there is no power in Congress to override the decisions of the Supreme Court. They have basically taken the position that 'money is speech' and that you can't control millionaires. I don't agree. Speech is about independent expressions of opinion. The Tea Party makes use of that freedom of speech.

'The majority of the people in West Virginia oppose mountaintop removal. President Obama should look to what Abraham Lincoln said in his Gettysburg Address: 'Ours is a Government of the people, by the people and for the people.' Not of the corporations and special interest groups. Advocates say that if they put enough billions of dollars into it, they can come up with clean coal', but it has never been proven. The alternatives – solar and wind energy – should be utilized! There is only one thing that is keeping the American public from doing that: Money. We're all suffering the corruption of bought bosses and officials. That's about it. Justice is what every public official ought to regard as his moral compass. And justice is on the side of those that want to protect the people against mountaintop removal.'

Many people can afford not to mind, especially if they live far away where they don't feel the consequences. But if they did, they would feel differently. Most of my conversations with government representatives or people from the EPA's Office of Surface Mining are a fight just to get through to them. It feels like your mouth is moving, but they're not hearing you. Over the past 12 years, one conversation always stands out to me. 'I will never get in the way of passing the Clean Water Act,' Congressman Nick Rahall told us when he took office. But after he got in some trouble with the coal industry, one of the first things he came out with was: 'Well, I'm the person who got in the way of the Clean Water Act!' He blatantly lies to us. Shortly after the flooding happened here in 2003, I was getting phone calls from Rahall's office every day: 'Is there anything we can do to help?' Nothing was being done, but they kept calling to the point where it got annoying. 'Yes,' I said. 'We need to start on that mountaintop removal site behind my home, and work our way out.' They hung up. Once I had figured out what had caused all this and told Rahall's staff that I had, they wouldn't talk to me anymore. That absolutely says it all.

Lobby power
The powerlessness of the EPA is a story in itself. Let's not beat around the bush: they're in the pocket of the coal and energy industry. They're only employed by Congress to mask the real problems at hand – the 'scientist' in this mad science project. They do more to justify mountaintop removal than to admit their mistakes and move to correct the problems, protect the American people and ban the practice. This ultimately relates to the power and predominance of lobbies in the US Government, which includes the leftover of rule changes by the Bush Administration. The coal and energy companies have the billions of dollars that they stole from the people of Appalachia to buy lobbyists and politicians. On Christmas Eve 2008, the Bush Administration did away with the buffer zone rule

which protects our streams from mining. This was nothing other than a repayment to the coal industry for their campaign contributions. The Obama Administration is a welcome change and is reviewing that decision. Even the EPA is hearing us now. But in the meantime streams are being buried forever. They still seem to think that they can find a balance somewhere. But there is no balance to be found in blowing up mountains. We're not just aiming for mountaintop removal to become better regulated. We're aiming for a complete ban.

Our Senator Jay Rockefeller also really surprises me. 'I never want to look at another aerial photo of mountaintop removal,' he said. 'Those are ugly photos.' How the hell does he think we feel? We have to live in it. Meanwhile however, he continues to support it. For another reason, I have been very surprised at our Senator Byrd and very pleased by the switch he has made. In the past, he used to preach at our Capitol in Charleston: 'Stop them crazy environmental extremists!' But in 1996, when a lawsuit ruled in our favor saying that the coal companies had to stop valley fills, all hell broke loose. Senator Byrd was one of the politicians that beat the podium down. 'They're trying to destroy coal, but we're here to protect your jobs!' They fired the coal workers up in a frenzy. In reality, we were only trying to stop mountaintop removal. This time, when the EPA made the ruling, he sat back quietly and didn't say a word. In the last couple of years, Senator Byrd and his staff have lent us a very close ear and I firmly believe he cares about the people of the southern mountains.

As a matter of fact, there were two recent public statements that weigh heavily in our favor. One talks about the biblical connection between our culture and our mountains, the other about the fact that the people in West Virginia need to embrace the future. Basically what that says is: coal is on its way out, and the time has come to explore alternative sources of energy. Those statements are very promising. I think the first was partly inspired by some Bible scriptures that I had been sending to his staff. There are many mentions of mountains and wilderness in our Bible. Moses came down from Mount Sinai with the Ten Commandments, and Jesus spent 40 days and 40 nights in the wilderness. The spiritual connection between people and the land and between the land and God are prevalent throughout the Bible. To see the mountains being destroyed – how can anyone do something like that and pretend that they care about the Creation or the Creator? I met a miner one day who had a sticker on the back of his vehicle: 'Jesus forgives strip miners.' Does that mean He does? I don't think so. We may have a forgiving God, but He also recognizes evil when He sees it. And mountaintop removal is absolutely evil. If you don't know what you're doing you may be forgiven. But once you do, it's unlikely. We call that 'hypocrisy'.

Obligation to the future
At times my life has been in danger, and I certainly feel the pressure of coal company workers that shout at me in gatherings. At the end of an argument in a convenience store, I told a man: 'My name is not Bitch. I'm called Maria.' Then we both had to laugh. In a way however I feel that this is what success must feel like. But after the flooding, I sat here on my porch literally for three days holding my head in my hands. It built something in me that nothing will cure and that nothing will make go away. It's a determination beyond any I ever had before. Right now, I would lay my life down for the cause of stopping mountaintop removal. It means that much to me, because I know that the future of my children and grandchildren and the future of Appalachia are based on it. Also, it's our obligation to the retired and laid-off miners and those who would have been the new generation of miners coming up.

The opposition is powerful. But there have also been Massey Energy workers who came up to me saying: 'We hope you'll stop mountaintop removal.' It's unbelievable. When together with other people, they're willing to kill me. But one-on-one it's a different thing. Not only do they want me to win the battle against the coal companies, but they know it is very important not to let Appalachia slip through the cracks this time. We've depended on coal now for 200 years. This place has been mined to death. Hundreds of thousands of coal miners have been dying in these hollers, and I firmly believe that as a country we are much smarter than this now.

We can have wind farms, solar farms, geothermal energy, hydro dams and so on. We can do this a different way! I've been to many colleges and the kids there know that the United States of America can have clean, renewable energy ahead of them! But huge corporations and very greedy politicians oppose us, so first we have to get the rich white fogies out of the way.

One of the most thrilling things I ever experienced was when I talked to a young man during a panel discussion at Virginia Tech back in 2001. He must have been 19, and was going into mining engineering. But being on the panel and learning more about the impacts of mining made him rethink his decision. A couple of years ago, I came across him again. He is a wind engineer now. To me, that's perfect! If I could just go to a panel now and then, and have a wind engineer come out of it, we're winning. That's the real promise of it all. It's just about the only thing that encourages me, because those young people know what they have planned for this country and it has nothing to do with fossil fuel. They are extremely concerned about the state of our country, and fortunately they're learning about ways by which we no longer have to depend on coal in the future.

My generation and my mum and dad's generation sat back and allowed the Government and corporations to take over our country and to make decisions for our children's future that just aren't feasible. Like carbon sequestration. The coal industry is talking about capturing – it sounds really nice – capturing the carbon as it comes out of the top of the coal-fired power plants, and then storing it in underground voids. There it will be 'sequestered' for all time. Now, do you believe that? The earth moves, the sequestration leaks. It's a mad experiment. But they're throwing billions of dollars of this stimulus package towards 'clean coal' technology. There's no such thing! Coal is black through and through. Down around Charleston you'll see signs that say 'Truly Clean Carbon-Neutral Coal'. When my 12-year-old daughter saw that sign for the first time, she turned to me: 'Mom, ain't coal carbon?'

How can coal be carbon-neutral when it is made of nothing but carbon? King Coal however will try and convince people that carbon-neutral coal is a real possibility. Likewise, President Bill Raney of the West Virginia Coal Association recently said to miners at Beckley Pocahontas in Raleigh County, when that facility received a conservation award: 'Today we recognize the real, true practicing environmentalists of this state and nation.' All we've got to do is tell the truth and use the industry's own facts against them. They just keep proving us right. The youth is absolutely going to change things. Shame on us for allowing their future to look as bleak as it does right now. The United States could very easily turn around. But as long as we depend on a fossil-fuel-based economy, that's all we're going to have.

Sustainability is doable

The amount of intelligence and alternatives available is huge. When I talk about sustainability, I often end up referring to a town in New York State called Ithaca. It's a college town and Cornell University is nearby. Everything in the town is made locally. There's one thing you'll never see there: a truck transporting anything from the outside. They make their own beer, they have their own dairies from their own cows. That's the amazing thing about its history: it has been self-sustaining all these years. It's a really nice, really cool town. And it's just a bunch of Cornell college students that brained all this up. Ithaca has never been a part of what most of us believe communities should be like, such as connected to the Government, resources, power plants and so on. It is a freestanding community. The people that attend college respect the rules inside Ithaca. That's how it stays true to what it is. My point in telling that is showing the fact that it is doable. It doesn't take a massive amount of money. It takes intelligence and dedication, and that's it.

Wasn't it Eisenhower that warned us all against the dangers of the military-industrial complex? That seems to be exactly what is happening here with the energy companies. Their power is based on the fact that they provide goods that everyone has to have, because they have no other choice. They are the ones that exercise control over our country, not our Government. Somehow, the United States has become really good at hiding its dirty secrets. It reminds me of the so-called 'treatment ponds' to clean the runoff from coal operations step by step. Visually, it looks good. But it doesn't wash. It's like a Band-Aid on a hemorrhage. My great-grandmother used to say: 'If you get to thinking about something, and it leaves you confused, there's usually something messed up about it!' What's messed up in Appalachia is mountaintop removal. And what's messed up in the United States is that our country wants other countries to believe that we live in a democracy. That's not what I'm seeing from my front porch.

Robert Kennedy Jr. wrote Crimes Against Nature in which he criticizes the failings of the Bush Administration and he refers to the practices of lobbyists and coal companies as 'the subversion of our democracy'. He is very much in support of our work, and so is Al Gore. I sat down with him after receiving the Goldman Environmental Award. He's very concerned about mountaintop removal. Our conversation centered on the disappearance of the trees, and that it is necessary to keep them, as they naturally absorb the carbon from the air. As a matter of fact, all the trees in West Virginia alone would be enough to sequester carbon, as long as we're not putting out massive amounts of it. Other outspoken celebrities are country-music singers Emmylou Harris and Kathy Mattea, and actress Ashley Judd who is originally from Kentucky. Their support is a big step forward, when you come from a time in which you couldn't even get a letter to the editor of the local paper. Even the media are blinded to the facts. They've stopped really investigating. When we first started back in the 1990s, it was a nightmare. You stood on your own without anyone to protect you. We used to say to each other: 'Are you nuts?!'

Every single day, I connect to what my children and grandchildren will be doing in the future. The flooding hurt my children too, but they have stood by me, put up with problems at school, with their peers, teachers and total strangers. I don't want them to have to fight for water. I want them to live a peaceful life, to enjoy Mother Nature and preserve their family history. That's the life I'm looking forward to, and look forward to leaving behind. Each day we make moves to prevent a footprint on our planet's ecosystem. At the same time, I'm constantly thinking of ways in which I can increase the size of the footprint of my activism with OHVEC. Hopefully, someone somewhere will recognize that clean water and a healthy environment are connected to healthy people and a healthy economy.

Sleepless nights
At first, our work was totally ignored and we were ostracized in our own community. But when more and more people started supporting it, others started with open criticism and threats of violence. In 2006, it got really bad. After I had testified in federal court to stop that valley fill, apparently some people thought that killing me somehow or other might help. They threatened me everywhere they ran into me. Many of them see me as an enemy, mainly because they fear losing their jobs. One day, my neighbors overheard people planning an arson attack on my home. My daughter's dog was shot dead, and 'wanted' posters with me on it appeared in convenience stores. I even gave one of my friends a bullet-proof vest, because he has been driven off the road and shot at. Because of the threats, I tried to stay out all night and sleep part of the day. My son wouldn't go to sleep anymore, because he was afraid that someone would burn the house down. I made a deal with him. 'I will stay up all night, so you can get some sleep and graduate from high school.' I couldn't back down on that deal. If he had woken up and caught me catnapping, I would have been in trouble. But after two weeks like that, I had to call in reinforcements. Some local union miners volunteered to watch over us while we slept at night. It was very stressful, but unfortunately very necessary.

One night at 2.30 in the morning, a man was standing in front of my home. He had something in his hand that looked like a coffee can, but it was too dark to see. And then there was another occasion that happened before this valley fill ended up on the road in front of my house. At that time, the bridge nearby my home was still accessible by foot. A young man was racing back towards my truck, which was parked down there at the time. But a volunteer guard was keeping an eye on us and our house from the garage. We communicated with a CB radio link. 'Somebody is at my truck!' That young man was ready to break something when the guard came out yelling from the garage, so he turned, ran away and got into a car. After that, I had a chain fence installed around my home.

Just recently, there was a family, the Greens, who intended to move out of the community and never come back again, because they were so upset about this valley fill. But as we managed to stop it, they decided to stay. Now, slowly but surely, the atmosphere is changing. I believe that if it wasn't for what we've done in stopping that valley fill, not only would the Greens have left, but so would everyone downstream. We literally stopped the depopulation of that community, and with that we preserved a portion of this very important culture. If we let the culture that we're trying so hard to preserve here escape, it will be lost forever. Everything dies in a bad environment – fish, animals, people, and crops. Our environment is all we've got. Our lives and health depend on it. I hope I'm young enough to see all the things that OHVEC wants become reality. We have to do this. Our only way to salvage anything is to grab onto it, hold onto it with everything we've got, and never give up.

On 5 April 2010, I was on a mountain slope with some companions to mark cemeteries, to protect them from the activities of mountaintop removal. Suddenly, I almost lost my balance, because there was a blast that shook the earth under our feet. 'That wasn't a normal blast,' I said. Normally, when they explode ANFO to get at the coal seams, you only feel it in your chest due to the shock waves in the air. But this time we felt it both in our feet and in our chests at the same time. 'It felt like an earthquake!' one of my companions said. Later, it turned out that what we had felt was the underground explosion in the Upper Big Branch mine in Montcoal. The explosion and underground fire killed 29 men. It's impossible to survive such a blast. The air itself catches fire. That mine should have been shut down long ago, because in the preceding month alone there were 57 violations. Now, if I get 57 speeding tickets, I'm not going to be allowed to drive. Any other industry – cotton, cabbages, you name it – would be shut down. Not the coal industry. Don Blankenship has enough money to the point where he can just do anything he wants and get away with it. Especially here. Following the disaster, Massey Energy in no way diminished its activities. The number of trucks hauling out coal from the mountains didn't slow down one bit. A fire raged for days, because the explosion had generated so much heat that the slopes caught fire.

Justice up for sale and the Upper Big Branch mine

A federal grand jury indicted Don Blankenship, Chairman and CEO of the Massey Energy Company, in November, 2014, for conspiracy to violate mandatory federal mine safety and health standards, impeding federal mine safety officials, making false statements to the Securities and Exchange Commission, and securities fraud. The charges derived from circumstances that led up to the Upper Big Branch mine disaster. Blankenship came under increased scrutiny.

Donald Leon 'Don' Blankenship (born in 1950) headed Massey Energy, the sixth largest coal company in the U.S., and was known for frequently speaking out about politics, the environment, and coal production. He features unflatteringly in Laurence Learner's book The Price of Justice: A True Story of Greed and Corruption (2013). A USA Today editorial stated that Blankenship 'has vividly illustrated how big money corrupts judicial elections. It puts justice up for sale to the highest bidder.'

A 2005 memo reflects his attitude towards his employees: 'If any of you have been asked by your group presidents, your supervisors, engineers or anyone else to do anything other than run coal... you need to ignore them and run coal. This memo is necessary only because we seem not to understand that coal pays the bills.' Blankenship faces 30 years in prison if convicted of all charges. While his board continued to support him, President Obama and Vice President Biden paid tribute to the 29 miners at a memorial service in Beckley, WV.

Pro-future argument
We really need to weigh up the benefits of what we're doing, I'd say to the wives of Massey Energy's workers: There is no chance that your children will have the same kind of jobs that their daddies currently have. You can only blow up a mountain one time, and you can only take the coal out one time. The 25 years of minable coal that's left might be enough for your husbands to retire, but what jobs are your sons going to have? We have got to make this transition. It's not a pro-coal, anti-coal argument anymore. It's a pro-future, anti-future argument now. If we don't make a move immediately, we're leaving our children in a wasteland. What are we going to have to hand over to them after that? Nothing. We, as Appalachians, have got to make a plan to sustain future generations or the coal barons will just walk off and leave us holding the poverty bag again. Perhaps I should add that all mining laws were written in blood. They were only ever updated after accidents and disasters. But we don't need more laws. We need enforcement of those that already exist. Had they been enforced, these 29 men would still be alive today.

'Corporate America controls Administration after Administration.'

Jack Spadaro (born in 1948), former head of the National Mine Health and Safety Academy, revealed on the weekly news program 60 Minutes how the Bush Administration had covered up a coal slurry spill in Martin County. The Office of Special Counsel and the Merit Systems Protection Board failed to protect him, but in 2010 Spadaro received the Lifetime Achievement Award from the US Government Accountability Office. Today, he works as a consultant and expert eye-witness.

'As a young mining engineer, I began working in the coalfields of West Virginia back in 1968, when the Farmington explosion killed 78 miners. Four years later, in 1972, a coal waste dam failed in Buffalo Creek and killed 125 people, left 4,000 people homeless and wiped out 17 communities. I reported on the failure of the dam and interviewed survivors, many of whom had lost almost their entire families. The thing that saddens me is that most of these disasters are completely avoidable. Many mine operators violate the law with impunity.'

'In October 2000, when I was making my reports about the Martin County coal slurry spill, all I wanted was to get the truth out. It was the largest environmental disaster in the history of our country: more than 300 million gallons of toxic coal slurry had polluted a hundred miles of streams as far as the Ohio River, killing everything downstream. But the Bush Administration thwarted the investigation. On Inauguration Day 2001, they ordered us to close it. The energy industry had contributed a lot of money to the two campaigns of the Bush Administration. The pay-off was pretty good. They were allowed to run freely for about eight years with virtually no limitation. The Bush Administration was the worst that I have seen since 1966. They were totally corrupt and actually enabled the industry to violate the law.

'That is one of the great disgraces of this country. We've had good environmental laws since the early 1970s, but they simply have not been enforced. I know the laws pretty well, because I helped to implement the Surface Mining Control and Reclamation Act that was signed into law by Jimmy Carter. He was a good environmental President. But during the Reagan and first Bush Administrations, the officials of the EPA, the Office of Surface Mining and the Army Corps of Engineers were beholden to the Republican appointees that ran the agencies. They allowed the industry to bypass the laws. Unfortunately that continued through the Clinton Administration. It was only under Obama that the EPA began finally seriously looking at the environmental consequences of mountaintop removal. Of course, the mining industry and politicians such as Senator Jay Rockefeller and Congressman Nick Rahall are trying to weaken the EPA. Governor Joe Manchin went to

Washington twice to lobby the Obama Administration to get them to not enforce the Clean Water Act in West Virginia.

'Mountaintop removal was supposed to be the exception rather than the rule. But not one operation in Appalachia is done within the confines of the Clean Water Act and the Surface Mining Control and Reclamation Act. They're all in violation of the law. There's a lot of corporate lawlessness in our country and it nearly destroyed our whole economy in the past few years. I don't think that most Americans yet realize just how close we were to utter collapse because of the abuses of corporate America, which pretty much controls Administration after Administration. That's not really democracy at all and I wonder whether we will survive as a democracy.'

An important new study conducted by researchers at Washington State University and West Virginia University (see box) finds significantly higher rates of birth defects in mountaintop removal coal mining areas compared to non-mining areas in Appalachia. The study was based on analysis of over 1.8 million birth records. One of the writers, Dr. Melissa Ahern, said that the study 'is evidence that mountaintop mining practices may cause health impacts on people living in those areas, before they are even born.' Her co-author, Dr. Michael Hendryx, said that it 'is significant not only to people who live in coalfields but to policy makers as well.' This report confirms we have a problem. Yet in West Virginia and Kentucky our governors and federal legislators are protecting the coal industry at any cost. Shame on them for shutting us out of decisions that mean the life or death of our communities.

'At substantial expense to the environment, to local economies and to human health.'

In the United States, birth defects occur in about 1 in 33 births. In an article in Environmental Research of June 2011 about a health study that focuses on Kentucky, Tennessee, Virginia and West Virginia, researchers however say that:

'Rates were significantly higher in mountaintop mining areas for six of seven types of defects: circulatory/respiratory, central nervous system, musculoskeletal, gastrointestinal, urogenital, and 'other'. There was evidence that mountaintop mining effects became more pronounced in the latter years (2000-2003) versus earlier years (1996-1999).'

The researchers from Washington State University and West Virginia University conclude: 'The findings documented in this study contribute to the growing evidence that mountaintop mining is done at substantial expense to the environment, to local economies and to human health.'

Source: Ahern, M.M., et al., The association between mountaintop mining and birth defects among live births in central Appalachia, 1996-2003, Environ. Res. (2011), doi:10.1016/j.envres. 2011.05.019. Quotations printed with permission.

My son recently went into the navy. I had pleaded him not to go, but as a child he grew up with the feeling that he had to fight for our freedom, because that is what he had felt all along having to fight for our home. My children paid the price and have suffered being harassed at school and fearing grown men of coal companies. I think a lot of Mother Jones. She was a union organizer. She was only a little tiny woman, but she had great fortitude and was really concerned about the living and working conditions in the coalfields. To a certain degree I feel that I am continuing the work that she began. I think though that each one of the women that strives for a better life in Appalachia shares a connection with Mother Jones.

The people of Appalachia have sacrificed everything for energy in America. For many, that sacrifice included their lives. For years, this land has given America its steel, its coal and its men to fight in our wars. The least our Government could do is to honor these people for the sacrifice they have made. We must put a stop to mountaintop removal and make the transition to renewable sources of energy.

Don't we already know that it works!? That will allow us our Homeland Security and the preservation of our rightful place and culture in the mountains.

We're not giving up. We won't compromise on banning the practice of mountaintop removal. One day, it will stop. I just hope it will be soon enough to keep our culture. We don't want regulation. We want abolishment. Of it, and of dirty politics. All of it.

Pablo Fajardo - Ecuador
Fighting for justice against an oil giant in the Amazon jungle

'One of the problems with modern society is that it places more importance on things that have a price than on things that have a value,' says Pablo Fajardo, lead attorney in a landmark lawsuit against oil company Chevron. The company has a track record of pollution and malpractices in the Amazon region. In Fajardo's view, 'the lawsuit is a fight not just about oil companies in the jungle, but about 500 years of South American history.' As a child, he witnessed 'an oil-world hell'. While working as a laborer and teaching evening classes, he did a distance course in law, enabling him to eventually become the lead attorney for the Frente de Defensa de la Amazonia on behalf of 30,000 affected people. 'We are in a collective fight for justice, for the people, the earth, and the environment.'

Pablo Fajardo

'Immoral, inhumane and criminal,' says Pablo Fajardo about Chevron's oil operations in Ecuador. Pablo (born in 1972) is the lead attorney in one of the largest environmental lawsuits in history. Working with the Amazon Defense Coalition, he represents the rights of about 30,000 Amazonian settlers and indigenous people, Los Affectados, the Affected Ones.

Context

Will a landmark billion-dollar environmental lawsuit establish a global precedent? Or will this David-and-Goliath story fade away, and leave the people in the Ecuadorian Amazon with a problem the size of Rhode Island for generations to come? Chevron, which incorporated Texaco in 2001, has progressed worldwide since 1911, making profits of $14 billion in 2006 alone. But if you sell a commodity needed by almost everyone, can you get away with almost anything?

So fabulous are the corporate values of Chevron, the third largest corporation of the United States, to read them is to join them. 'At the heart of The Chevron Way is our vision... to be the global energy company most admired for its people, partnership and performance.' Fabulous or from the realm of fables? Chevron aspires to conduct its business 'in a socially responsible and ethical manner' that 'respects the law, supports universal human rights, protects the environment and benefits the communities where we work.' But Steven Donziger, one of the lawyers advising on a monumental class-action case against the oil company, would say: 'Chevron really is the oil giant that gives US companies a bad name.'

On the plane to Quito, a promotional video shows the beauty of the rivers, rainforests and wildlife, and a sunset that takes your breath away. Ecuador is one of the most bio-diverse places on Earth; the Amazon, the Andes Mountains and the Galapagos Islands contain natural wonders beyond imagination. Something else is hard to imagine too. This pristine corner of the earth is being destroyed at a rapid pace. Yes, there are others, such as Occidental Petroleum and Maxus Energy, but Chevron is the major one. Due to Texaco's sub-standard operational practices over a 26-year period, Chevron now faces a $27.3 billion liability. With little restraint, and even less conscience, the company chose not to re-inject into the ground the wastewater and 'drilling muds' generated by its oil operations. Instead, it dumped it into the waterways, and left crude oil and toxic waste in open pits. 'Oil is the dirtiest industry in the world,' said The Guardian's environmental editor John Vidal, 'and Chevron, one of the world's largest companies, must be the oiliest.' For lead attorney Pablo Fajardo it is not the money that matters, but the principle. 'One of the problems with modern society is that it places more importance on things that have a price than on things that have a value. Breathing clean air, for instance, or having clean water in the rivers, or having legal rights. These things don't have a price, but they have a huge value.'

From the plane, into the bus. For most of the 9-hour journey from the capital Quito to oil town Lago Agrio, a huge high-pressure pipeline snakes through the jungle. Oil spills happen frequently, as it is easy to swerve off the road and hit a section of the Trans-Ecuadorian Oil Pipeline System (SOTE). Built in the 1970s, it was later joined by another, the Heavy Crude Pipeline. Ecuador produces 500,000 barrels of oil a day, making it Latin America's third-largest oil supplier to the U.S., behind Mexico and Venezuela. Lago Agrio means Sour Lake, so called after the Texas town where Texaco was founded in the early 1900s. It is only a short distance from the Colombian border. Its current inhabitants include local oilmen, oil workers, drug dealers, and families with children. But there are also shootouts between Colombian FARC rebels and anti-rebel paramilitaries, kidnappings, and drug-related crime. You are advised to 'avoid side streets and sketchy bars'. During the night there are gunshots, but the following day children play on the sidewalk, and all seems quiet in the Oriente.

From the truck into a canoe – after checking that anacondas and piranhas do not frequent this particular river. This region is the one that is most affected by the contamination resulting from oil operations. Around Lago Agrio, the environmental and indigenous rights organization Amazon Defense Coalition provides 'toxic tours'. Expecting paradise? The sight of former Texaco operation sites, better described as disposal pits, Lago 1, Lago 5, Lago 20, is shocking.

Some pits are hidden, others covered up, and some even 'remediated' by Chevron. The inverted commas here are not without reason. Standing in front of just one of these pits will probably fill you with dismay or outrage. Next, you won't be able to keep count. There are more than 900 of them.

The ecological disaster and human tragedy are of massive proportions. 'The fish from our river tastes like petroleum, so we don't eat it anymore,' says a Cofan elder. 'We have to go further into the forest, while many of us are getting diseases we never had before.' The scale of Chevron's neglect makes you wonder how things could go wrong for so long. Legal loopholes and lawyers' acrobatics is just the short answer. Decades ago, the region was pristine. Now, plants, animals and human beings can no longer live.

Forty-eight inhabitants of the Oriente, representing about 30,000 residents from about 80 villages, joined forces in el Frente de la Defensa de la Amazonía, the Amazon Defense Coalition. Their lawsuit, Aguinda v. ChevronTexaco, is a struggle on behalf of the people of the Amazon, and of Ecuador against Big Oil. The lawsuit takes its name from the first plaintiff listed, Maria Aguinda, a Quechua Indian. Next to Quechua Indians, the lawsuit also represents the grievances of the Cofan, Huarani, Secoya, and Siona tribes. Over the course of the past few decades another tribe, the Tetete, have died out. The plaintiffs allege that between 1964 and 1992, Texaco dumped 18 billion gallons of toxic water, and is responsible for a disaster that did not just result from one accidental spill, but from 28 years of employing cost-cutting and sub-standard technology.

These days, South-American governments act with new vigor, and newly elected presidents are finding left-wing soul mates that are not as forgiving towards foreign investors or oil companies as they used to be. Moreover, many foreign oil companies have recently been forced to rewrite their joint-venture contracts or find that different countries nationalize their oil companies. 'The lawsuit is a fight not just about oil companies in the jungle,' a Quito-based law professor said, 'but about 500 years of South American history.'

On a poster-sized black-and-white cartoon at the Frente's office in Quito, a Chevron official pours out an oil barrel full of accusations. Another wall poignantly illustrates their position: Chevron Texaco Basta Ya. No Mas Pressia Ni Corrupcion. It is the place where Pablo Fajardo, the lead plaintiff of the class-action lawsuit against Chevron, works half the week; the other half is spent in the Oriente. Without exception, the Frente's employees have made personal sacrifices. Their offices have been robbed of case-related computer files, and there have been threats and attacks on their lives. Their level of commitment to the protection of the earth, the air, the water, the health and dignity of Ecuadorians? Forever.

Meanwhile, in the Amazon region south of the Oriente, Argentinean, Brazilian and Chinese consortiums are already lobbying to drill for oil. Promises abound. The rainforests will remain clean, the Indians will prosper, cultural identities will be respected, and communities will thrive with schools and hospitals. Really?

Personal narrative — Pablo Fajardo

A story about me? Why? I don't mind telling you about myself, but the most important thing is that you understand the whole problem with Chevron. The problems they are causing are very big, and it is causing many people great distress. Many people from Ecuador, and from its indigenous communities, have joined together to fight them. I'm only one of them.

I was born into poverty, in a rural area of the coastal province of Manabí. The day of my birth was only a few days after oil started flowing through the pipelines across the Andes Mountains, and into the tanks at the port of Esmeraldas. I was the fifth son, one of 10 children. Perhaps my parents had so many children because they didn't have television. Nor much else. My father is illiterate. All of his life he worked in the field as a farmer. My mother dedicated herself to taking care of the home, her children, and was skilled in medicine. She is not a professional, but when she was young she learned to cure many illnesses with plants and vegetables, and she is also a

271

midwife. They struggled and had to work very hard to raise us. For this reason, since we were young, my siblings and I also had to work in the fields.

When I was six, the land in our region dried up, so our family moved to the northern province of Esmeraldas. There I finished primary school, and the first year of secondary school, while working in the fields. When I was nine or 10, my mother opened a tiny shop selling basic food items and put me in charge. I did what my mother asked and ran the shop. But in the 1980s, drought came to Esmeraldas as well and money was scarce. We heard that there was work to be found in the east, the Oriente. By this time, some of my older brothers had already traveled to the Oriente, or the Amazon, to look for jobs. My parents hoped they could find a better life there, with more opportunities to work so their children could finish school. So, in groups we got on different buses heading for the Amazon. We passed through Lago Agrio, and traveled another 80 kilometers, and settled near the largest of the oil fields in a small town called Shushufindi in 1987. It's a place with a bad reputation. There is a lot of violence that usually goes uninvestigated. Sometimes gunmen appear in the streets or bars, and there are more brothels than schools.

'Welcome to Houston' read a sign when entering town, because it had arisen around Texaco facilities. By that time, 1987, Texaco's operations were in full bloom. My father and mother settled in a shack on the edge of town, near a dirty, stinking stream. Here, I realized for the first time how big the problems were. The stream had no fish in it anymore. Another stream was covered in oil, so we had nowhere to bathe. We did have a well, but the water tasted like acid. We had to wait for rainwater. But that too contained many black particles. Wherever you went, the water was dirty. 'An oil-world hell,' is how a Spanish priest from the Apostolic Vicariate of Aguarico described it. Upon arrival, I went to work with my brothers in a palm-oil grove called Palmeras del Ecuador, clearing jungle growth with a machete. For two years, I lived in a 'camp' with the other workers of the company. During these two years, I was not able to study at all. However, I did start getting more involved with social work in the Catholic Church. I wanted to continue studying, so in 1989 I went to live in the city of Shushufindi. I immediately enrolled in secondary school, but still had to continue working in order to survive. My only option was to study at night.

My rhythm of life was again altered when my parents separated and moved away, leaving me, only 16 at the time, in charge of my younger brothers and sisters. With the little income I had, I managed to buy a shack in the poorest part of town. Now my duties also included cooking and keeping a watchful eye on my brothers and sisters. I had to wake up at 4 o'clock in the morning in order to make breakfast and send them to school. Then I would leave for work, return at around 3 or 4 in the afternoon, eat the lunch that my siblings made me, and prepare for my evening classes. Moreover, all of the students in my school elected me to act as their president and I assumed leadership of the community group in my neighborhood. I also found the time to play soccer, and charm a number of girls. At some stage I took some driving lessons, but I was less successful in that. I also enrolled in a correspondence class for computer technician. It didn't really interest me, but there wasn't much else to study. With this routine, it would take me another seven years to finish school. At that time I didn't know it, but all these challenges prepared me for the upcoming battle with Chevron.

Life was hard. There are many things I remember from this period that used to make me cry. For instance, the thought of confronting life alone, the responsibility of being a father to my younger siblings and, of course, the injustice faced by the people in my town. However, today when I remember these difficult times, I do not do so with sadness, but happiness. I learned so much from every moment, from my elders, from illiterate men and women like my father that do not have money and do not know how to read or write. They taught me the greatest life lessons: to be persistent, honest and hard working. The truth is: I have absolutely learned the most in my life from this time of suffering and pain.

I began attending meetings of a Catholic group, not because I was religious, but because the Spanish priest urged all of us to stand up for our dignity. In those days, the Catholic Church represented 'liberation theology'. 'You are all human beings,' the priest said, 'equal to any other. People should not exploit you just because they are in positions of power. Look upon others eye to eye, on the same level.' I cherished his advice and began to deepen my involvement with the social work of the Church. My parents believed in God. During my childhood in the bosom of my family, this belief was always present. Nevertheless, as soon as challenges arose and I saw how so many people suffered, I knew the only way to create real change in society was to work and fight together for justice. The changes our planet needs, the justice that so many dream of, and a life of dignity, will not be obtained with only faith or hope in God.

It was easy for me to adapt to the life in the Amazon with the workers and indigenous people, because I knew the hardships of trying to provide for one's family. I understood the pain and suffering that they lived with everyday. I believe that the family is the main social base and it is what always motivates and helps one to continue on the path of life and justice. One of the first things that I became aware of in the Amazon was the people who suffered due to the pollution of the environment by Texaco. I saw how the company contaminated the water, the air and the land. I witnessed many of my friends becoming sick and dying of cancer. In 1989, I helped found the Human Rights Committee of Shushufindi. It took me by surprise that my fellow members elected me as their president. The goal was to stand up against the abuses towards laborers and the contamination by oil companies. Many people in the indigenous communities were already well aware of all the problems. They suffered ill health, various kinds of cancer, their crops wouldn't grow, and their livestock was dying. We started to investigate the problems, and look for solutions. But there was no one to turn to. The Government did not reach out to them. They had nowhere to go. They were on their own.

Search for solutions
One of our first goals was to create a space in which people's grievances could be heard. That revealed another problem. The extent of the problems was becoming clear, but we had no idea what

274

to do about them. Often, in our search for solutions, we encountered officials and institutions that left us with one resounding advice: 'Look for a lawyer to defend you.' We realized we needed a collective effort to improve education and awareness of our rights. We needed to continue to reinforce the hope and belief that it is possible to achieve what at first seems impossible. So, we decided to motivate each other, and become those defenders and lawyers ourselves, so that we could help the communities that we lived and worked in.

When I was working at the palm-oil grove with my two older brothers, there too they asked me to be their leader. The work was grueling, unsafe, and poorly paid. The wages were only $50 a month. I didn't starve, but it was hardly enough to live on. The workers didn't consider themselves to be slaves, but when the company didn't pay them, or didn't provide them with protection from the chemicals they had to use, they turned to me. 'Can't you help us, go to the managers to complain, and ask for raises?' I challenged the company's rough treatment of the workers and the bad working conditions. Immediately, they labeled me a subversive and accused me of being a labor unionist. To the best of my knowledge, they put a spy on me to follow my movements. Not long after, my brothers and I were called into the office. 'You are fired,' they said. It came as no surprise.

But I could not let this stop me. My dream has always been to live in a more just world, where everyone respects each other, and we all understand that a dignified life is the most important thing we have, not money. But in order to have a dignified life, we must have an environmentally healthy world. A world without injustice. While I continued night school, I signed on as a laborer performing maintenance in the oil fields, cleaning storage tanks and pipelines, and pouring concrete. It made more money than in the palm-oil groves, but I was still poor. It became more difficult to find work. Although I cannot be 100 per cent sure, I believe at that time I was blacklisted by oil companies, so I went to work fulltime at the human rights office, still making only $50 per month. I endured the poverty, but it was hard just to feed ourselves, and my family suffered from it.

The presence of the oil companies could be felt everywhere. While the North-American oilmen lived in a compound where they played tennis at night, the people outside the fence couldn't even afford electricity. Day and night, the air was thick with black smoke from gases and waste oil being burned at one of their 22 separation stations. These receive crude oil and formation water from 356 well sites. Most separation stations have elevated flares, part of the process of separating the crude oil into gas and water, before the oil is led into the pipelines. Some of these flares burn permanently. If you stand near them, they'll give you a headache. When it rained, the soot or oil particles fell down too. People collected the rain anyway, often in discarded Texaco drums, and for lack of choice they drank that water. Town streets were sprayed with oil from waste pits to suppress the dust. It made the streets very slick, especially when it rained. Oil-company pickup trucks roared through town without slowing down, and on a number of occasions people got injured, and some pedestrians got killed.

Our house was about 500 meters from one of Chevron's central separation stations. At first I wasn't aware of the fact that it could poison us. But shortly after, I visited many communities. I saw all the damage, and how the poor suffered. No clean water, dying animals, and a lot of sick people. I became more and more convinced that it is everyone's duty to fight for this cause, and to have a better environment. There was no recourse to the police or to the army. The police were criminal themselves, and completely without power. The Ecuadorian Army was there as well, but primarily to protect the oil operations. Their relationship with the oil industry continues to this day. Notably, during the first few years of the trial that is now underway, Chevron's attorneys stayed in a house on the local military base. Yes, Texaco's managers deplored the violence as well, but they felt they couldn't do anything to stop it. And after all, they were there for one reason only, and it wasn't to solve Ecuador's social problems. They blamed the Government for encouraging too many settlers, but the pool of the poor and unemployed provided them with an ample supply of laborers willing to work for low wages, and easy to replace.

When we saw that the health problems, the poverty, and the death of our animals affected my family just as much as the families next to us and the whole community, finally we realized that there was an overarching environmental problem that was causing it all. This problem was affecting the entire region. It was caused by the large oil company, and the State was not capable of fixing things. What's more, it was difficult to unite the different cultures, traditions and ways of living of the indigenous tribes and farmers. But as we were confronted with the same problems, we realized that we would have to unite and organize ourselves to fight and work together in order to confront the large and powerful oil company. Now it has been more than 16 years since we began the process of organizing a campaign and lawsuit against ChevronTexaco, and to this day we remain united, despite the enormous differences that exist between the towns and peoples.

Class-action suit
In 1992, Texaco pulled out of Ecuador when its contract expired. It handed over its substandard operations to Petroecuador, including the entire flawed infrastructure that was intentionally designed to dump toxic waste directly into the rivers and streams of the jungle. A year later, in 1993, an Ecuadorian-American attorney named Cristobal Bonifaz filed a class-action suit in a New York federal court on behalf of the settlers and Indians. At this point, the New York lawyer Steven Donziger joined the case to give advice. The class-action case was the same as the one that would be filed a decade later, in 2003, in Ecuador. The reason for this was that Texaco had petitioned for years to have the case relocated to Ecuador. They even praised the integrity of Ecuador's judicial system. As a condition of the removal, the company promised to submit to the jurisdiction of the Ecuadorian court, and to abide by any judgment in the trial, meaning that any judgment against them in Ecuador will be enforceable in the United States. At a Lago Agrio meeting, an organization was formed to serve as the plaintiff's voice, the Frente de Defensa de la Amazonia, the Amazon Defense Coalition. But we simply call it la Frente.

'These are international crimes subject to punishment.'

As seen in the documentary 'Crude: The Real Price of Oil', chief American legal adviser Steven Donziger can be direct and relentless. On camera, he repeatedly accuses a Chevron lawyer of corruption in open court. What does he think himself?

'For the past 16 years or so, I have been part of the joint Ecuadorian- American legal team that represents the plaintiffs in the case Aguinda v. ChevronTexaco. While a major humanitarian crisis is unfolding in the Amazon because of deliberate pollution caused by Texaco, the major line of defense of Chevron thus far has been to spend millions of dollars on lobbyists, legal advisers and public-relations consultants. Their aim is to keep the full details away from the public, from journalists, and even from their own shareholders. Their defense strategy is to delay an outcome as long as possible; they have concluded it is cheaper to litigate than it is to properly remediate the damage. US Congresswoman Linda Sanchez of California recently referred to Chevron as engaging in 'a lobbying effort that looks little more than extortion'. In my opinion, the company is completely abusing the legal system by filing redundant motions, raising frivolous arguments, and filing multiple actions in various jurisdictions that deal with the same issues. It is unfair that after 17 years we do not have a resolution of the claims at the trial level.'

'In Ecuador, Chevron engaged in the worst kind of malfeasance. To cut costs, the company violated industry standards, Ecuadorian environmental law, and international regulations. Last but not least, it violated its own agreements with Ecuador's Government not to pollute and betrayed its own internal standards that it touts on its website. What else could be said about a company whose operations leave behind a legacy of oil-related and carcinogenic deaths, miscarriages, and genetic birth defects? People are dying of cancer of the kidney, stomach, spleen, skin, uterine cancer and so on.

I know or knew many of these victims personally; the level of tragedy is astounding. What's worse, this is the result of a deliberate policy to pollute, rather than the effects of negligence stemming from some accident. Chevron even tries to manipulate the US Government to protect its ill-gotten profits in Ecuador. To do so, they pay enormous fees to employ high-powered lobbyists like Mack McLarty, former chief of staff to President Bill Clinton, former Senators John Breaux and Trent Lott, and Wayne Berman, who served as the national finance chair for Senator John McCain's presidential campaign. These people have an incentive to keep the litigation going so they can continue to reap personal benefits at the expense of the Amazonian communities.

'The indigenous groups of the region had prospered for centuries before oil began to be extracted. There used to be six such groups: the Cofan, Huarani, Quechua, Secoya, Siona, and Tetete. The Tetete are gone now. Having made numerous trips to the toxic waste sites across the rainforest, I have seen firsthand how the rights of these vulnerable peoples are being violated by intentionally reckless practices to extract oil – intentionally, because instead of re-injecting the toxic wastewater in order to minimize environmental impact, Chevron designed a system to dump the toxic waste directly into the streams and rivers used by local people. Reinjection of waste is more expensive than dumping it. So despite the known harm to the environment and people, the company chose to cut costs to the bare minimum and that is how the toxic waste ended up in open rivers, in the ground, and in 916 unlined pits gouged out of the jungle floor. Soil samples taken during judicial inspections at all of the former Texaco sites in Ecuador that Texaco claimed had been remediated, revealed extensive contamination. The company's so-called remediation was a sham.

'This is what Chevron did. Clearly it was well aware of proper practices as laid out in the 'oil-field primer' published by the American Petroleum Institute as well as the company's own patent on reinjection technology. Chevron's violations of human rights, of regulations regarding environmental protection and of standards in the oil industry are indisputable. We consider them violations of international human rights law as enshrined in various treaties, legal instruments, and general custom. We believe these actions should be subject to punishment and accountability.

'Thousands of people are at risk of illness and death, or have died preventable deaths, because of Chevron's ongoing cover-up and general failure to take responsibility for its actions. In 2009, a Chevron lobbyist created a major stir when he was quoted anonymously in Newsweek. With regard to Chevron's potential environmental liability in Ecuador, he said: 'We can't let little countries screw around with big companies like this – companies that have made big investments around the world.' That is pretty much an accurate reflection of how Chevron's management privately thinks about this problem. Occasionally, the truth slips off their own lips.'

After 1993, the Human Rights Committee of Shushufindi joined forces with the Frente. Many people and groups wanted to join: Indians, women, laborers and so on. Step by step, I became more involved. In 1995, I got my diploma as a computer technician. I disregarded it however, and with about a dozen other leaders started taking correspondence courses from a Quito university on the environment and human rights. The following year, I founded a free night school for adults, and began to teach literacy classes. Also, I began to work with Indian communities. I met my future wife, Fanny Vilares. She's really cute and funny. We met in the human rights group, and we moved in together in my little house. Between

1996 and 2000 I was working with the Catholic Church, the only organization that had a point of view, and that stood up for human rights. All other organizations were influenced or controlled by Texaco in one way or the other. For us, however, the Texaco case was only one of many others that we fought.

Throughout all of these experiences, I learned that it was impossible to win these fights on my own or as a single individual. Together with all of my friends and companions, we fought together for a very long time. However, despite everything we were doing for the people of the Amazon, we finally realized that we needed to find a lawyer to defend us in court. Of course, there were some lawyers in our town, but they were either working for businesses or for the small number of functioning public institutions. There were no lawyers that could dedicate themselves completely to the human rights work that needed to be done.

Shortly after, it felt like the sun came out. In 1997, my daughter was born, and a few months later the Catholic priest that had been helping me for years found the resources to provide me with a law-school scholarship. It only covered books and tuition, but eight of my friends committed themselves to supporting me for the whole period of a six-year correspondence course. So, with a little help from my friends, I managed. Once again, it started a strict regime: I woke up at 3.30 in the morning, ate something quickly, studied law books until 8.00, rushed to the human rights office, and worked on cases until midday. Next, I sat down in the Shushufindi radio station where I read the news that I had prepared myself, rushed back to the office, worked until closing time, prepared a lesson plan for the evening class, went to night school and taught. I got home at 11, slept a few hours, and did it all over again the next day.

Eye to eye
A few years ago, a team of settlers and indigenous leaders proposed that I take over as lead attorney on behalf of the Frente. 'I need time to think it over,' I said. 'Can you give me a month?' 'You can have three days,' they said. I was worried about my lack of experience, as I had only been a lawyer for a year. In contrast, the Chevron attorneys

had 30 years of experience, and usually worked with a team. Sometimes they would come down to the Lago Agrio courthouse with eight of them, while I was by myself, often afraid of making mistakes. However, I practiced the advice the priest had given me: look at people on the same level, eye to eye. So, when someone is old or very poor, I do not feel above them. When someone appears to be superior, I do not feel below them. I realized that I was not inferior to the Chevron lawyers. In fact, I had one advantage over them: I know the problems as they really are, because I live here. If I took on the case, all I would have to think about is how to tell the truth to counter their lies. And I'm still here.

Around 2003, I finished my law studies, and I started to work with the Frente. By coincidence, that same year the case came to Lago Agrio, and I assisted several other lawyers who were working on the case. I became 'their man' in Lago Agrio. A year later, I became a licensed lawyer, and in 2005 I took on full responsibility for the case. The whole process of developing the class-action case has taken almost 20 years now, while this lawsuit against Chevron is actually my first. What makes things hard is the fact that Chevron is represented by lawyers from Ecuador's ruling class. They wield a lot of power, while the Frente only has a small house with office space, and limited facilities. It is just enough for the members of our team, and for keeping the records of the lawsuit. The documentation now amounts to almost 200,000 pages, the equivalent of a library with about a thousand books.

Those pages provide detailed evidence of the fact that the pollution you see in the Oriente today is left over from the original drilling operations. Even though the oil company has withdrawn, and is now working in other areas, the contamination will still be there for years to come. Texaco drilled most of its wells in the first few years, when Gulf Oil was its financial partner. Often, the drilling rigs were built on flat terrain, and on high ground, where clearings were created by bulldozing, and which would drain into the streams and rivers. The water table is usually about 10 feet under the surface, and the topsoil consists mostly of organic matter and clay. On hilltops, the water table may be deep, but naturally in swamp areas, it is close to the surface. The oil however lies about one and a half kilometers down.

Shortly after taking on the case full-time, my best friend Freddy Raul Valberde was killed. He was a taxi driver, and one of the eight people that helped me financially to get through law school. He was shot four times, and his car disappeared, but the police never investigated. I began to notice that there were people following me in cars and on motorbikes. I don't know who they are. One morning, shortly after I had arrived by bus at the office of the Frente in Lago Agrio, I received a phone call. 'Wilson has been murdered!' My brother! I was in shock, and so was the rest of my family. Wilson was a decent man, an evangelical minister with no ties to crime or even to the social issues that I am fighting for. It may have been a regular crime. But it may also have been a case of mistaken identity. In any event, I believe they targeted him rather than me, because of my relative prominence in the region. After this, at times I lived like a hunted man, sleeping in different places. One time, I narrowly escaped an attack, simply because I was in the company of two women. I sold the house in Shushufindi, and my wife, now with an infant son as well, remained in Sacha for safety. But the pressure is still on. 'There will soon be a cleanup,' an anonymous man said on the phone. 'We will cleanse the land of people like you.' Other members of our team have also been threatened or attacked, sometimes by men using a car with dark windows, and no license plates.

Crude oil, crude practices
Drilling for oil, and extracting it, involves noxious fluids that are known as drilling muds. Once used, they become waste, and the soil in Texaco's concession areas has been found to be contaminated with unusually high levels of chromium VI, cadmium, barium, and lead. Crude oil also contains many toxins. The resulting sludge was slopped into unlined open-air pits on the sides of jungle clearings. More crude oil was added once the wells became productive, and during the necessary testing of its quality. Most of that is normal. Not so normal was the fact that the pits were abandoned after the drilling, and the wells were hooked up to a system of small feeder

lines. According to regulations existing in the United States that would have been totally unacceptable. At many well sites, settlers and indigenous people live close by. Their livestock slipped into the pits, trees began to die, plants and fruits proved to contain toxic chemicals, and many people began to develop health problems.

Chevron maintains that the pits were universally self-lining, because almost everywhere the soil consists of impermeable clay. The Frente and independent experts however maintain that this is far from the truth. Soil samples from around the pits show that elements of the toxic waste had drifted into the nearby soil. In the United States, unlined pits have been restricted to locations where they cannot contaminate freshwater supplies. But these regulations were not respected in the Amazon. Here it is also harder to contain, as the Amazon is a very watery environment, and the poor and indigenous people that live here don't have any choice but using the water for drinking, cooking, bathing or washing their clothes. In 1980, Texaco did consider lining its pits or transferring the wastes to new, concrete-lined pits. They calculated that this would cost them $4,197,968. They decided to leave things as they were.

Water is heavier than oil. In the pits therefore, during rainfall the oil drifts to the top, pushed up by the water. Texaco put in pipes or 'siphons' at lower places through the sides of the pits to drain them down slope, and keep them from overflowing in the tropical rains. This didn't work, and there is ample evidence of it from at least 45 field inspections. Even after 30 years of drilling, hundreds of meters away rainbow patches float down the stream. When you stir the ground around the streams, you see the oil bubbling up. If you can't see it, you will certainly smell it. For decades, Texaco officials were aware of the problems they were causing. Already in 1972, a confidential memo had surfaced. 'No reports are to be kept on a routine basis,' it read, 'and all previous reports are to be removed from Field and Division offices and destroyed.' It related to the reporting of spills, was signed by R.C. Shields from Texaco's office in Coral Gables, Florida, and sent to Texaco's manager in Ecuador. Five years later, the Ecuadorian Government accused Texaco of negligence in the maintenance of pits and oil wells around Lago

Agrio. Believe it or not, they were fined the sum of $3,650. Absolutely nothing. Instead of accepting responsibility, Texaco maintains that the problem with the water is that it has been tainted by the settler's latrines.

We have another great concern. Over the 17 years that Texaco has operated the 502-kilometer Trans-Ecuadorian pipeline, the oleoduct, it suffered 27 major breaks that spilled nearly 17 million gallons of oil. It's more than the 11 million that were spilled during the grounding of the Exxon Valdez in 1989. Most of it was never cleaned up. Compare this to the spills of the 1,287-kilometer Alaskan pipeline. That one spilled 1,675,000 gallons, almost all of which was cleaned up. In other words, other players in the industry know very well how to handle spills, much better than Texaco ever did in the Amazon. In the view of the Frente, the contamination that exists today resulted from choices Texaco made in the past to maximize its profits. They achieved top revenues by disregarding the environmental standards that it maintained at the same time in the United States. Also, we believe that the fact that the Exxon Valdez disaster still hasn't been settled and paid for 20 years later, strengthens the Chevron lawyers in their belief that they too can get away with the worst of negligence.

The Chevron lawyers that work on the class-action case are very clever. Even the single issue of selecting a technical expert to survey the total extent of the pollution in the former Texaco concession area was impossible. We couldn't agree on it. I proposed to have only Ecuadorian experts, all of which Chevron's lead attorney, Adolfo Callejas, rejected. Callejas is a man who has served Chevron for more than 30 years, and who comes from a wealthy and powerful family. He proposed only foreign experts, which in turn were all rejected by me. In the end, the judge intervened, deciding that he himself would select the expert, in order to break the impasse and move justice along. He selected technical expert Richard Cabrera.

The Cabrera Report
In 2008, Cabrera released a 4,000-page report that analyzed all the evidence, including more than 62,000 scientific sampling results,

most of which were submitted by Chevron. Cabrera had been assisted by a team of 14 scientists. The results conclusively proved that 100 per cent of Texaco's former well sites had dangerous levels of carcinogenic hydrocarbons. The report found Chevron responsible, and estimated the damages to be as high as $27.3 billion, a possible record for an environmental case. The Cabrera Report also estimated that the oil contamination had caused 1,041 excess deaths from cancer in Texaco's operational area. Other studies confirmed that the levels of cancer were above the norm with phenomena such as child leukemia, miscarriages and birth defects.

One also has to take into account that when a person dies, the victim is not only this one person. Their death and suffering extends to their children, their family and the community who all suffer psychologically, in a way that is irreparable and economically unquantifiable. Furthermore, the indigenous groups in the region where Texaco operated have lost 95 per cent of their ancestral lands, and the social impacts are devastating. Undaunted, at a later stage Callejas submitted a document to the judge with 30 pages of legal points raised by the Chevron lawyers. The judge doesn't have a clerk to assist him, and I think he already works eight days a week. Along with the thousands of pages of trial documents, having to go through those additional legal points is a massive task of judicial inspections, environmental surveys, associated arguments and maneuvers.

'Before writing the decision,' the judge once said, 'I would have to isolate myself in a Tibetan monastery for two years, just to get the reading done.' Under Ecuadorian law, we have a system of rotating judges. But for each of them, the reading list is endless. It is delaying the case, which is part of Chevron's strategy. Chevron however insists that delay is not its object. In an interview with Vanity Fair, Steven Donziger explained the cold logic of delay. 'Take $6 billion as a figure. Simply by sticking the money into a savings account, Chevron could make $300 million for every year that it doesn't pay. That sum multiplied by the four years of the trial so far would amount to $1.2 billion, which is far more than, say, $50 million spent on legal fees, even if Chevron now loses the case.' What if Chevron wins? What would be the calculation then?

By now, it is clear that I've had to pay a price for this work. It is taking its toll on me, my friends and family. I was married, but now I'm divorced. My ex-wife and my children live in a safer town called Sacha. My ex-wife runs a grocery store. As for myself, I often sleep in my office, as I cannot afford a house. I can also not afford a car. I like driving, but I'm a poor driver, so usually when I'm in Lago Agrio I get around on a mountain bike. The streets have potholes, but I maintain the bike well, and it has shocks for comfort. But when I have to appear before the judge, I take the bus. Sometimes, when I meet with Chevron lawyers, they arrive in the company of heavily armed bodyguards. It's intimidating. We don't engage in conversation, as Chevron doesn't allow Callejas or other Chevron attorneys to speak with me.

'My responsibility is the whole case. Every part of it.'

Luis Yanza, coordinator of the Amazon Defense Coalition, is also a human rights activist, community leader, and founder of the Confederation of Indigenous Nationalities of Ecuador (CONAIE).

'Most of my life I have lived in the Amazon. The first 16 years were in the south, where even now the environment is clean and without contamination. After that, I moved north, where everything – the whole environment and all the communities – is dominated by the contamination caused by oil companies. When I arrived in 1977 it hit me very hard. The moment I descended from the bus, I stepped on oil. Those were the days that Texaco sprayed oil onto the roads, as you can see on photos and videos on YouTube.'

'Before I joined the class-action case against Texaco, for many years I had already been working as a social worker with local organizations. My experience of the region is very broad. I have been a community worker, and I formed CONAIE, a coalition of social organizations, in 1990. In 1993, when the case was put before the court in New York, we created the Frente to fight Texaco. This was necessary, because Chevron applied a strategy of divide and rule, and separating the different communities in the Amazon from each other by causing rumors and antagonism. But we worked hard to overcome those tactics, and now the Frente is strong and well organized. I have come face to face with Chevron representatives, and attended some of their shareholder meetings in San Ramon. They have no interest in listening.

'Every time after working for the Frente, I return to Coca where I live. I visit the communities, the places where the consequences of Chevron's activities are clearly visible. I keep the communities informed, so that they are aware and part of the whole process. Sleepless nights have become part of my life, because I keep thinking about every aspect of the case, such as a demonstration that we are preparing in Lago Agrio with marches, and speeches by indigenous leaders. We do this to show people that we are here, and that we are active. It gives a clear signal to Chevron: look, we are aware of what is going on, and watching you. Chevron's attitude is dominated by the desire to maintain their financial power. Their world is governed by money, and doesn't allow them to see beyond their own interests.

'We believe in the judicial system of Ecuador. We also believe that the appointed judge will take a good decision, and that justice will prevail. At the same time however, we are worried about Chevron's power, and that they might do anything to avoid justice, and steer the case in such a way that they get away with impunity. Right now, they might even be thinking of actions worse than putting out that video that they put on their corporate website. It shows two men who try to trick the judge into making wrongful statements, but they didn't manage to do so. I think the appearance of the video however is a good sign. Apparently, Chevron now even needs sting operations to derail the trial. It shows that Chevron expects to lose, and that they are becoming desperate. It shows that we are moving forward in the right direction, that we have done our work well, and that we are very close to a final decision. The court case is coming to an end. In other words: Chevron has to beat the retreat.

'For now, the most important result of the class-action case is straightforward: the reparation of all the damage, and the health of the people. It would be good if Chevron is severely sanctioned for neglecting its responsibilities, because it may give many other people and regions the hope of doing the same. But remediation of such magnitude? Never. Many places are now beyond repair. There are only a few parts that can be remediated by improving the environment, the health of the people, and their quality of life.'

Corruption and social exclusion
There have been problems with the Government of Ecuador for decades. For many years, it didn't recognize the peoples of the Amazon. They saw it as a far-away, mythological jungle, and only began to recognize it when they realized they could benefit from the natural resources beneath its soil. This was perfect for Texaco. They could simply go about their business without any obstacle. Even the Ecuadorian armed forces were serving the oil company. The problem wasn't just corruption, but especially the social exclusion of the people that lived there. There still is hardly any contact. The Government cannot be counted on.

Historically, the story of Chevron has never changed. I don't think they were ever honest. Perhaps they will be forced to become honest now. They are loyal to the principles they always had – their principles. Their victories and profits were always achieved by a mixture of racism, human rights violations, exerting pressure on local people, and serving their own ambitions and economic interests first. Even today, their Ecuadorian lawyers claim that the Amazon is an industrial area, without any recognition of the rights of the Indians that live there. This whole case is such a mixed bag! The main problem was caused by Texaco, but other factors play an important part. Big oil companies are very skilled in manipulating weak governments like we had then. Chevron issued many internal documents that prescribe how their employees should influence and manage the different ministries and departments of the Government of Ecuador. So when we speak about corruption, it isn't just about the prior Government. It's also the company that corrupts the Government. They are linked. So in this context, it is understandable why Chevron worked the way it did, and neglected their respect for life and nature. It suits them.

Fifteen years ago, people didn't know about the problems that Texaco was causing, nor did they know about the fight that the Frente was organizing against it. But thanks to a lot of work by many people in different organizations, both from Ecuador and from other countries, the case is becoming widely known. Amazon Watch, as an example, has been of great support to our struggle, and to making the issues known to the world. One way this has recently been done is by the documentary *Crude: The Real Price of Oil* that had its premiere in Los Angeles in 2009. The class-action case is a very important tool for growing people's awareness in Ecuador and in the world. Struggling together, we hope to find justice. And as the damage that was caused in the Amazon is experienced collectively, the fight for justice should also be conducted collectively. This is why the people in the Amazon have joined hands with the people in other parts of Ecuador and the world. We are in a collective fight for justice, for the people, the earth, and the environment.

Over the years, this struggle has left some very strong marks in me. It has affected me considerably. I have encountered some very bitter experiences, some of which are very personal or relate to my family. The disintegration of my family life is a direct result of my work on this case. I live with ongoing stress, due to the uncertainty of what is going to happen with me, and the fact of being chased by people that shadow me. But my commitment is rock solid, and that's why I will continue doing this.

The worst part of it all is that we don't know what result we will get. The video that Chevron recently put on their corporate website and posted on YouTube is just one more thing in a long series of actions they have taken. Chevron claimed that the footage implicates the Ecuadorian judge Juan Nuñez, who presides over the trial, in a $3 million bribery scheme. But their 'smoking gun' looks more like an elaborate hoax. In fact, it reveals that a former Chevron contractor, Ecuadorian Diego Borja, and an American businessman called Wayne Hansen, try to entrap the judge, while recording their meeting using micro-cameras hidden in a watch and a pen. Later, it turned out that Hansen is a convicted felon and drug trafficker. They can't manage however to make Nuñez reveal the verdict. The appearance of the video is a strange turn of events, but it fits the pattern of how they work. A few months later, Nuñez said he was set up by Chevron. To avoid any appearance of impropriety he withdrew from the case, and another judge has replaced him. But what else is Chevron up to? What else might they come up with?

When we first took up this struggle, right away Chevron tried to stop it by bribing leaders, and making alternative arrangements with the Government and the communities of the region. But it didn't work. The next five years, they accused the communities of ignorance and creating terrorist trouble. That didn't work either. Next, they attacked the struggle of the Ecuadorian people with all the strength they could muster. I think we have now reached the last phase, the top rung of the ladder: attacks of every kind – media, judicial, and economic attacks. They may even contemplate personal attacks. It means that no one that works for the Frente is entirely safe. One of my greatest personal concerns is my children. I feel sure that Chevron won't hurt me personally. But they may do things indirectly, and hurt people that are dear to me or close to me. That worries me. We understand now: this is how Chevron operates. We have to be ready for any kind of tactics that they may come up with. If this step doesn't work out for them either, maybe the next step will be Chevron saying: let's do something about it.

Chevron's problems
So far, Chevron has never indicated the wish for any kind of settlement. But it would cost them a lot less. As the case develops further, it can only grow. The class-action case now demands more

than $27.3 billion. What do they want? They have enough money. The first problem Chevron has is arrogance. The second is the fact that they cannot accept that simple people like us Ecuadorians will make them pay. They cannot tolerate that one little country like Ecuador annoys and disturbs their grand enterprise. In a single year however, Chevron earns more than six times the entire gross domestic product of Ecuador, so there is no doubt that they could settle the matter outside of court. But they show no sign of giving up. Chevron's third problem is their concern about their image, and what this whole class-action case will do to their reputation in the world. Especially if we win. Why? Because what Chevron did here, they have also done in other places around the world. And so have many other companies. They don't want to clean up the Amazon; they want to clean up their image.

If we win this case, or make a favorable agreement for all the participants in the class-action case, it will mean that Chevron or other companies will be held responsible. If so, they will be sued, and will be asked for reparations, remediation, and compensations in other parts of the world as well. They're afraid of that. Especially as they are aware of the fact that this crime is not only being committed in Ecuador. This is why they will fight until the end, so they won't feel that they are losers or lose face. If an agreement was reached now, Chevron's condition is that the Government of Ecuador accepts responsibility for the damage caused by Chevron. In that case they will pay money, but the State of Ecuador will be forced to say that it is responsible for the contamination and its consequences. Think about it! They want to make our Government responsible for a problem that it didn't create, but that Chevron created itself! That's what all the international pressure is about. In a nutshell: it's immoral, inhumane and criminal.

I believe that more and more people in our country are beginning to see that the Frente is working for a good motive. We have been very clear about the fact that neither the Government nor any of its representatives can interfere in the judicial process. We demand that the different powers of the State – legislative, judicial, and executive – should be respected. Our President has also repeatedly said that

Ecuador's Government will not intervene. This is right, because intervening would undermine the independence of Ecuador's judiciary, and ultimately allow Chevron to circumvent a binding court decision. But we did ask the Government to assist immediately in the humanitarian crisis in the area, for example in housing programs and the relocation of families whose houses were built on top of or next to pits full of toxic chemicals and move them to safer places. Those are not final solutions, but it helps a lot of people, and solves at least some of the most urgent problems.

There are many studies regarding the health of the Amazonian people that clearly demonstrate the ill effects of the pollution in the air, and the contamination in the ground. Those studies prove that the toxic chemicals in crude oil and in 'formation water' – water pumped underground to force out the crude – cause cancer. Two medical doctors, San Sebastian and his wife Anna-Karin who lived in the Amazon for 10 years, wrote a book about it. Their investigation details the impact of the operations and contaminations caused by Chevron. But there is another problem: the difference between using science in a hard way, and in a human way.

One of Chevron's arguments is that the contamination found in the Amazon, and the oil dumped by Texaco, does not cause cancer. They continue to assert this, even though there is ample evidence that lays the blame at Chevron's doorstep. In the water you find benzene, toluene, and hydrocarbons that are all carcinogenic, and the people in the Amazon fall victim to more and more diseases on an ongoing basis. Human science would tell you about the importance of precaution, and how to avoid coming into contact with chemicals that are harmful to your health. Chevron itself has never conducted any health-risk assessments. It will twist the truth to the point where it's comical. In the United States, they accepted that chromium causes cancer. But in Ecuador? No.

A game of smoke and mirrors – Chevron's 10 biggest lies

'When one connects the dots of Chevron's behavior in Ecuador,' says the Amazon Defense Coalition, 'what emerges is a coordinated series of misinformation and frauds designed to deceive courts, the public, shareholders, and the financial markets.' While experts refer to the environmental devastation as the 'Amazon Chernobyl', Chevron employs spin doctors to misinform people. The Frente debunked the oil giant's myths.

Lie nr. 1: Texaco's operational practices caused no harm to the environment.
Chevron has admitted that Texaco dumped over 18.5 billion gallons of toxic produced water into the rainforest near Lago Agrio from 1964 to 1992. Worse still, much of the harm inflicted upon the rainforest residents was lethal and irreversible.

Lie nr. 2: Scientific evidence at trial proves Chevron caused no harm.
The Cabrera Report conducted by 15 independent scientists found that 100 per cent of the Chevron sites examined had illegal toxin levels. Moreover, Chevron's own scientific evidence is proving the case against the company itself.

Lie nr. 3: Texaco's operational practices were customary for the industry.
Texaco's operational practices in Ecuador violated industry practices and a host of laws, some of which date back to the 1920s. Requirements to 'employ modern and efficient machinery' to 'avoid contamination of waters, airs, and lands' were ignored.

Lie nr. 4: The dumping of toxic 'waste water' poses no health risk.
Health risks from being exposed to oil and oil wastes are well documented in the scientific literature. Several studies have found high cancer rates where Texaco operated. Scientists from 17 countries signed a letter criticizing Chevron's lack of scientific integrity in Ecuador.

Lie nr. 5: Texaco remediated the damage.
The 'remediation' covered less than one per cent of the damage. Texaco dumped dirt over a small number of waste pits – the equivalent of using makeup to treat skin cancer. Its 'remediation' was no more than a choreographed fraud designed to evade accountability.

Lie nr. 6: The Ecuador trial court is biased against Chevron.
Texaco fought to avoid trial in the US by claiming Ecuador's courts were fair. When the evidence showed it was culpable, Chevron started to attack the court process by distortions, politicized lobbying, intimidation, and creating fake laboratory test results.

Lie nr. 7: The plaintiffs are undermining the due process rights of Chevron.
In Ecuador, Chevron has probably been afforded more due process than any other defendant in history. It has tried to undermine the rights of the plaintiffs, and has repeatedly violated the due process rights of Ecuadorian citizens to forestall a resolution of the case.

Lie nr. 8: Soil samples collected where Texaco 'remediated' show no contamination.
Soil sampling evidence from each of the 'remediated' sites shows significant contamination, often thousands of times higher than norms. Like the tobacco industry did for decades, Chevron attacks legitimate science and manufactures fake results to support its claims.

Lie nr. 9: The responsibility for clean-up rests with Petroecuador.
Texaco exclusively designed, built, and operated the oil production infrastructure in Ecuador. As operator, it is responsible for the environmental damage it caused. The law is clear. An oil operator cannot absolve itself of responsibility simply by abandoning a nuisance.

Lie nr. 10: The damages report is biased.
More than 25 scientists have reviewed the report and found
its conclusions reasonable. Chevron attacks any judge or
journalist who does not agree with it. Its list of 'liars' also
includes lawyers, indigenous leaders, doctors and
environmental consultants.

We are aware that we will never be able to repair all of the damage
that Chevron has done to the people nor the ecosystem of the
Amazon. The biggest part of the crime committed by Chevron is
absolutely irreversible. No matter what sentence Chevron receives
for their crimes, it will always be unjust for the victims. No amount of
money in the world can recuperate the cultures of the indigenous
villages that are now extinct. I am referring to the Tetete and
Sansahuaris people. These people lived in the Amazon when Texaco
began their oil extraction activities there and five years later they no
longer existed. Hopefully, one day someone will explain to us and
show us what happened to these people. Who exterminated them?
Why did they disappear? We can easily compare this to the
ecosystem. The rich amounts of fish, flora, and fauna have been
slowly chipped away at. The quality of the soil has plummeted,
making it impossible to live in many places. These natural resources
and areas will never return to their original condition.

Despite this very adverse reality, what we do believe should happen
as a result of the case can be summarized in seven points. That
Chevron is ordered to cover the costs of remediation and reparation
where it is possible to repair and that this is done in a way that is real
and effective. That the people recognize that Chevron committed a
crime against humanity. That the people recognize and remember
that when poor people unite to fight for justice, it is possible to win,
despite their small numbers or how much time it takes to reach the
end. That the people do not allow crimes like this one to repeat
themselves anywhere in the world. That everyone recognizes that
oxygen, clean water, forests, indigenous cultures, and life itself, no
matter what country you are from, has intrinsic value and is worth
much more than oil, gold, or other 'precious' metals. That this
example serves as a lesson for all the companies in the world and

obligates them to work with more responsibility and respect for human rights and nature. That the United States and other Governments assume responsibility and do not allow for those in power to abuse this privilege.

Together with Luis, I have been touring the region and the country, because we feel that the trial is an issue of national importance. It concerns our dignity as a people and our sovereignty as a nation, and the trial has become part of the national collective consciousness. In 2008, we hosted former President Chávez to show him Texaco's former operations, and the damage that has been caused. It led to a pledge by the Government to relocate several communities that were living in dangerously contaminated areas. But even though there is some recognition, we're still fighting. I am convinced changes are not produced by the upper-class nor by the high hands of the Government. Changes are made at the bases, from the everyday, working population. It is these people that live the reality of exclusion, injustice and poverty. Consequently, this same society is obligated to organize itself to fight. But, it's not without danger. We, and many of our colleagues, have received death threats, and experienced harassment and intimidation. I don't know where it will all end. If Chevron loses the court case, its officials promise they will present us with a 'lifetime of litigation' by dragging out the appeals process.

We have met with Chevron lawyers in Washington. But what is there to discuss? What is there to talk about? Usually the atmosphere between us is like boxers in a ring. What do they want? We have different positions, and we will never accept any decision against the indigenous people, and the people of Ecuador. The way Chevron representatives talk reflects an arrogant and racist attitude towards our people. 'The people are sick,' they say, 'because they don't wash their hands.' They make many derogatory statements, and their attitude is insulting to our people. It's unacceptable. Chevron is fighting for their reputation and for money. What we are doing today is trying to boost the conscience and education in the communities in order to ensure that this process of demanding justice does not end when we win the trial. But rather, it begins a true process of reconstruction of the social fabric that for 40 years has been shattered. We are fighting for life, and we stand together. I agree with Luis: 'We will continue fighting for rights and justice until the last days of our lives.'

'Recognition' and ruling of the International Court of Justice

At the end of 2014, Swiss environmental organizations crowned Chevron for its efforts to evade justice with the Public Eye Award. "Chevron is a recidivist toxic polluter that deserves condemnation from the world community for its horrific acts against the vulnerable indigenous peoples of Ecuador," said Paul Paz y Miño of Amazon Watch. Chevron has used more than 60 law firms and 2,000 lawyers, spending an estimated $2 billion on its legal defense. "Chevron is making a mockery of the rule of law around the world," said Humberto Piaguaje, an indigenous leader who has fought Chevron for almost two decades.

Four years ago, judge Nicolás Zambrano had found Chevron responsible for damages of about $8.6 billion. Chevron officials immediately rushed to court in New York to obtain an order to shield the company anywhere in the world from collection efforts relating to the case. True to their word, Chevron representatives "will fight until hell freezes over and then fight it out on the ice." Paying lawyers is cheaper than paying the damages. In March 2015, however, the International Court of Justice in The Hague ruled that the decision of 2011 should be upheld. Ecuadorean Attorney General Diego Garcia Carrion called it 'an important step in the right direction.'

Liliana Ortega - Venezuela
Providing legal aid and education in a land of impunity

'We try to wake people up about human rights,' says Liliana Ortega. Ever since the Caracazo riots of 1989, she has worked for the Committee of Family Members of Victims (COFAVIC) against impunity and for human rights awareness in Venezuela, a nation that sees around 900 extrajudicial executions per year. With her team, she gathers testimonies, keeping track of human rights violations, and educating people as diverse as school children to police officers. After Caracazo, the scales had fallen from her eyes about the conditions in the barrios, Venezuela's slums. 'We defend people. We defend principles. We don't know and don't need to know whether you are left or right, catholic or protestant, from the upper class or from the barrios.' To bring about change, she leaves no stone unturned.

Liliana Ortega

'In short, we try to wake people up about human rights.' Liliana Ortega (born in 1965) has been active as one of Venezuela's foremost human rights defenders since the Caracazo riots of 1989, trying to bring about change, especially for those in the line of fire, the women. 'Our situation is an anomaly. It's outside of the rules.'

Context

When in 1498 Christopher Columbus sailed near the Orinoco delta, he thought of the region as heaven on earth and called it Land of Grace. But it remains undecided whether Venezuela owes its name to a local tribe called the 'Veneciuela' or to navigator Amerigo Vespucci's 'Little Venice'. Colonized by Spain in 1522, it took the efforts of national hero Simon Veneciuela' Bolivar to bring Venezuela full independence in 1830. Local military strongmen, caudillos, dominated Venezuelan society well into the 20th century, but the country has been democratic since 1958.

In the course of the 20th century, the exploration of oil and natural gas deposits transformed the economy. Today Venezuela consistently ranks as one of the top-ten crude oil producers in the world. 'Black gold' to some, to others it is 'the devil's excrement' because corruption is always on its heels. Omnipresent in Venezuela and much of Latin America, former President Hugo Chávez called it 'a cancer that has metastasized in all directions.' Since the Corruption Perceptions Index began in 1995, it always ranks Venezuela near the bottom.

Oil companies were nationalized in 1973, and now Petróleos de Venezuela (PDVSA) dominates 80 per cent of Venezuelan exports. The recovery of the oil prices after 2001 boosted the economy and facilitated social spending. But as per 2010, a third of the population still lives on less than $2 a day. Whatever the rhetoric both ways, and the fact that China now comes second, the United States still is Venezuela's leading trade partner. But it remains vigilant. Long ago, Simon Bolivar warned in one of his letters: 'The United States seems destined by Providence to plague Latin America with misery in the name of liberty.'

To face its external debts, the Government devalued the currency in 1983, causing the standard of living to fall dramatically. Rising poverty and crime brought people to a threshold leading to the Caracazo riots of 1989, 'the big Caracas blow'. The turbulence continued. From the end of the 1990s onward, many people would lose their lives at the hands of 'death squads' or 'anonymous avengers' beyond the control of the State. The relatives of victims suffer profound psychological trauma made worse by the permissiveness of the judicial system and the silent acceptance of public opinion. In a macabre vicious circle 'presumed delinquents' or 'pre-delinquents' – mostly young people from the most vulnerable parts of society – are eliminated. As Padre José Virtuoso, rector of the Andrés Bello Catholic University, puts it, they suffer 'the penalty of poverty'. They are always only one step away from 'special measures of security', a euphemism for killing. 'Rather than addressing poverty as a social problem, action is taken to cleanse society of poor and disadvantaged people.'

In 1992, there were two attempted coups d'état, one of them by Hugo Chávez. After negotiating surrender and addressing his companions in arms on live TV from the Ministry of Defense, Chavez said: 'I take responsibility... for now', which catapulted him forward as a national leader. He was pardoned in 1994 by President Rafael Caldera with a clean slate. Confidence in existing parties was at an all-time low when in the 1998 elections Chávez launched the Bolivarian Revolution, 'an alternative to neoliberalism', beginning with the rewriting of the Constitution. Chávez instituted a reform program aimed at redistributing the benefits of Venezuela's oil wealth by funding a variety of social, health and literacy programs.

The former establishment however protested it vehemently and in 2002 Chávez himself suffered a coup d'état. But thanks to popular demonstrations and actions by the military, he was returned to power within two days. Chávez also survived an all-out national strike, a strike of state oil company PDVSA and a referendum, to be reelected in 2006. 'Vivir en Socialismo', the current political climate, is advocated on billboards everywhere. Often dressed in a costume representing the Venezuelan flag, Chávez used to address the nation on Aló Presidente, with a record of airing his words for seven hours.

'I haven't traveled much, but I have been to Cuba,' says a Venezuelan businesswoman. 'It is one of Venezuela's greatest allies and Fidel Castro used to be one of Hugo Chávez' best friends. But if Cuba is to give us an idea of the future, I don't want to be part of it. They have no freedom whatsoever.' Asked about the benefits of the Bolivarian Revolution, taxi drivers have a lot to say too. 'Progress? It's totally ineffective. Nothing but demagoguery.' And: 'Look around. What do we produce? Nothing except oil. Where are the public works, the new infrastructure and the projects the Government talks about? Words, words, words. False promises and propaganda. It's all petro-dollar socialism. This whole Revolution is a deception.'

Troubles caused by torrential rains at the end of 2010 coincided with WikiLeaks' 'Cable Gate', which seem to have opened the floodgates of criticism of the Government. Readers' letters and editorials are surprisingly candid. In Tal Cual, José Rafael López Padrino accuses the Government of 'Bolivarian social-fascism'. In El Universal, Elides J. Rojas suggested that Venezuela is 'on the road of Zimbabwe': 'Confiscations, money laundering, elimination of administrative and judicial controls, total dominion of the powers, persecution of dissidents, surrounding himself [the President, ed.] with flatterers and imitators, attacking private property, legal insecurity for investors, administrative opacity, turning the corrupt and thugs into tacit allies, to govern for the cream of society, to work with accomplices, to squander all the money that falls into his hands. Centralism. Easy. The difficulties will emerge later.'

Now, turning to this chapter, its starting point was the Caracazo riots mentioned above. In its aftermath, members of 45 families set up the Committee of Family Members of Victims (COFAVIC), led by Liliana Ortega. The walls of the NGO reflect its quarter of a century history with photos of exhumations, but also emblems of recognition from the Caracas Metropolitan Police. A small sign says: Sin las mujeres, los derechos humanos no son humanos – Without women, human rights are not human. Next to Liliana's computer screen is a little blue book, the Constitución de la Republica Venezuela. In Caracas' busy centre with an almost permanent traffic jam and matching noise levels, she deals with computer problems and a stream of interview requests, holding a cell phone in one hand and a Blackberry in the other.

In 2010, extreme rainfall caused floods and mudslides throughout the country, which later turn out to have caused the death of 35 people and the destruction of 5,000 homes. Seventy thousand people fled their homes taking refuge in emergency tent camps, hotels, and government buildings including the presidential palace, courtesy of the then President Chávez. Power outages are common, and on the last day of interviewing we speak in darkness with the light of a single candle.

Personal narrative — Liliana Ortega

I grew up in a well-off middle-class family in Caracas. My mum and dad were both Catholic, so together with my older sister I attended a Catholic school. We used to do the regular things people do in the city. When I was a little girl, things were mostly peaceful.

My dad always insisted that all people are equal and that we have to respect everybody. It was not only because of his Catholic faith, but because of his own attitude towards life. He had been working clandestinely for Acciòn Democràtica, Democratic Action, a party that fought against the last military dictatorship of Marcos Pérez Jiménez. He was not a leader, but he did suffer political persecution and was jailed because of his membership of Democratic Action. The dictatorship ended in 1958, and since then our country has been a democracy.

I was well aware of my dad's former activities, because people talked openly about the dictatorship and about the value of freedom and human rights. Overhearing the conversations of grownups influenced me, and of course my dad proved by his own life that these values are important. But it wasn't a big issue in our home, because my dad focused most of his attention on his work as an engineer. When I was about 12, my dream was to become a journalist. On Sundays, I read the newspaper with great interest, particularly the political news. Later, when I finished high school, I went to London for a year and studied English, while staying at my cousin's family. Upon my return to Caracas, I enrolled in law school. Two of my uncles were lawyers and I felt that it might offer me a career in the future.

In retrospect, my studies prepared me for my current work, but at that time I thought that after studying corporate law I would be working for a private company and litigate cases. Nothing predicted that I would be running an NGO later. My awareness of the problems facing my country was still limited, but thanks to my curiosity in reading the newspapers, I did know about the corruption and other unlawful things happening in Venezuela. In the 1980s, when I was a teenager, issues of corruption and impunity dominated the front pages of every newspaper. These same issues led up to what came to be known as the Caracazo riots in 1989.

'The days that shook the country' happened in early 1989 and I finished my studies at the end of that year. After more than a decade of deteriorating living conditions, many people had become desperate and they took to the streets. Demonstrations of students and workers spilled over from one city to another, and the live television coverage of the events caused many other disgruntled people to go out, making the riots even more widespread. The riots lasted for only two days, 27 and 28 February. Ninety per cent of the shops in the center of the town were destroyed, torched and looted. But worse than the physical damage were the many psychological scars.

After those two days, the Government declared a state of emergency. The military immediately filled the streets and started shooting at people indiscriminately. Most of the victims were innocent. One person was changing their clothes, another was smoking a cigarette and yet another was sitting in a chair. Many of the victims were children that were simply playing. Young or old, they were killed because they happened to be close to the window where the bullets entered. Three women who lost relatives during the riots later became founder members of COFAVIC (Committee of Family Members of the Victims), which was established with members of 45 families. Yris lost her husband, Maritza lost her brother, and Hilda lost her son. They have been working alongside me ever since. They still live in the barrios and their stories are more interesting than mine (see Testimonies 1-3). With about 600 people killed, Caracazo became the turning point in the recent history of our society. It still is an open wound.

Eyewitnesses and victims of the Caracazo riots – 28 February through 3 March 1989

Testimony 1 – Yris Medina

'For me, the time of the Caracazo riots was very disturbing, because I was only 18 and didn't understand what was going on. The name 'Caracazo' suggests that the events unfolded in the capital only, but really it affected many cities throughout our country and began in Guarenas, 30 kilometers east of Caracas. The rise in living expenses and public transportation triggered a totally spontaneous social explosion. At first, people tried to find fruits, vegetables and groceries at the supermarkets, but after a while it deteriorated and some of them started looting furniture, televisions and so on. On the second day, President Carlos Andrés Pérez declared a curfew and people had to stay at home between 6pm and 6am.'

'My husband Wolfgang died on 2 March. We were at home talking, while he was holding our 3-month-old daughter in his arms. Vehicles with policemen and soldiers poured into the streets of the San Juan district and they began to shoot randomly. One of the bullets entered the window and hit my husband in his chest. He quickly put our daughter on the bed and shortly after collapsed and died because of his wounds. Wolfgang was 20. It was a miracle that our daughter survived. Waving a white T-shirt I tried to go out, but police officers and soldiers stopped me as they couldn't guarantee my safety. When we eventually arrived at the hospital, a lot of people had died there as well. There was no opportunity to hold a ceremony for my husband. I was alone and my family members didn't have the means to come to Caracas. Nobody knew what to do. It terrified me. Next, my family members assumed that Wolfgang and I must have done something wrong, because they couldn't understand why he had died in a safe place, our own home.'

Testimony 2 – Maritza Romero

'My brother Fidel Orlando Romero Castro was killed on 1 March and I was living in barrio Ojo de Agua in Baruta. My brother was 24 and employed as a construction worker. As we were watching television we realized that it was too dangerous that day to go to work. So he went out to make a phone call near our home to inform his boss and colleagues that he would stay at home. At 6pm I received a phone call from neighbors that someone had died on the street. With some difficulty we walked to the scene where a number of injured people were, because there were police officers and soldiers everywhere shooting at anyone that moved. We found Fidel near the telephone booth. Together with family members, I took his body and put it into the car of someone I knew. They took him to the hospital where he was operated on big wounds in the stomach area. The surgery took the whole night, but he died in the morning. When I arrived at the hospital, my brother's body was no longer there. Hospital staff explained to us that they had to take the body, among many others, to the morgue.'

'At the morgue, they informed us that Fidel's body was no longer there, so we returned the next morning. My other brother was allowed to enter and saw a lot of bodies piled up. Among them, he recognized that of Fidel, so he carried the body to a table for autopsy. Again, we were asked to go home and wait. A day later we found the morgue completely empty. As we later found out, they had put my brother's body in a mass grave in Southern Cemetery, in an isolated area high upon a hill called La Peste. In the morgue we got to know other bereaved family members, as well as Liliana. They helped us understand what was going on. Twenty-two years later, we're still struggling for justice.'

Testimony 3 – Hilda Páez

'On 3 March 1989, I lost Richard, one of my sons. At that time I was living in barrio Maca. That day, the television announced that order had been restored. As it was calm, we went out to buy groceries. While my son was next door in the house of his godmother. Metropolitan Police officers arrived and began to shoot. A few of them appeared at our door. 'We're going to take your son to the police station,' they said, but they gave no reason. I went next door and ran into another police officer. 'Are you this boy's mother? He has fallen out of the house's terrace.'

'Other family members arrived and the police officers asked them to have a look at Richard's body to confirm that his death had not been caused by shooting. My family members were also scared and the police officers walked off, leaving his body behind. Around 6pm they took his body to the Perez de Leon Hospital. They said to my husband: 'Tomorrow, go to the hospital to claim the body of your son, because today it is too dangerous.' Richard was 17 and had been attending high school here in Caracas. He was loved in the neighborhood, and I drew much comfort from the fact that the neighbors were with me to help me through these difficult moments. I think that the police officers wanted to handle the case as quickly as possible, because there was a lot of evidence showing that they were guilty of his murder.

'As we don't want this kind of thing to ever happen again, we educate people about the values of human rights. You can't do without. At the time, many of us were housewives and we had no idea how to deal with institutions, judges and Attorney Generals. Although people told us that it would be difficult to win a victory against the Government, the pain of those days turned us into human rights defenders. There is a different Government now, but the State is the same that caused us harm in 1989. Even if it takes another 25 years, we will still be here to fight for justice. Besides the Caracazo case, there are many others in Portuguesa, Aragua, Falcón and Lara. Attorney General Isaias Rodriguez stated that there have been more than 7,000 executions by grupos parapoliciales between 2000 and 2007. It's like a war zone here. Caracazo is in the past, but every weekend there is a small Caracazo.'

Two sides of the coin
At the university I became very concerned about social justice. I voted for the Movimiento al Socialismo (MAS), the Movement for Socialism, supported their candidates and visited many places and barrios. Shortly after the Caracazo, some deputies of the MAS formed a Disappearance Committee in Parliament to inquire into the deaths and disappearances. 'Where are our husbands, wives, brothers and sisters?' relatives asked them. 'What happened to them?' Many students were helping the Disappearance Committee and I also volunteered. I went around and interviewed perhaps a hundred relatives, taking notes about where they lived, what had happened and what was known about those who had disappeared. It was very emotional and moving. You can imagine that these people were beset with fear, distress and bereavement. This all happened in March, 1989.

After collecting people's testimonies, I felt that I had to return to my regular life, because I still had to do my exams. I finished interviewing victims and bereaved family members at 6.30pm and said to the deputies:
'This is my last day here. I have to go back to my studies.'
I took the mechanical stairs of the Congreso Nacional and ran into a number of women.
'Liliana! Hello! We hear you are leaving.'
'Yes, I am.'
'But we will see you on Monday, no?'
'On Monday?'
'Yes! We need to talk to you!'
'Okay, we will see on Monday.'
They drew me in, and I'm still here. The contacts with so many people from disadvantaged communities of our society impacted me

tremendously. I decided to change my professional focus to defending these people's rights.

Workers of a body shop, Venezuela 2007 (photo by Peter de Ruiter)

Two months later, the relatives took the position that they didn't want to be involved in political affairs. They set up COFAVIC, independent and free of any doctrine. I joined them. After all, I was there for them. Not having a political agenda allowed us to have good relations with other NGOs, the Catholic Church and so on. Initially, our main objective was to establish the truth of what really happened and to seek punishment for the guilty. But this changed when it emerged that shortly after the riots the Government had dug mass graves, in which they had buried many people without anyone knowing who they were. Our major concern then became to identify those who had been buried there. One of the main mass graves turned out to be the Southern Cemetery in Caracas, just 10 minutes from here. We could go and visit it now, but it is a very unsafe area.

Two years later, in 1990 the prosecutor and the judge decided to have the graves dug up and to have the bodies examined. We brought in a team of forensic anthropological experts from Argentina and physicians from the United States. They helped us a lot. In the

Southern Cemetery, the forensic experts found 68 bodies from the Caracazo riots. Most of them had been shot at close range in their heads or in their backs. It was terrible. Next, the Government closed the investigation and until today we still haven't been able to identify the vast majority of the bodies. All this was very hard to do.

Then, the scales fell from my eyes. All along, both during the conflict and in the following years, there had been two sides of the coin. In my own neighborhood, people had been generally happy, because the military were in the streets to keep everything under control. But on the other side, in the barrios, the people had been dying and were still suffering. There was a clear distinction between the privileged and the disadvantaged. 'Liliana, my son was a good boy,' they would say to me. 'He looked after himself, he played baseball and did his best at school. We are good people!' It was hard for me to listen to their pleas for help. Having been raised in the privileged middle-class and with a sense of respect for all, I had never realized how bad things were in the barrios. During the criminal proceedings, I witnessed how they were being treated. They meant absolutely nothing to the judges and Attorney Generals, who didn't ask them any questions. They didn't even address or acknowledge them. Nothing.

Continuing the work resulting from the Caracazo riots, every day I became more involved. We made new plans regarding the objectives of our NGO such as justice and fighting impunity. First we needed a license as an NGO, to find our way in dealing with the many lawyers and to strengthen the team of volunteers. One year later, many family members realized that their problems were not unique, because every year people die in the streets at the hands of police officers and soldiers. 'We need to support all the relatives, not just those victimized by the Caracazo riots,' they said. I understood their concern then as I understand it today, because last year alone 60 police officers were killed. They too are from the barrios.

Fighting impunity
During the 1990s, most of our work centered on the promotion and protection of human rights. We felt that it was our fate to work on

these issues. Impunity was at the top of our list of priorities and we started a lot of cases. All my contacts with the Inter-American Court stem from this period. Caracazo was the first case we presented, even though until today we don't know the real number of victims and casualties. The Government never revealed it.

In 1992, we supported the relatives of people of a massacre that had taken place in the Reten de Catia prison, costing the lives of 63 inmates and causing about a hundred casualties. Human Rights Watch later stated that most of them had been shot while locked in their cells and about 20 of them were killed in a ravine. One case resulting from the massacre and emblematic of impunity was that of Montero-Aranguren. It eventually appeared before the Inter-American Court of Human Rights. On the one hand, the impact of the Court's decision was substantial. But the State has yet to fully comply with the Court's judgments. In fact, the level of violence in prisons has only increased.

That same year, Hugo Chávez and a number of army officers staged a coup d'état. At COFAVIC, we attended to the relatives of people involved, because the Government at that time had begun extrajudicial procedures. A lot of NGOs sought out the media to publicly state that these procedures were illegal and that they had to be reviewed. Our position at the time was very complicated. We stood by these people, but they forgot. Today, they simply seem to think that we are too critical and they want to limit the power of NGOs. Since that time, COFAVIC has been monitoring about 700 cases. We have a lot of contact with the relatives, gather evidence as much as possible, and send some of them through to the Inter-American Court. This is proving to be very productive.

In 1999, after two weeks of torrential rains, flash floods and mud slides buried tens of thousands of people in the coastal areas of Vargas Province. More than 100,000 people lost their homes and livelihoods. It was a devastating blow to the whole province and to our country. The police took control of the area. But this added to the tragedy. On top of the already high number of lives lost, some of the people that had survived began to disappear. It turned out that most of them were young drug addicts with police records. The police arbitrarily detained them and held them incommunicado until the devastating truth emerged: they had been killed. Because of this, we presented and litigated cases at the Inter-American Court, in particular the case of three young men – Oscar Blanco Romero, Roberto Hernandez Paz and José Rivas Fernandez. Accused of looting, paratroopers had burst into their homes and they had been taken by force right in front of their family members.

During the 1990s, the media used to follow the human rights cases that we fought more or less in support. But this has changed. Here at COFAVIC, and of course at many other NGOs, we try to disseminate the values of human rights and mutual respect. We hold a lot of workshops to mobilize people from various backgrounds and professions and we give a lot of interviews. In short, we try to wake people up about human rights. But the number of threats and even the criminalization of NGOs and human rights defenders have increased. Since 2002, people follow us in the street, make abusive phone calls and send hate mails. Police officers stop my car: 'What are you doing?' they ask me, while four men are holding me at gunpoint. At the end they will say: 'No, no, no. It was a mistake.' But it is scary and intimidating.

On national television, there is a program called La Hojilla, The Razor, which criminalizes the work of human rights defenders. On several occasions I have been named in that TV show. At this moment, there are 34 human rights defenders in Venezuela for whom the Inter-American Court has had to take special protective measures. In the light of similar measures in 2002, the Inter-American Court provided COFAVIC with protective measures and some of the NGO members were protected by a bodyguard between 2002 and 2009. This too demonstrates the impunity in our country.

Our work is very hard, because the Government doesn't like the fact that we have an independent voice. If you have some form of autonomy, you are considered to be an enemy. It is a war dynamic, a military dynamic that has existed for the last 10 years. The fact that they are so much against our work implies that they want to keep things hidden under the carpet. They don't want to hear things that are not 'popular'. But human rights defenders are critical by nature, whether they are in Norway, Spain, Argentina or Venezuela. Except that in most other countries, the government supports NGOs in doing their work.

Our objectives are all interlinked, so I don't know which one comes first. Perhaps the foremost thing is the fact that the political forces of the Government, the judges and the Attorney Generals have to change their minds. They have to think according to the needs of the people and the needs of justice for the people. 'In 2009, only 3.29 per cent of human rights cases appeared before the judge,' said Attorney General Luisa Ortega Díaz. That gives you an idea how high the level of impunity is. An overwhelming 96.71 per cent of cases never go to trial and the perpetrators are never brought to justice. Those cases just vanish in the files and archives in silence. They mostly concern those who are poor and from the barrios.

Mothers, daughters, grandmothers, aunts, sisters – 70 per cent of those who denounce human rights violations are women. They suffer a lot of abuse, because we live in a male-dominated culture. It's an endemic problem in Venezuela. It's just that now we have a higher level of impunity than ever before. Not only is there impunity because there are hardly any decisions in the legal system, there is additional impunity because those who seek justice are threatened and persecuted. Most of them are women. Did you notice that most of us here at COFAVIC are women too? In my view, the women are always the first to be in the line of fire.

Public order
The most important problem facing our country between 1989 and now is that the police and the military are unwilling to stay in the streets to maintain public order. They have no plans and are not intent on maintaining human rights standards. It is a big mistake, because nobody benefits from this state of affairs. If you want to live in a safe city or village, you have to respect human rights, no matter who you are. Public order is not against human rights; it is a precondition for it.

For police officers, we developed training that focuses on respecting human rights. Some of the trainers themselves lost relatives at the hands of police officers or the military. Those who experienced the price you pay when human rights are not respected are well qualified to lead the workshops. They know what they're talking about. We need to keep those trainings going and involve more police officers, lawyers, journalists and people in the street. Some trainers may come face to face with workshop participants that were involved in the death of their own family members, but we don't know who they are. We don't discuss it. Our only goal is restoring the values in society. If no one is concerned about human rights, who will do it? Where is a sense of human dignity and personal integrity to come from?

Sometimes I take part in the training myself. I explain the work of the Inter-American Court, the Universal Declaration of Human Rights and respect for human rights. The most frequent question that police officers ask is: 'Don't we have human rights?' 'Of course you do,' I tell them. 'Everyone does.' Police officers work under very difficult conditions and get paid very low salaries. This also makes law enforcement so difficult in Venezuela, because the temptations to make some extra bucks on the side are multiple. At the same time, they are often confronted with *malandros* – delinquents. To do their work, the police officers have to leave behind their homes. But if the malandros know them, they show up on the doorstep of their families threatening them with retribution.

Naturally, I dedicate a lot of time to COFAVIC. Sometimes I work 13 hours a day, but there are also days when I do much less. When we began in 1989, things were much harder, because today the COFAVIC team assists in many activities. I'm no longer the executive director and no longer responsible for all the administrative problems that we face. That's why now I can do the things that I love: the Inter-American Court, the various cases and the workshops. I am deeply concerned. There is no death penalty in Venezuela, but there are 900 extrajudicial executions per year. Most of them are young men of 18 to 23 years of age with drug problems and police records. Sometimes the police officers extort them, put them in arbitrary detention, torture them and then kill them, apparently with a view to 'cleanse' society of these persons.

In 2003 and 2004, we investigated 71 cases of human rights violations, deaths and disappearances by parapolice groups throughout Venezuela. We interviewed family members and gathered testimonies and 'itineraries of impunity' in Anzoátegui, Falcón, Portuguesa and Yaracuy and published a book called The Parapolice Groups in Venezuela. We have a collective mission to fight against impunity or the lack of justice, because it transmits all the human rights problems to the rest of society. It works like a multiplying factor, because it just never ends. For the victims' family members, it also never ends (see box).

Vanished without a trace

The story of Henry Omar Sánchez Méndez, who disappeared on 17 October 2000 in the State of Portuguesa, exemplifies hundreds of such cases throughout Venezuela.

'The relatives of Henry Omar Sánchez Méndez know that he was born on 14 December 1971, that he was a hard-working farmer, that he had a son and that he didn't have any outstanding accounts with the police. What they do not know is his whereabouts, whether he is detained or whether he was assassinated. Consequently, they don't even know whether they should mourn his death. In the afternoon of 17 October 2000, Henry Omar was arbitrarily arrested by three plainclothes civil servants of the Police of the State of Portuguesa, in front of the Brasilandia Restaurant in the Avenue of Agriculture of Acarigua. A policeman who witnessed his arrest, said that he was apprehended by three policemen who argue that Henry Omar was wanted for stealing vehicles. Although the Public Ministry has acted diligently, the case has never been resolved. The three civil servants are still free, and have only been given precautionary notice.'

Ana Sánchez Méndez, sister of Henry Omar: 'Ever since Henry Omar disappeared, my mother is like a walking corpse, just like my father. They keep thinking that my brother is alive somewhere near a river and keep asking about it. Psychologically, it has been the worst thing that ever happened in my life. I don't know what hurts more, the disappearance of my brother or seeing my mother and my father suffer so much. My mother has completely changed. This whole crisis has locked her into herself. She has blood clots in her legs, there are days that she doesn't want to eat and days on which she no longer has the desire to live. During such times, she gets up at 4am in the morning to visit the cemetery. There are days that she doesn't sleep at all... it's horrible. My father no longer wants to know anything about the subject, he only wants my brother to reappear. Living with this constant uncertainty is hard. When someone is killed, at least you have a gravestone to go to and put a rose beside it. My brother was not a delinquent, he simply paid a high price because he looked like someone else. Really, his disappearance has destroyed my family and it is like torture.'

Polarized society
From the first few years of his mandate, the Government of Hugo Chávez stood up for COFAVIC and for NGOs in general. A few months before he was President, the NGOs invited him to a workshop and a number of ministers and Government officials also attended. They know about our work. Caracas is a big city, but it is also like a village.

The Government acknowledged its responsibility in relation to the operations that cost the lives of so many people during the Caracazo riots. It recognized the sentences of the Inter-American Court to some degree and paid out reparations to the relatives of 45 victims. In itself that is a good sign, but it is only a small part of doing justice. Think of this: decades after the event nobody has ever gone to jail for the human rights violations committed during the riots. After all these years, the prosecution of those who were allegedly responsible for the deaths and disappearances is still in its 'investigation' phase.

To the Government's credit, COFAVIC and many other NGOs were invited in 1999 to participate in the re-drafting of the Constitution. A coalition of Venezuelan NGOs called the Forum for Life presented a series of proposals to the Constituent Assembly. Representatives of COFAVIC assisted in discussions and lobbied for the acceptance of several proposals with regard to impunity, civil law, the investigation of human rights violations and excluding the option of amnesty for serious human rights violations. The Constitution made important progress in the area of human rights, most of which was based on the work done by the Forum for Life. The new Constitution was adopted on 30 December that year.

Despite the excellence of our Constitution, our greatest problem is the lack of due process. That has to be addressed. More than 90 per cent of investigations don't go beyond the initial stage, because those in charge of administering justice impede the process. Moreover, the practical application of our national laws insufficiently mirrors international human rights conventions. Jurisdiction can easily be bypassed. If a defendant doesn't like the judge, they ask to be tried by another. Another reason for the deficit of the legal system is the fact that many decisions are politically motivated.

In a healthy democracy, the powers of the legal system are separated. But in Venezuela the division of the executive, legislative and judicial powers is confused. Many officials accept bribes, another structural problem. If you walk on the street and wait for a red light, you may be the only one. Wearing a helmet when riding a motorbike is mandatory. How many do you see that wear one? How many cars go against the direction of the traffic? How many drivers talk on a cell phone while driving? Our traffic reflects our predicament. Our situation is an anomaly. It's outside of the rules. Rules and principles don't have a value in this country.

In 2002, there was a coup d'état by the opposition. The coup failed, but for 47 hours President Chávez was ousted from office, after which he was restored by a combination of military force and mass demonstrations of popular support. Following these events, we defended a lot of ministers and deputies from the chavismo. Even until this day, there are members of the National Assembly that are grateful to COFAVIC and Provea, another NGO, because we supported them after the coup d'état. Our work is to defend everyone's human rights, regardless of your political background, whether you support chavismo or the opposition. We defend people. We defend principles. We don't know and don't need to know whether you are left or right, catholic or protestant, from the upper class or from the barrios.

A few years ago, former President Chávez tried to implement a new law, the Law of Intelligence and Counterintelligence. It obliged people to cooperate with intelligence agencies. Refusal to do so would be made punishable with up to six years in jail. Whether they had any political views or not, that law touched the hearts of people. It was quickly nicknamed the Toad Law, because 'toad' is a colloquial term for 'snitch'. This touched a nerve. Friendship and bonds among family members and neighbors are strong and you don't betray those relationships. Even young drug addicts in the barrios wouldn't go up to a police officer to betray their friends. It just wasn't the way forward for Venezuela and might have led to the disintegration of society. People could not swallow the idea of welcoming people in their home, having a beer and watching TV and then talking about them to the Government. The NGOs in Venezuela, including COFAVIC, were strongly opposed and made it known in letters to the Government and public speeches. The Government felt the social pressure and was forced to retrace its steps. The President recognized that the law would have breached our Constitution. It was good that he changed his mind and abolished it, for no one wanted to be a toad!

Sometimes the media do pay attention to NGOs, but the current social climate is very polarized. But of course, human rights are not about this or that Government, and the people in the streets have a lot of problems such as the levels of violence, the insecurity, the corruption of police officers, the impunity and so on. It is incomprehensible why these issues are not on the agenda of the political parties. The media however are very open about human rights. They are the most important window that the victims and relatives have against the impunity.

At the beginning of the Bolivarian Revolution, the Government strongly promoted the participation of the general public in the political process. That's a good thing and we applaud it. But outside of the National Assembly and the Government, public institutions are crumbling. To strengthen public participation from the grassroots, we also teach human rights issues at primary schools. Although we do get some assistance from the Catholic Church, there is a lot of resistance from the Government. They are not interested in working with NGOs in this field and usually they don't even acknowledge our proposals to work with children or train police officers. But we are like water. We have 25 years of experience. If one mayor doesn't want to cooperate, we write another proposal to another mayor. We have learned to explore every possible route to reach our goals and leave no stone unturned.

Cooperation?
When the Government proposed the so-called International Cooperation Law, we had to deal with it right away. We felt that some of the space that the Government claimed to have created was lost again. But all our work happens within the legal framework enshrined in the Constitution of Venezuela. If the Government has any concerns, they can use the penal law, the Attorney General and the judges. The Chairman of the Foreign Policy Committee, Roy Daza, stated that the International Cooperation Law would close all NGOs that are politically engaged. 'Are human rights NGOs political?' journalists asked him. 'Yes,' he answered. The Government sees the funding of NGOs by foreign nations as direct meddling in the internal affairs of Venezuela, especially of the 'imperialist' United States, which it is very much against. NGOs that focus on human rights issues have come under attack, and so have deputies of the PSUV, the United Socialist Party of Venezuela. Feliciano Reyna, the director of human rights watchdog Sinergia sees it differently: 'The law would give the Government discretional power to restrict the work of some NGOs or eliminate them.' I believe that the law is meant to control all financial support from abroad. The name is misleading, because it is

actually a law against international cooperation. However, COFAVIC has no position on the Government, only about the human rights situation in Venezuela, the same we had in 1989 or in 1995 under other Presidents.

Living in a slum in Venezuela, 2007 (photo by Peter de Ruiter)

President Chávez said in 2010: 'How could we permit political parties, NGOs and leading figures of the counterrevolution to continue to be financed by the millions and millions of the Yankee Empire?' He wanted swift parliamentary approval of the law. But if it is passed, it would make the work of independent NGOs and that of human rights defenders very difficult. Imagine, if from 1989 the Government had to give us permission to do our work. It would have been impossible to do the Caracazo case. Without independence and international cooperation it could never have been done. That's why it is so important.

In Venezuela, human rights are confronted with a lot of problems. The problems are not new, but that is all the more reason why they should be addressed and why the situation must be improved. True, most NGOs in Latin America are supported from abroad. But what alternatives do we have? The private sector of Venezuela hardly supports NGOs. Some may give money to breast cancer, HIV or child issues, but it is not very common. They don't raise funds however for human rights or addressing impunity, torture, extrajudicial killings or disappearances. In the case of COFAVIC, more than 90 per cent of our budget comes from European countries. If we no longer have access to this way of raising funds, we will be prevented from working. Yes, we can have volunteers, but in reality it is very difficult to work with volunteers only. The Government's decision affects all Venezuelan NGOs.

We consider it to be very important to have a dialogue and always offer a bridge to the Government. But we cannot walk across that bridge when it isn't supported on both sides. We are a human rights NGO and a committee serving relatives. That is our responsibility and that is our work. A bridge between the people and the Government can only be completed by dialogue. But it is difficult when the other side remains silent. We're looking for members of the Government that are open to dialogue, but at this moment it is very hard to find them. Each side says: 'If you're not with me, you're my enemy,' leaving us in the middle. We're not of the Bolivarian Revolution and not of the opposition. We're human rights defenders. For everyone. Whether you live in the barrios or whether you are a Member of Parliament.

Because our society is so polarized and divided, each opinion that you express is very sensitive with regard to how the public will perceive it. One unfavorable or misrepresented story can ruin years of hard work. Many problems in our society exist because people suffer from poverty, lack of good housing, lack of good education, lack of good sanitary conditions and lack of medical support, especially in the barrios. On top of that, people's most immediate concern is the street violence, a lot of which goes unreported. Venezuela is a very unsafe country. The Government stated that in 2009, 19,000 people died in the streets. It is too much! Most of them are young people aged 18 to 23 who run into problems because of police records, extortions and drug-related issues. It's the highest number of people that get killed in a country that is not at war, a death toll that is even worse than that of Mexico's drug wars.

To stay alive
What depresses me most about the violence is the effects it has on young people. Just a few months ago, we did workshops for teenagers at schools in the barrios Antimano, Catia, Valle-Coche and La Vega, to the west of Caracas. They were between 15 and 17 years old. For an exercise, we had prepared a newspaper with articles on human rights. 'What are your dreams?' we asked them. 'What do you want to be in the future?' Wouldn't you expect answers like nurse, doctor, lawyer, President, racing car driver? Something like that? You know what most of them answered? 'To stay alive. To survive.'

They grow up in fear. They have very few possessions and when they do have an MP3 player or a cell phone, they don't know whether they will be killed by someone who wants to take it from them. It goes against my heart to see young people in such conditions. Sometimes, if they survive a fight, they cannot find access to medical support. So you see people with broken arms or legs that never heal well and young people on crutches. But these teenagers should be playing soccer or baseball, enjoy listening to music or go out with their friends. The normal life of children. There again, you see the weakness of the institutions, because who can they turn to? In some places there is medical assistance and some NGOs try their best, but the presence of the Government in the barrios is very limited.

The people of Venezuela are my greatest hope, because they endure this very polarized situation. The people in the streets go on regardless and many of them are more democratic in character than some of our political leaders. They live hard lives. They wake up at 5am to get ready, take a jeep that takes them from the barrios into the city to catch a bus or the metro, begin their work at 7am and continue until 6pm, after which they return to the barrio again. Next to their work, they spend hours in the traffic, they don't have enough money, but still they smile or at least they are in good spirit.

The current situation looks desperate and living in Venezuela has become very risky. It is especially sad that the oil industry generates so much money and yet there is so much poverty in our country. You would expect that those revenues are invested in poverty alleviation, better housing, social and employment projects. There are some, but they are not very efficient. Our country's wealth remains beyond the reach of the people in the barrios.

When there is excessive rainfall, whatever precarious houses and possessions people in the barrios had, much of it is simply flushed away down the mountain slopes and they end up on the street with their children. I don't know where we will be in 10 years time, but I hope that we will have a real justice system that is more efficient. We have to start somewhere.

Disregard for human rights

Under President Nicolás Maduro, human rights guarantees seem to have evaporated, enabling the government to control, intimidate and prosecute its critics. According to various reports, notably that of Human Rights Watch, in 2014, security forces used excessive force against peaceful demonstrators, and denied them due process rights. Routine use of unlawful force, killings and impunity are chronic problems. The judiciary has largely ceased to function independently. Some members of the Supreme Court have openly rejected the principle of separation of powers, and have pledged their commitment to advancing the government's political agenda.

Sheila Watt-Cloutier - Nunavut
Safeguarding the future of the Arctic and its people

'The Arctic is the barometer of global environmental health, and we Inuit are the mercury in that barometer,' says Sheila Watt-Cloutier, former Chair of the Inuit Circumpolar Conference. She champions issues ranging from education to climate change. Raised by her mother and grandmother, Sheila started her life traveling by dog team or kayak, worked as an interpreter in a hospital and for the Kativik School Board. Her experience caused her to seek ways to bring about change for the Inuit and the Arctic region. One success was the Stockholm Convention on persistent organic pollutants that cause health problems in the north, caused by industries in the south. Putting things in perspective, she said: 'I'm more afraid of not taking the right action for the future of my grandson than of the Bush Administration.'

Sheila Watt-Cloutier

'When you're small in number, it's really: strategy, strategy, strategy,' Sheila Watt-Cloutier (born in 1953) used to say in her former role as Chair of the Inuit Circumpolar Conference. As one of the foremost Inuit representatives at the regional, national (Canadian) and international levels, she has championed issues ranging from education to climate change. 'The Arctic is the barometer of global environmental health, and we Inuit are the mercury in that barometer.'

Context

One thing is certain. Our deep ancestry – great grandfathers and great grandmothers – stems from hunter-gatherers in the mists of time before us. But for some people, those days are not so remote. Hunting and gathering still is a way of life for millions of indigenous peoples, some of whom live in the circumpolar world. And while undergoing a time of rapid transition – from the ice age to the space age in one generation – it is the Inuit in particular who have a message that transcends the Polar Regions.

The changes happening in the Arctic are momentous. Under the Great Bear constellation (Greek 'arctos' means bear), a helicopter pilot recently spotted a strange animal. Flying over Canada's Northwest Territories, he lost sight of it. Was it an unknown species? A hunter came closer, proving the rumor to be true. He had shot an animal that was a cross between the grizzly and the polar bear: the polar grizzly. Some indigenous Inuit call the polar bear *pisugtooq*, the great wanderer. But clearly, grizzlies wander too.

Part of the changes for the Inuit are the transition from their traditional way of life to living in communities and going to the supermarket, while their staples of course used to be 'country food' such as seal, whale and other animals. Due to the remoteness of the region and the fact that most of the products are flown in, the store prices are astronomical. The effects of global warming – and global pollution – are not a theory to the Inuit. They are already feeling it and some of them call people from southern regions 'the people who change nature'. Writer Melanie McGrath expresses her concern: 'The

Arctic is the last place of innocence in the world. To lose that would be devastating.'

There are also many other new arrivals on the Arctic horizon, and the Inuit do not have names for such species as barns owls, robins and wasps. The changes in fauna and flora life are causing many scientists to wave the red flag, both for the endangerment of species unique to the Polar Regions and some 155,000 indigenous people, but also for its significance in relation to global warming. In 2005, a massive chunk of ice 500 miles (800 kilometer) south of the North Pole broke free from the Ayles Ice Shelf. It was about the size of Manhattan and the rupture registered as a small earthquake.

Another aspect that highlights the speed of change is the interest in geopolitical issues and sub-soil resources. In the summer of 2007, the Russian Government sent two icebreakers to the North Pole on a 'scientific' mission. When the ships got to the top of the world, Arctic explorer Artur Chilingarov, member of Russia's Lower House of Parliament, planted a small titanium Russian flag on the sea floor, after having descended 14,000 feet (4,300 meter) in a deep-sea submersible. Broadcasted around the world, it announced that the seabed under the pole is part of the 1,200-mile-long Lomonosov Ridge, an extension of Russia's continental shelf.

Meanwhile, the sea ice is melting and the outlook of the quiet circumpolar world may change. An open Northwest Passage in Arctic waters seems to become reality within the foreseeable future. This would shorten the shipping times from Europe to Asia by two weeks. In any event, whatever will happen in the north matters not only to Inuit culture, wildlife and the environment, but also to the security and sovereignty of Canada, Denmark (Greenland), Russia and the United States. And thus, it matters to the rest of the world.

But let's return to the Inuit. Imagine a kayak gliding towards the coast. After an Inuit man gets out and steadies his kayak, his wife emerges, and next a whole series of children of ever-decreasing size. And finally a puppy. Thus opened Nanook of the North, the film made by intrepid traveler Robert Flaherty in 1920. For most of the

20th century, this was people's introduction to the people in the Arctic, even for those who needed explanation about what snow is. Up till the 1950s, the Inuit were still regarded as 'refugees from the Stone Age', and treated as such by forced relocations and residential schooling designed to assimilate them with southern Canada. Oversight varied by region and was done by Federal Government administrators, the Hudson's Bay Company, missionaries and churches and the Royal Canadian Mounted Police (RCMP). It is common knowledge that RCMP officers still suffer an unfavorable reputation today.

In the 1960s, the Canadian Conservative Government of John Diefenbaker had a view 'to enrich the nation by making available the Canadian Arctic's golden cornucopia of minerals, fossil fuels, and other valuable resources'. It was called the Northern Vision. But over the last four decades, the Inuit have found ways of bringing about a monumental change in the status of the region, even while some concerns remain, notably about offshore oil drilling, uranium mining and the further exploration and exploitation of the region's sub-soil resources. Today however, the Inuit have a voice.

After more than two decades of negotiations, on 1 April 1999 the territory of Nunavut – 'Our Land' – came into being. With one fifth of the Canadian land surface – eight times the size of the UK or five times that of California – it is the world's largest self-governing territory in which the indigenous population forms the majority. Iqaluit became the territorial capital. In return for the land, Inuit formally relinquished their right to the other half of the Northwest Territories. There are about 30,000 citizens, 85 per cent of whom are Inuit, while 33 million Canadians live in the other four fifths of the country. Nunavut has fewer than 50 kilometers of road.

One of Iqaluit's residents is Sheila Watt-Cloutier, whose life mirrors that of many other Inuit. But she has emerged as one of the most recognized voices of her people and of Canadians at large. Markers of her efforts include Silaturnimut – The Pathway to Wisdom (on education), the Stockholm Convention (on trans-boundary pollutants) and the Petition to the Inter-American Commission on

Human Rights (on human rights violations caused by global warming). Perhaps no image better represents Sheila's intimate connection with the issues she represents than her gift to the executive director of the United Nations Environmental Program in 1999: an Inuit carving of a mother and child.

Sheila has managed to put the human face on the map in relation to climate change by showing the human dimension of environmental issues. That face is not just that of the Inuit. It is also ours, the face of the car-driving, television-watching consumer. While the polar bear wanders on, human beings often wander from their principles or those enshrined in declarations and conventions, at a high price. 'Our emotional, spiritual and cultural well-being and health depend on protecting the land,' says Sheila. 'We cannot find our way with Band-Aid solutions. For Inuit, the environment is everything.'

Personal narrative — Sheila Watt-Cloutier

My beginnings were humble. I was born in a small Inuit family in a tiny little place called Old Fort Chimo. It used to be a trading post of the Hudson's Bay Company that was first established there in 1830 to trade furs. It was situated across the river where New Fort Chimo is now, although that name has not been used for decades. In our language, Inuktitut, Fort Chimo has always been called Kuujjuaq, which means Big River. In the 1950s it wasn't even a community, because most Inuit families lived out there on the land and ice in outpost camps.

The parents in the household I grew up with were my mother and my grandmother. Then there was my older brother Elijah who was adopted from another community when he was 12, my brother Charlie and my sister Bridget. That was it. We were one of the rare families that lived permanently around the trading post, due to the fact that my grandmother was a single mother. There was no hunter at the time, although my grandmother hunted from time to time to feed her family country food, until my uncle became a teenager and was able to provide for the family. The same with my two brothers. When they became old enough, under the good training of my uncle, they were then able to provide for our family. My grandmother stayed close to the post where she worked for the Hudson's Bay Company cleaning, doing dishes and all kinds of domestic work. Ever since she was 10, my mother was helping her. Except for the Hudson's Bay Company and the missionaries, there was nothing else there.

After my Scottish grandfather left, my grandmother was left with three children and she had to give up her middle child, in order for that child to be fed and raised by another family and survive. Other families were struggling to survive as well, so they couldn't help a single mother with three children. Most other families were living in the outpost camps, still hunting and fishing and living off the land. They only came in to trade or during the summer, when they set up their tents around the Hudson's Bay Company – tents in summer, igloos in winter. Igluvigaq is the real Inuit name for igloos, but white men shortened it, as they couldn't pronounce it properly. At the time when I was young, there were no igluvigaqs around Kuujjuaq, but the other communities further north still used them.

A decade before I was born, during the Second World War, the Americans had come in to build an air strip across the river. After a while it became too cumbersome to be constantly transporting supplies and mail by kayak across the river in summer or by dog team in winter. Now that it had become more convenient to live closer to the air strip, things started to slowly move across the river. When I was four, we crossed the river by kayak to Kuujjuaq. I remember that time.

The first 10 years of my life, we only traveled by dog team or kayak. We lived traditionally, as much as we could. Our life was characterized by hunting, fishing, gathering and travelling by dog team to the hunting and fishing grounds. Being outdoors in the snow and the ice was a big influence on my life. The fishing in particular: out of the ice, while being out on the ice. Being the youngest, the baby of the household, I was always in the box part of the big sled that was pulled by the dogs. I completely trusted that my brothers, who were leading the dogs, would bring us all to safety and that we would have food at the end of the hunt.

Unlike today, when you can go for a few hours and come back with caribou, the animals were very far away. In those days the caribou were so far away that the women didn't always accompany the men. 'Charlie and Elijah are off hunting,' I remember hearing, thinking that we would soon be eating caribou. But even after three days or weeks, my brothers came back without having found any. It was much harder in those days, also because travelling by dog team made it slower to go and find the animals. Their whereabouts changes over time.

There's a great power that young Inuit learn in the hunting process. It's not just the technical ability to harvest and bring home food to your family; it's the character that is built during the process of the hunt. When waiting for the weather to clear, the snow to fall, the ice to form, the animals to surface, you really learn patience. You also learn to take survival-based risks. If you don't learn and integrate how to be courageous at certain times, how to withstand stress and be bold under pressure, how to be very focused and ultimately to have some judgment and wisdom, you'll be lost. Living on the land requires a high level of independence and self-confidence. That's what a hunting culture teaches.

Although the men went out on the caribou hunt on their own, we would all go fishing and hunting ptarmigan as a family together: men, women and children. Around Kuujjuaq there are lots of fowl. Goose and ptarmigan are the two huge staples. It was very different from Nunavut where I live now, where the main staples are caribou and marine mammals. We had marine mammals too, but they were much harder to find, so seal and beluga whale became a delicacy for us. But most of the time we would have ptarmigan, goose, trout, Arctic char and salmon. All that delicious food! That's our organic farm out there. There are quota systems today, but we never had marine mammals such as seal and whale as plentiful as Nunavut has now.

Bonding experience

The early memories of bonding with my family, my culture and our small community, are the very fondest I have of Kuujjuaq. Living the traditional way of life in a hunting culture gives you that immediate connection to nature and the environment around you. You grow up knowing and appreciating that the land and the ice offer this wonderful bounty of food and resources. You can't underestimate our connection to our food. Eating together from the same animal is a very powerful experience, not just in terms of how nutritious the food is, but also in how it bonds families and communities. 'We're going to have country food supper!' When that happens there's almost euphoria in the air.

To this day, I'm well known to be an avid country food eater and 'sharer' – I cannot say 'provider' as I don't hunt. In my current home in Iqaluit, my two freezers are always full and my friends come over for country food suppers all the time. I'm known to offer great tasting country food, a lot of which is still being sent by my brother Charlie, even though we are now in different communities. Sharing country food together feeds you physically, but also spiritually. You not only connect to the food that you are eating, but also to the hunter who harvested the animal and to your ancestors. When you're eating alone, it doesn't give that same connection to others and to history.

I hadn't learnt English until I was six, when I started school. Four years later, at the age of 10, I was off on a plane and sent for school with another girl, Lizzie Saunders, first to Nova Scotia, then to Churchill Manitoba and next to Ottawa. It was a big change. Having been very connected to our families, our language and our country food, it was very traumatic for us. Lizzie and I cried to come home for weeks, but that was not going to be the case. And not eating our country food, we had to adjust to milk. O! Fresh milk. We had grown up with canned milk that could be diluted in our cereal or tea, but for us fresh milk was a horrible experience. And peas! O, my God. Who would ever want to eat such food!

While I was away for school, my grandmother, whom I had always been very close to, died. She had been a very traditional Inuk woman and some of my earliest memories are of eating country food with her. The Federal Government would fly us home in the summer, but wouldn't allow us to return home for Christmas and my mother couldn't afford to bring me home. I would not see winter at home for five years. When I finally returned, Kuujjuaq was crisscrossed by snow mobiles. That too was quite a shock and at first I was quite afraid of these very noisy skidoos that were now all over the community.

At school, my only thought was: o, my God, I want to go home and be with my family. I was caught in the expectations of the Federal Government, the family we lived with and the southern community we were now a part of. Lizzie and I were staying with a really strict family who had worked in the north before. I was too young to get to the root of it, but I did wonder: how was it that they had convinced our parents to send 10-year-olds away from home? I think it was because of this idea that we were going to be leaders one day and we need these young Inuit children to be well educated. My mother and my friend's parents must have been convinced of this. They had sent us away, so we had to accept that. The family that took care of us drilled us so much to study that we surpassed all the other kids whose first language was English that we were in class with. There was that kind of enforcement: you're going to be an A student when you're here. And we were.

When I went home after eight years of being away, I said: 'I don't want to go away again for now.' I stayed home. I had wanted to become a doctor, but I was terrible in math, chemistry and physics. Numbers and all of that was not my strength at all. In hindsight, it would have been fair if the Government of the day had said: 'You're struggling in those areas. We understand you want to be a doctor and that's important for your path and your people, so perhaps we need to help you get there.' Instead, a government official told me: 'You're aiming too high. Perhaps you can be a nurse's assistant.'

Microphone for my people

I stepped into an elevator feeling totally crushed. Shortly after I came home however, I got a job working at the Ungava Hospital as an assistant and interpreter to the doctor. It was the next best thing to being a doctor and I just loved that kind of work. I really enjoyed helping the people that were coming in sick and who couldn't speak English. I was their microphone. Perhaps I'm still a microphone for my people on a larger scale today. I could relay what they were trying to say to the doctor and translate back and forth. The health issues gave me a window into the reality of the struggles and challenges we Inuit were facing. We suffered poor housing, the lack of food security and clean running water, and struggled with alcoholism, domestic violence and the impact of these things on the children and the families.

From the age of 18 until the time my daughter Sylvia was born when I was 22, I worked as an interpreter at the clinic. I was very pregnant, eight months, when I finished working. I wanted to work till the last day. In fact, the doctors, who were connected to a hospital in Quebec City and knew I wanted to be a doctor too, tried to make a tailor-made program for me to go down for four, rather than seven years. But the provision was that I would only work in the north. They were very gracious to try to do this for me, but I was very young and getting married, so that plan went out the window.

For a number of years, I was very busy with my children. In Montreal I took courses with the Kativik School Board through credits from McGill University on counseling, education and human development and I was trained as a student counselor to work in our Nunavik schools. When we moved south, I went to work for the Kativik School Board head office and coordinated student services in secondary education for a total of 10 years.
'The programs are weak,' I would say.
'O, are you against our Inuktitut programs?'
'No, that's not the point. The point is that Inuktitut materials do not make a program and a program does not make a curriculum. A lack of curriculum without a framework and a vision does not take you anywhere. We're trying to hold on to an institution that isn't even of

our making, because Inuktitut language and culture are just add-ons to a structure that we've inherited from somewhere else. This is not ours. We can't think that it's ours and say that because we worked hard as Inuit teachers or curriculum developers that all of a sudden this is the Inuit education system that allows a meshing of the two worlds – traditional Inuit and modern Canadian – to best prepare our children, because clearly this is not the case. You can't have powerful legends in a coloring book, thinking that this is an effective empowering program. It's through an elder telling the story and sharing the meaning behind it that you will grasp it. It's through observation in the Inuit way that you learn all of these things.'

At the end of 10 years I realized that I was bumping against too many walls. The administrators were very defensive. Even though in our Inuit world we don't have hundreds of years of institutional hold, very quickly we've learned to become very institutional. But there was also a personal perspective. It had been the best training ground for me in leadership in terms of asserting who I was and what I stood for in terms of my beliefs, my principles and my ethics. It was a tough turning point. These years were very tumultuous, very difficult and very lonely, but absolutely necessary for the establishment of self.

I went on to be part of the review of the education system in the Nunavik Education Task Force from 1990 to 1992. We tried to assess, 15 years after the James Bay Agreement (see box), why the education system didn't seem to be working. Why were our kids not making it in school? Why did so many of them have self-destructive patterns? Many students were already coming down with a load of baggage. On top of that, they now had to adjust to city life. You can stay in Kuujjuaq and be the best cashier of the Hudson's Bay Company store. That's fine. But if your dream is to be something else, then you have to be realistic and make sure you are prepared effectively.

James Bay Northern Quebec Agreement (1975)

In the 1960s, Quebec began developing huge hydroelectric projects in the north, and in 1971 created the James Bay

Development Corporation to pursue the development of mining, forestry and other resources. This undertaking was opposed by most of northern Quebec's Cree and Inuit. At the same time, it accelerated the awareness of their rights and later contributed to the negotiations with the Canadian Government.

The James Bay and Northern Quebec Agreement is a land claim settlement for indigenous peoples, approved in 1975 by the Cree and Inuit of northern Quebec, slightly modified in 1978 when Quebec's Naskapi First Nations joined the treaty. The Agreement established provisions ranging from land ownership, environmental and social protections and financial compensation (CAN$ 225 million for native economic development) to education (the use of native languages is explicitly encouraged), local government, health and social services. In 1982, the Agreement was entrenched in the Constitution of Canada.

Pathway to Wisdom
The report that we came out with in 1992, Silaturnimut – The Pathway to Wisdom, had 101 recommendations for change (see box). It is a powerful read, because as a team of people we had thought very deeply about these things, even while we had been under a lot of pressure from the School Board. Its officials, Inuit and non-Inuit, had always known me, but when I really started to push all their buttons, they first tried to muzzle me, and then they tried to put me in a place where I was doing this out of spite or frustration. They were simply trying to protect the status quo, because the report would reflect badly on them. But the communities really understood what this was all about.

'For thousands of years...'

'The effectiveness of education is measured by how well it prepares people to handle the problems and the opportunities of life in their own time and space. For thousands of years our people had a very effective education. We knew how to prepare our children to handle everything they would face when living on the land. Then things changed. The path of education we had followed for countless generations could not prepare us for all these new things.'

'We had no experience with the southern institutional way of doing things... We inherited an institutional system of learning that was designed and controlled elsewhere... the system never had enough program development capability to design and produce effective programs. What it provided was a watered down version of the official Quebec curriculum. Creating an education system is a necessary step to self-government in Nunavik.'

These paragraphs introduced the 101 recommendations for change in the report Silaturnimut – The Pathway to Wisdom. Source: Nunavik: Inuit-Controlled Education in Arctic Quebec by Ann Vick-Westgate (co-published by University of Calgary Press and Katutjiniq Regional Development Council, 2002).

The report made a big impact at the time, but to this day I don't know if the many recommendations have been implemented. Things have improved, but there's a lot more that needs to be addressed. As I left the School Board, the report became very contentious and controversial, and the School Board was trying to prevent me from being involved in the Task Force work. I was seen as 'biased' and 'not objective'. I sent them long letters. 'You know, 'biased' is one heck of a word. If you want someone unbiased, ship somebody in from Japan, because any one of us in our Inuit world has biases. You want someone objective? Send somebody in from another part of the world! And even then, they'll have their biased views.'

The Task Force Committee contracted me as the Inuk advisor as they had hired a *qallunaq* advisor – qallunaq is the Inuit word for white people – to help bring in the inside perspective and they felt I was a valuable player in seeing the entire picture. A couple of years after all the dust settled with the politics playing itself out, the Kativik school Board started another process called *Satuiriarniq*, 'Reclaiming'. The whole idea was that Silaturnimut would lead the way back to reclaim the life that we once had with our own education, judicial system, health and so on based on the values and principles of the Inuit tradition. It's not to say that everything was to return to being traditional again. But in the context of modern institutional schooling, how do we do that?

It was during that process of implementation that I entered into the arena of politics. Even though I had always been saying that it was not my path and not my passion, I came from a family that was very verbal and they were leaders in their own right. My mother was one of Kuujjuaq's best-known elders because of her skills working in the health field as an interpreter and accordionist. My uncle was for many years a mayor in Kuujjuaq and my brother Charlie Watt had negotiated the James Bay Northern Quebec Agreement and was appointed to the Canadian Senate in 1983.

As for me, politics wasn't something I felt comfortable with. But I needed a platform, some kind of power base for trying to do something with the youth issues. These were really just escalating. I just felt that the modeling that was happening at the leadership level was not helpful to the choices that the youth were making, especially in the areas of alcohol and drug addiction. How were we ever going to break free from these self-destructive patterns? So I decided to run for Corporate Secretary of the Makivik Corporation in 1993 and I lost. In 1995 I ran again, won, and that's how I entered the arena of politics.

In July of the same year, I was asked to go as a Nunavik delegate to the assembly of the Inuit Circumpolar Conference (now: Council), the ICC, which was being held in Alaska with the four participating nations – Canada, Greenland, Russia and the United States. I expressed certain things at the meeting and got elected to run the Canadian office. 'I'm green in politics and I don't think I'll be able to do this,' I said to my fellow delegates. 'No, no, no. We want you to do it,' they said. So I came home with two mandates, the regional one and the international one. I combined these, going between Ottawa and Montreal.

Global issues

The Presidency of the ICC was not a full-time job per se. But at the time I got elected, the global issues were just starting to really bubble up. The ICC Canada used its UN observer status to lobby and educate participants and intervene officially during the international intergovernmental negotiating sessions sponsored by the United Nations Environment Program (UNEP). One of the main issues was that of trans-boundary contaminants (see box). It needed focus and effectiveness. I did the two mandates for three years and then, when nobody else ran against me, I was reappointed in 1998 and held that position for another four years.

During that same time, I became the spokesperson for the Coalition of Northern Indigenous Peoples in the global negotiations that led to the Stockholm Convention on persistent organic pollutants (POPs), commonly known as the POPs Treaty. So I hit the ground running. As a mother and a grandmother, the POPs issue was a no-brainer. Toxins in our mothers' breast milk? There was no way that that was going to be an acceptable way to live for anybody. We were being poisoned from afar and we were the net recipients of these toxins. It wasn't just an environmental issue. The Arctic is the barometer of global environmental health, and we Inuit are the mercury in that barometer – an early warning system for the rest of the world. So with that, I put myself on the global map.

Trans-boundary contaminants

Long-lasting, persistent organic pollutants (POPs) are carbon-based byproducts of the world's industrial countries. The most serious contaminants are sometimes referred to as the 'Dirty Dozen'. Through a process of evaporation and condensation – the 'grasshopper effect' – POPs travel by wind and water currents and are deposited when encountering low temperatures. The pollutants gather in algae and shrimps, then in fish, then in seals, whales and walruses, worsening higher up the food chain. At the top of the food chain are humans.

During the mid 1980s, POPs were detected in alarmingly high rates in the breast milk and blood of Inuit mothers in northern Quebec and southern Baffin Island. Research revealed that POPs accumulate in the fatty tissues of marine mammals, the mainstay of the traditional diet of many northern peoples. Eating these contaminated foods has devastating consequences for human health, including neurological, endocrinological and behavioral disorders. POPs have been linked to high rates of breast cancer and reproductive disorders, transferred through the placenta and breast milk.

The Stockholm Convention on Persistent Organic Pollutants is a global treaty administered by the United Nations Environment Program to protect human health from chemicals and requires parties to take measures to eliminate or reduce the release of POPs into the environment. It was adopted in 2001 and entered into force in 2004.

Fortunately, we had incredible science to back us. We armed ourselves with it and translated that into international policy by getting involved in all global negotiations that culminated in the signing of the Stockholm Convention. Our focus had to be very intense, because it wasn't just about going to Nairobi, Geneva or the other countries where the negotiations were happening. It was also about preparing for the interventions and working with our Government to ensure that their stance was going to be as solid as we wanted them to be, and working with other governments to try and influence them. Giving effective interventions to allow these 150 countries or so to take the right action required a lot of energy. But our mandate was not just focused on the toxins issue. We also had teams from the ICC that were working with the Convention on Biological Diversity to try to incorporate indigenous knowledge into almost every chapter, and to instill ourselves into the UN processes.

The work of the ICC Canada, being one of the eight permanent participants of the Arctic Council (see box), kept us all very busy.

Arctic Council

Established in 1996 by the Ottawa Declaration, the Arctic Council affirms the commitment to the well-being of the inhabitants of the Arctic, sustainable development and the protection of the Arctic environment. Member states are Canada, Denmark, Finland, Iceland, Norway, the Russian Federation, Sweden and the United States. Except for Iceland, all have sizeable indigenous communities living in the Arctic.

Covering all 24 times zones, the Arctic represents one sixth of the earth's land mass. Its collective population is about 4 million people, including more than 30 different indigenous peoples. The Arctic States form a high-level intergovernmental forum with the involvement of the Arctic indigenous communities and peoples, though 'the use of the term 'peoples' in this declaration shall not be construed as having any implications as regards the rights which may attach to the term under international law.' Canada and the United States rejected the UN Declaration on the Rights of Indigenous Peoples. Nonetheless, the Arctic Council's Working Groups, Programs and Action Plans have been very effective.

The Arctic Council meetings were painfully diplomatic. Painfully! I remember sitting at one of these meetings, still jetlagged, looking at one of my advisers and whispering: 'What am I doing here?' It was all consensus based. We did not represent the Government, but we were permanent participants, so even though we could intervene, we couldn't vote. It was a way and style of meeting that was very difficult for me to adjust to. Not that I can't be diplomatic. But eventually, the work for the Arctic Council was actually very powerful, and its strength to this day is the assessments its members produce. One of the results was the Human Development Report, but of course the Arctic Climate Impact Assessment was the biggie. These were so important to the communities back home. That's what made me stick it.

Russia and Belize
Even though we have many challenges in the Inuit world, as a result of the very creative and innovative way in which ICC Canada was involved, we have become a people with a vast amount of experience. The last 25 years we've been running our own businesses, we've become very shrewd negotiators in land-claim issues, and we have co-management regimes with our Government in issues of wildlife and so on. There are things that we Inuit have developed and learned where other indigenous peoples of the world are just at starting points. The Inuit experience on these issues has become very marketable to other places in the world. We would get funding from the Canadian International Development Agency (CIDA) that deals with development issues in underdeveloped countries, and started projects in Russia and Belize.

Inuit en route *(photo by Wilfred E. Richard)*

It was a natural fit to be working with our fellow Inuit in Chukotka, Russia. As President of ICC Canada, I coordinated a large and highly visible humanitarian mission to indigenous peoples there and we helped them in issues of co-management and setting up small businesses. But CIDA said: 'If you want to have a project with your fellow Inuit in Siberia, it can't be just Inuit. It has to be all the 31 indigenous peoples.' But those peoples span 10 time zones! Working with Russia is no easy feat. On top of language problems and bureaucracy, the country was nearing the end of the communist era, but still functioning in the old ways. But we were able to travel in and out safely and managed to help our fellow Russian indigenous peoples develop their voice.

The other project we sometimes called 'Ice to Spice'. It was in Belize, where we implemented sustainable development projects with Mayan and Garifuna Indians. We engaged in dialogue with them to start them on their way in terms of co-management regimes with land and so on. When you have CIDA funds, you really need to be focused and be accountable for every penny. That almost turned into a project in itself and that became the problem in the end. It required so much management of the funds and reporting to Government to be able to be effective, you lose the focus needed to deal with other matters.

After the successful campaign on POPs leading to the Stockholm Convention, we had that experience under our belt. It had prepared us for the even greater issue of climate change and how to tackle and strategize that. We knew it wasn't going to be as easy as the POPs Treaty, especially because the United States wasn't budging whatsoever in terms of being a team player with the rest of the world. They didn't sign the Kyoto Protocol and their rhetoric didn't address any of these issues, including the Arctic Climate Impact Assessment. Pff, I was running back and forth to Iceland for that one. It was very, very difficult.

Not only was ICC Canada accountable to its elected executive council, we were also accountable to our own boards in our own countries. My Canadian board and my direct bosses were the four regions of Inuvialuit, Nunavut, Nunavik and Labrador. On top of that, I was also accountable to my communities. For a number of years I virtually lived on an airplane. Being effective with your voice in the global world is one thing, but making sure that your people are with you is another. You really get your strength from knowing that they understand what you're doing. I made a lot of effort to be on the radio and to walk people through the steps of the process.

During one of our board meetings we were discussing the effects of the breakdown of the ozone layer. The Arctic is most negatively impacted. At the time, there was almost an epidemic of cataracts, sunburns and blisters, skin cancer and immune system disorders, because there was less protection now from ultraviolet radiation. Plus the toxins of the POPs, and now our climate! The environment is changing so quickly! 'What recourse do we have?' said one of the board members. 'We're such a small number of people. What do we need to do? Launch a law suit? What?' I was observing all of this, and when you're elected to lead you're thinking all the time of ways in which to take action, to get the world to pay attention.

Another level of hunting
I would go home and think about this at night. For me, when you're small in number, it's really: strategy, strategy, strategy. It's another level of hunting. You're scouting. When the man of the family wakes up in the morning and scouts the horizon and checks the conditions, he tries to put everything in his favor, so that he can be successful in his hunt. One of our great leaders, Zebedee Nungak, said: 'This is another level of hunting that we do with our briefcases and in our suits.' I pushed that a little further, staying with the image of the hunter on another level of hunting, you scout the horizon, you have to know who and what you're dealing with, you're focused and you're strategic, because your community expects you to come home with something that will alleviate some of the challenges we face. You don't just go up to the meeting, sit down and cry about the problem. You offer help, solutions and actions, so that you can tell those that you lead that you have much to offer in helping them to do their jobs better. That you're not a thorn in their side or some ball and chain they have to carry around, but that you have certain ideas and solutions as to how together we can make this a better world, not just for the Arctic, but for the planet.

Meanwhile in the United States, Earthjustice in San Francisco and CIEL in Washington were already making linkages between climate change and human rights. They think like lawyers. That's how they spin. While I'm thinking of the other end. How do we place ourselves on the map to say that this is such a serious issue and that indeed our right to exist as an indigenous people is being violated through the arrogance of countries that already know the damage they're doing, but choosing not to take action on it?

When in 2000 the Arctic Climate Impact Assessment started, the science of climate change was still almost non-existent. There was a huge void. We realized that we needed to have this assessment be on the circumpolar world. But meanwhile, the work plan had to be approved officially and politically by the top guns of the eight Arctic nations, the ministers of Foreign Affairs of Canada, Denmark, Finland, Iceland, Norway, Sweden, Russia and the United States. We also insisted on having a policy document attached, so that the countries involved would have some kind of marching order to push them to take action. We didn't want anyone weaseling out of their responsibilities.

From the Arctic and Inuit outlook, we knew that our hunters had been observing monumental changes. Snow generally falls later in the year and the average snow cover has decreased by 10 per cent over the last three decades. The spring thaw comes earlier and more sudden than in the past. The polar ice-cap ice forms much later in the year and breaks up earlier in the spring, causing havoc for both man and animals. The sea-ice season is a lot shorter than it used to be. As a result, we have less time to hunt on the ice. Our wildlife, and most noticeably the polar bear, has a lot less time, so in some regions they are struggling to survive. Streams on traditional hunting routes that were once fordable have become torrents that claim lives every year. The ice packs have become so unpredictable that even seasoned hunters have fallen through and drowned. Sometimes with their skidoos. That is the reality we knew. But the work plan was approved. 'This is great stuff!' we said.

But then, two years into the work, we started to hear that the United States officials didn't want the policy recommendations attached to the report. 'You can't change the game plan,' we said. 'It's been approved by the ministers of Foreign Affairs and it's all consensus based.' 'O, yes we can,' came the response. The headache, the drama of it all! The State Department sent its senior Arctic officials, the Dobermans as some call them. Paula Dobriansky was the head of their department under Secretary of State Colin Powell. 'O boy,' we said, 'we're in for a ride.' When this really started to escalate, Iceland was chairing the Arctic Council. There were several meetings that year in Iceland and Greenland to deal with this dilemma, and I flew there to try and influence the way in which this needed to be changed.

It was very strenuous. In between it all I was invited to testify at Senator John McCain's Senate hearing on climate change in Washington DC. 'A golden opportunity,' we said in our team. 'We can't miss this.' Not just to tell the American officials about climate change, but to be bold and tell them what's going on with the Arctic Climate Impact Assessment and that this State Department is changing the rules of the game in the middle of this very important work. And so I testified to that whole effect and encouraged McCain to write to Colin Powell to tell them to get on side. He did. Three Senators wrote to Powell and I can tell you that the State Department went ballistic after that. With us. One day, when I was speaking at an event in the United States, a State Department official stood up from the audience. 'This is not true!' There was some intimidation, but I just looked at this person and didn't say much.

During that dark period when the Americans were very much in denial about climate change, John McCain was one of the rare leaders – and he happened to be a Republican – who was open to looking at these issues. 'We are the first generation to influence the climate and the last generation to escape the consequences,' McCain said. He and Hillary Clinton were probably the US Senators that were the most helpful to our work.

Eventually, back in Iceland at the final meeting, we reached a certain agreement that we could live with at the time. And yes, the policy document would be attached. In the reception hall, where there was a kind of elation because we had come to some common ground, someone approached me from behind and grabbed me. It was the American negotiator whom we had had many challenges with. 'We did it!' she said. 'It's all OK!' O God, I thought. She had made a U-turn in her mind. I suspected it was more because she had been outnumbered and had no choice but to change her stance. Now she was acting as though she had 'bought' into the process willingly. Aaah, the joys of politics!

The power of science
The Arctic Climate Impact Assessment report was presented at the Arctic Council in Reykjavik at the end of 2004. It offered a synthesis of knowledge on climate variability, climate change and increased ultraviolet radiation and its consequences. Among its major findings was: 'Increasing global concentrations of carbon dioxide and other greenhouse gases due to human activities, primarily fossil fuel burning, are projected to contribute to additional Arctic warming of about 4-7C°, about twice the global average rise, over the next 100 years.'

The report was a highly detailed, comprehensive assessment of climate change and it was really groundbreaking on many fronts. Finally we had the science to prove it! And just when the problems with the United States were escalating, then synchronistically the right people came together to start to really dialogue and flush this out. 'What do we do?' one of my colleagues asked. 'No law suits,' I said. 'I don't want them to think that we want money or compensation. It should be on moral high ground and in a style that I can live with when I leave the campaign. Strong and powerful, but not aggressive or confrontational.' We scouted the avenues we could employ.

In 2003, I had had my first meeting with Don Goldberg of CIEL in a hotel lounge in Washington DC. It felt right, and I trust my intuition. But it would take us two years to prepare the 'Petition to the Inter-

American Commission on Human Rights Seeking Relief from Violations Resulting from Global Warming Caused by Acts and Omissions by the United States'. This was a good way to try to bring the United States on side in a way that wouldn't cost us fortunes, which we didn't have as an NGO. It was a very interesting process, because the right people would come forward offering pro-bono help as well.

I targeted the United States, while most members of my team were American. Two students, Rich Powell and Sasha Earnheart-Gold from Harvard and Dartmouth University, had heard about my work on connecting human rights and climate change. 'We both have fellowships,' they said. 'How can we help you out with this?' 'For free? Come on up!' I trained them in my own house with an Inuk lawyer named Sandra Inutiq. Martin Wagner of Earthjustice also flew up to work with us in Iqaluit. We trained these young men to be the chief interviewers gathering testimonies in Canada and Alaska. Sandra went along to some of the communities to ensure that they were doing it right and respectfully. All this work allowed us to file the Petition on behalf of 62 hunters, elders and women from Canada and Alaska to the Inter-American Commission on Human Rights (IACHR) in 2005. The testimonies can still be seen on the website of Isuma TV, the Inuit-owned station.

The work on the Petition was part of my mission to give climate change a human face. In fact, everything that I've ever done was to put the human face on the map, because these issues have always been so academic, you would never think that there was a heartbeat to any of them. Whether economist, politician or scientist, people in their comfort zone tend to keep the issue faceless. It's statistics and numbers, ice and snow, weather and wildlife. Every picture that comes up in terms of climate change is a polar bear. You never see the human face or the people involved in this. The key is to move the issue from the head to the heart.

'Aren't you afraid?' fellow leaders said to me. They felt that the Bush Administration might come at us, as they always seemed to be very reactive to whatever was going on in the world. 'What if we lose our funding as a result?' 'No, I'm not,' I said. 'I'm more afraid of not taking the right action for the future of my grandson than of the Bush Administration.' Simply put, it was that. I cannot think that when you fight for your rights, in an honorable way, with the best of intentions, that there would somehow be a punishment attached to what you do. And it has held true for me, because the reverse has happened. Not only has there been no punishment, in fact, the world has recognized this now as a human rights issue, and I have probably become one of the most decorated environmental and cultural activists in the world, including the 2007 Nobel Peace Prize nomination. It isn't about me getting all this recognition however. It's about the fact that people are getting it. That's the message. It is the resonance of truth with others that is the greatest honor I get from all the recognition I receive.

We filed the Petition based on the findings of the Arctic Climate Impact Assessment, which project that Inuit hunting culture may not survive the loss of sea ice and other changes over the coming decades. It alleges that unchecked emissions of greenhouse gases from the United States have violated Inuit cultural and environmental human rights as guaranteed by the 1948 American Declaration of the Rights and Duties of Man. Our human rights – to live our traditional way – are being violated by human-induced climate change. The IACHR decided against moving forward with the Petition, but representatives of our team, of Earthjustice and CIEL were invited to testify at a hearing in March 2007 to help the Commission learn more about the legal aspects of climate change and human rights.

Bringing it home
In our time, there is such a disconnect with environmental issues. But there's a real human dimension to them. They are, first and foremost, a human rights issue. Even though we have made a lot of progress, there are still many concerns, such as the exploration and exploitation of the natural resources of our land and all its possible adverse effects. Sandra Inutiq is still working on these issues, in particular with regard to the mining of uranium (see box).

'Imagine future generations'

'It is Makita's belief that once our lands are open to one uranium mine, it opens the door for others to open. Uranium ore and the waste tailings created by uranium mining and milling are known to be among the most toxic of substances found on earth. Once extracted this toxic nuclear waste remains for thousands of years. In the Baker Lake area alone, there are 18 uranium exploration sites. Imagine the waste lands that would be left for generations created by these mines. The consensus of medical professionals has long stated that there is no safe dose for exposure to radiation. Everyone knows what the exposure to radiation has done post Chernobyl nuclear plant explosion. Yes this is an extreme example. However, as stated, there are no safe levels of exposure to radiation, so the same effects would be faced in regions where uranium mining is allowed to happen, which is cancer, deformities in fetuses, mental retardation for humans, and other living beings.'

'It is also Makita's position that once a uranium mine is allowed to open in Nunavut, the door will then be opened for Government and industry to push to store high-level nuclear waste in Nunavut as well – a consequence that has been experienced by other regions. Imagine future generations asking why these activities were allowed to happen. After all, they are the ones that will be left with the mess left by us.'

Excerpt from a letter to the Inuit Circumpolar Conference of 24 February 2011, by Sandra Inutiq, spokesperson of Nunavummiut Makitagunarningit ('Nunavummiut can rise up'), an NGO that fosters informed public discussion about uranium mining in Nunavut.

I believe that it is the doctrine of collective human rights that really brings diverse cultures, peoples and countries together. A human rights approach to these issues is highly potent and much more effective than dry technical reports can ever be. When people talk POPs, they don't think about a young mother they know who cannot breastfeed her baby for fear of passing on toxins from her own body. But that brings it home. What a world we have created! 'It's not personal against the US Administration,' I said when we launched the Petition. 'It's personal when Inuit women have to think twice about nursing their babies due to toxins coming to the north as a result of industry and globalization. It's personal when my grandson may lose what I had as the foundation upon which I do my work.' That's the human issue here, and that's what drives me to do the work that I do.

Up to 2010, I had received many honorary doctorates from Canada. But in August, I started working as a visiting Tallman Scholar at Bowdoin College in Maine. Two years ago, I never knew it existed, until I received a letter from the President asking me if I would do them the honor of receiving an honorary doctorate there. When I received that invitation, I said to myself: 'O, America! Wow, this is new!' After going through all the struggles from within and from without, to come to that point of receiving the highest honor of academia in the United States was a real breakthrough.

So I went down and learned a little bit more about this private college that has the Peary-MacMillan Arctic Museum. A dialogue started and I talked to people there about The Right to be Cold (see box), the book I was writing, and so on. One thing led to another, my Nobel nomination went into the pot, and they decided that this would be great. And I felt it would be such a great opportunity. What a perfect audience to speak to about these issues! For me, it was a double plus. It offered me a great platform to influence the next string of leaders – maybe one or two will eventually be a scientist or Congressman. At the same time, it helped me to get a little more focused to complete my book.

Sounding the alarm

Sheila Watt-Cloutier's memoir, The Right to Be Cold: One Woman's Story of Protecting Her Culture, the Arctic and the

Whole Planet (2015), tells the story of how she rose from a life of dogsleds and canoes to become one of the most influential human rights advocates in the world. She argues that climate change is a human rights issue to which all world citizens are inextricably linked, not just the hunting culture of the Inuit. "Our own government and other governments and businesses around the world are trying to see it as an opportunity for business, for mining, for extracting the oil and gas and so on."

Climate change poses an existential threat. Especially for cultures that are embedded in ice and snow, the failure of the world to reduce its emissions to prevent that constitutes a grave human-rights violation. It worries Watt-Cloutier that Arctic politicians would lose their moral leadership if they adopt an "if you can't beat 'em, join 'em" attitude toward fossil-fuel extraction beneath the melting ice. Writer Naomi Klein sees her as "sounding the alarm that unless we change course – and fast – our collective home will become incurably sick."

As far as my spiritual journey is concerned, the main anchor of my personal feeling is that I have a really, really strong maternal instinct. Always have. Perhaps most women do, I don't know. But the wellbeing of my children and my grandson are the most important for me. I have a grandson who is growing up in the Arctic and I really want him to have the opportunity of seeing the richness of our culture in the way that I had as a child growing up. To have the love and the safety and a culture that I just find absolutely ingenious and brilliant in so many ways. It touches me when I talk about that, because growing up with my mother and grandmother so much has remained a part of me, even with all the struggles they had with the fathers of their children and having to raise their children on their own. The common thread that kept us together is the love of our culture and the love of our way of life. It is that which I'm trying to protect for our people and to move forward and beyond what we're struggling with today. That, I think, is what keeps me going, and not giving up.

As a leader you have to always make sure that you're leading from a place of strength, of focus, of clarity, and not from fear or victimhood. Because if you're functioning from a place of fear or victimhood, then you're not modeling effectively the possibilities for others. I try to check in as much as I can to ensure that I'm being real with myself and with the issues. I'm not religious per se. The only time that I will really go to church is when I go home to Kuujjuaq and I just want to come back to that place that I remember where everybody is under one roof, either singing or just being together. Unfortunately, most of the times that I have been in church for the last several years have been because of losses in my own family. But the spiritual aspect of it is about getting to know who you are, getting to know your own weaknesses and strengths, testing yourself on every level and ground, becoming more consciously aware of what makes you tick and developing a trust in the cosmic order to life. While embracing that in your own life, you try to model that for others, not just settling with a mundane life, but seeing that there are incredible, creative, innovative, and purposeful ways in which one can contribute to this life that we have.

Adaptability
Not so long ago, from 1941 until 1978, instead of surnames, the Canadian authorities gave Inuit disc numbers to organize us. The discs were made of leather and were supposed to be worn around the neck attached to a string. It was nothing like a social security number. It was more like a dog tag and every Inuk had one. Since the 1950s, the Inuit suffered tremendously due to government policies, without having outlets for the complete transformation of their lives. Each subsequent generation hasn't been able to heal or overcome the pain. It's not our inability to adapt – that couldn't be further from the truth. It's the speed at which things have happened. We are a people whose very foundation is the ability to adapt – to the seasons, to the settings, to the animals and their migration, all of those things. We are renowned for our adaptability.

Paving the way – unexpectedly

'I don't regret the experience, but I have never recovered from it,' says Inuit elder Zebedee Nungak. Together with Peter Ittinuar and Eric Tagoona, he was one of three 12-year-old boys who were shipped south in the early 1960s from their homes in the Arctic to attend public schools in Ottawa. The film The Experimental Eskimos documents that unusual attempt at social engineering.

Contrary to the expectation that their education would make them malleable to the desires of the Canadian Government, all three went on to pave the way for indigenous rights. Peter Ittinuar became Canada's first Inuk Member of Parliament. Zebedee Nungak became president of Makivik, the major Inuit economic and political organization. And Eric Tagoona became president of the Inuit Tapirisat of Canada, the first Inuit political organization. But all three had suffered profound disconnection, deprived as they were of their parents, their language and their culture. Part of their lives was marked by alcoholism, drug addiction and family breakups, an experience shared by many Inuit. Their legacy however is a victory.

As long as the ice remained frozen, no one much cared for the Arctic Sea but us Inuit. Now that it has begun to melt, however, everyone desires the new landscape for their own devices.

Because of all the rapid changes in the Inuit world, along with a lot of historical traumas such as the forced relocations and the residential schools (see box), our society has broken down very quickly. It is totally uncharacteristic of Inuit to be violent, to be addicted or to be suicidal. This is just not who we are. Addictions are really a substitute for wisdom. It's a way in which people try to alleviate the quality of their experience by trying to numb themselves. But in fact it gets worse. In 1971, when I was 18, there was the first suicide in my community. Except for the odd circumstance, and mostly for survival reasons, we never used to have as many suicides as we do now. Today, we are faced with the highest suicide rates in North America.

The skills of the hunting culture are very transferable to the modern world. You can learn those skills, and they can lead the way for creative thinking and trying to create positive judgment calls and choices for yourself. For example, if you have learned to take survival-based risks, you have learned to be reflective and not impulsive. Committing suicide is a very impulsive act. You're just overwhelmed by your immediate stress and pain and not thinking beyond that. It's not to take away the pain that people are going through who have been traumatized and violated – individually as a child, or collectively as a society.

You have to be really consciously aware of yourself to overcome these things and realize that it doesn't pay to be impulsive, because it puts you and your family at risk. If it is integrated within you to be reflective and to think twice about taking certain actions, that sense of judgment kicks in, no matter whether you're dealing with a boss at work or the breakup of a relationship. In fact, that's one of the big reasons why young people commit suicide: when they break up with their girlfriends or boyfriends. 'My God, you're supposed to break up at that age, you know!' we say. 'But you're not supposed to take it so seriously.' Instead of being in this wounded situation and vulnerable, the skills of the hunting culture teach you to be able to withstand that kind of stressful situation and to have a sense of confidence and worthiness about yourself and sound judgment. Then you can adapt.

The crown on my work would be the young Inuit finding their rightful place in this new world order of globalization that has hit us so hard. It would also be a tribute to the importance of maintaining Inuit culture, so that we can make it in both worlds. One way of life doesn't have to be at the cost of another. They can complement and strengthen each other. My grandson can be the great hunter if he wants to be. At the same time, if he wants to be a hockey player or engineer, he can be that. But hunting puts him in touch with nature. He will then always have that connection, so that the choices he makes in his professional life will be influenced by what he knows about the cycles and rhythms of nature and the changes that are happening.

'Well, we can't all be hunters,' many people in the south say. 'No, and I don't expect you to,' I answer them. But if you're living in an urban setting, when you go out hiking or canoeing and doing things outside, you'll learn more about what's happening to this planet. If you live in a vacuum, you might never know that there is anything terribly wrong with our planet. Learn about it, so that you can get more in touch with nature and with what it is you need to do as a citizen of the world, so that you don't live disconnected from the Inuit hunter falling through the ice if you're living in Toronto or in Washington. In my view, if you protect the Arctic, you will save the planet. We're all connected in so many ways.

Sources and further reading

Introduction and general

Arendt, Hannah, The Origins of Totalitarianism (1951)
Arendt, Hannah, Eichmann in Jerusalem: A Report on the Banality of Evil (1963)
Benda, Julien, The Treason of the Intellectuals (1928)
Douglass, Frederick, My Bondage and My Freedom (1855)
Douglass, Frederick, Narrative of the Life of Frederick Douglass, an American Slave (1845)
Loyola, Saint Ignatius of, Personal Writings (1522-1556)
Mackay, Charles, Extraordinary Popular Delusions and the Madness of Crowds (1841; edition of 1852)
Mundy, Talbot, Tros of Samothrace (1925-'26)
Orwell, George, Nineteen Eighty-Four (1949)
Woodward, Bob, State of Denial: Bush at War, Part III (Simon & Schuster, 2007)

Burma - Soe Myint

www.burmalibrary.org
www.dassk.com
www.dvb.no
www.mizzima.com
www.myanmar.com
Ball, Joseph, and Mizzima News Agency, Come Rain or Shine: A Personal Account of Burma, the 2007 Uprising and Cyclone Nargis (Mizzima News Agency, 2008)
Donkers, Jan and Minka Nijhuis, Burma Behind the Mask (Burma Centrum Nederland, 1996)
Haksar, Nandita, Rogue Agent: How India's Military Intelligence Betrayed the Burmese Resistance (Penguin Books, 2009)
International Press Institute, Brave News Worlds: Navigating the New Media Landscape (IPI, 2010)
Mizzima: On the Road to Media Freedom in a Better Burma (2008)
Myint, Soe, Burma File: A Question of Democracy (India Research Press, 2003)

Myint-U, Thant, The River of Lost Footsteps: A Personal History of Burma (Farrar, Straus and Giroux, 2006)

Chechnya - Khassan Baiev

www.chechnyaadvocacy.org
www.doctorswithoutborders.org
www.memo.ru
www.omct.org
www.physiciansforhumanrights.org
Baiev, Khassan with Ruth and Nicholas Daniloff, The Oath: A Surgeon Under Fire (Walker & Co., 2003)
Dunlop, John B., Russia Confronts Chechnya: Roots of a Separatist Conflict (Cambridge University Press, 1998)
Gall, Carlotta and Thomas de Waal, Chechnya: A Small Victorious War (Pan Books, 1997)
Karny, Yo'av, Highlanders: A Journey to the Caucasus in Quest of Memory (Farrar Straus & Giroux, 2001)
Lieven, Anatol, Chechnya: Tombstone of Russian Power (Yale University Press, 1998)
Nekrich, Aleksander M., The Punished Peoples: The Deportation and Fate of Soviet Minorities at the End of the Second World War (W.W. Norton & Company, Inc, 1978)
Nikolaev, Yu.K. (editor), Chechnya Revisited (Nova Science Publishers, 2003)
Nivat, Anne, Chienne de Guerre: A Woman Reporter Behind the Lines of War in Chechnya (Public Affairs, 2001)
Politkovskaya, Anna, A Russian Diary (Harvill Secker, 2007)
Politkovskaya, Anna, A Small Corner of Hell: Dispatches from Chechnya (University of Chicago Press, 2003)
Politkovskaya, Anna, Putin's Russia (The Harvill Press, 2004)
Seierstadt, Asne, The Angel of Grozny: Life Inside Chechnya (Little Brown Books Group, 2008)
World Organization Against Torture, Chechnya: No Means to Live: An Appraisal of Violations of Economic, Social and Cultural Rights in Chechnya (2004)

East Turkestan - Rebiya Kadeer

www.cecc.gov
www.chinaview.cn
www.iuhrdf.org
www.rfa.org/uyghur
www.uhrp.org
www.uyghuramerican.org
www.uyghurcongress.org

Bellér-Hann, Ildikó, Community Matters in Xinjiang, 1880-1949: Towards a Historical Anthropology of the Uyghur (Brill Academic Publishers, 2008)
Blackmore, Charles, Conquering the Desert of Death: Across the Taklamakan (Tauris Parke Paperbacks, 1995)
Hopkirk, Peter, Foreign Devils on the Silk Road: The Search for the Lost Cities and Treasures of Chinese Central Asia (The University of Massachusetts Press, 1980)
Kadeer, Rebiya, Dragon Fighter: One Woman's Epic Struggle for Peace with China (Kales Press, 2009)
Millward, James, Eurasian Crossroads: A History of Xinjiang (Columbia University Press, 2007)
Starr, S. Frederick (ed.), Xinjiang: China's Muslim Borderland (M.E. Sharpe, 2004)
Tyler, Christian, Wild West China: The Taming of Xinjiang (Rutgers University Press, 2004)

Ecuador - Pablo Fajardo

www.amazonwatch.org
www.api.org
www.chevrontoxico.com
www.texaco.com
www.texacotoxico.org
www.theamazonpost.com
www.thechevronpit.blogspot.com

Martin Beristain, Carlos, Dario Páez Rovira and Itziar Fernández, Las Palabras de la Selva: Estudio Psicosocial del Impacto de las

Explotaciones Petroleras de Texaco en las Comunidades Amazónicas de Ecuador (Hegoa, 2009)

Dematteis, Lou, and Kayana Szymczak, Crude Reflections: Oil, Ruin and Resistance in the Amazon Rainforest (City Lights Books, 2008)

Kimerling, Judith, Indigenous Peoples and the Oil Frontier in Amazonia: The Case of Ecuador, Chevron Texaco, and Aguinda v. Texaco In New York University Journal of International Law and Politics, Vol. 38 (2006)

Gerlach, Allen, Indians, Oil, and Politics: A Recent History of Ecuador (Scholarly Resources Books, 2002)

Shah, Sonia, Crude: The History of Oil (Seven Stories Press, 2004)

Sawyer, Suzana, Crude Chronicles: Indigenous Politics, Multinational Oil, and Neoliberalism in Ecuador (Duke University Press, 2004)

India - Martin Macwan

www.dalitfoundation.org

www.dalitstudies.org.in

www.navsarjan.org

www.safaikarmachariandolan.org

Freeman, James M., Untouchable: An Indian Life History (George Allen & Unwin, 1979)

Gill, Timothy, Making Things Worse: How 'Caste Blindness' in India Post-tsunami Disaster Recovery Has Exacerbated Vulnerability and Exclusion (Dalit Network Netherlands, 2007)

Guha, Ramachandra, India After Ghandi: The History of the World's Largest Democracy (Harper Perennial, 2007)

Macwan, Joseph, The Stepchild: Angaliyat (Oxford University Press, 2004)

Mangubhai, Jayshree, Aloysius Irudayam Sj and Emma Sydenham (editors), Dalit Women's Right to Political Participation in Rural Panchayati Raj: A Study of Gujarat and Tamil Nadu (Justitia et Pax, 2009)

Kurup, Stalin (director), India Untouched: Stories of a People Apart (documentary, 2007)

Moon, Vasant, Growing up Untouchable in India: A Dalit Autobiography (Rowman & Littlefield Publishers, Inc., 1995)

Rodrigues, Valerian (ed.), The Essential Writings of B.R. Ambedkar (Oxford University Press, 2002)

Thekaekara, Mari Marcel, Endless Filth: The Saga of the Bhangis (ZED Books, 1999)

Liberia - Samuel Kofi Woods

www.cental.org
www.emansion.gov.lr
www.liberianobserver.com

Best, Kenneth Y., Albert Porte: A Life Time Trying to Save Liberia (The Observer Publishing Company, 2010)

Ellis, Stephen, The Mask of Anarchy (Hurst & Co. Ltd., 1999)

Fahnbulleh, Boima H., Voices of Protest: Liberia on the Edge, 1974-1980 (Universal Publishers, 2005)

Johnson, Charles S., Bitter Canaan: The Story of the Negro Republic (Transaction Books, 1987)

Moran, Mary H., Liberia: The Violence of Democracy (University of Pennsylvania Press, 2006)

Paye, Won-Ldy and Margaret H. Lippert, Head, Body, Legs: A Story from Liberia (2002)

Smith, James Wesley, Sojourners in Search of Freedom: The Settlement of Liberia by Black Americans (University Press of America, 1987)

Walraven, Klaas van, The Pretence of Peace-keeping (Netherlands Institute of International Relations 'Clingendael', 1999)

Wreh, Tuan, The Love of Liberty: The Rule of President William V.S. Tubman in Liberia 1944-1971 (C. Hurst & Company, 1976)

The United Nations and the Situation in Liberia (UN Department of Public Information, Reference Paper February 1997)

Nunavut - Sheila Watt-Cloutier

www.acia.uaf.edu
www.arcticathabaskancouncil.com
www.arctic-council.org
www.arcticpeoples.org
www.gov.nu.ca

www.inuitcircumpolar.com
www.isuma.tv
www.itk.ca
www.manystrongvoices.org
www.nunatsiaqonline.ca
www.tunngavik.com
www.uranium-network.org

Bennett, John and Susan Rowley (editors), Uqalurait: An Oral History of Nunavut (McGill-Queen's University Press, 2004)

Byers, Michael, Who Owns the Arctic: Understanding Sovereignty Disputes in the North (Douglas & McIntyre, 2009)

Kolbert, Elizabeth (editor), The Arctic: An Anthology (Granta Books, 2007)

Lopez, Barry, Arctic Dreams: Imagination and Desire in a Northern Landscape (Charles Scribner's Sons, 1986)

McGrath, Melanie, The Long Exile: A True Story of Deception and Survival in the Canadian Arctic (Fourth Estate, 2006)

Mowat, Farley, People of the Deer: The Vanishing Eskimo – A Valiant People's Fight for Survival (Little, Brown and Company, 1951)

Saul, John Ralston, A Fair Country: Telling Truths About Canada (Viking Canada, 2008)

Struzik, Ed, The Big Thaw: Travels in the Melting North (Wiley, 2009)

Vick-Westgate, Ann, Nunavik: Inuit-controlled Education in Arctic Quebec (University of Calgary Press, 2002)

Wheeler, Sara, The Magnetic North: Travels in the Arctic (Vintage Books, 2009)

Wilson, Simon, Janine Murray and Henry Huntington (editors), AMAP Assessment Report: Arctic Pollution Issues (Arctic Monitoring and Assessment Programme, 1998)

Nasivvik Centre for Inuit Health and Changing Environments at Université Laval and the Ajunnginiq Centre at the National Aboriginal Health Organization, Unikkaaqatigiit: Putting the Human Face on Climate Change (Inuit Tapiriit Kanatami, 2005)

South Africa - Vuyiseka Dubula

www.botshabelo.org
www.gcis.gov.za

www.gov.za
www.nkosishaven.org
www.tac.org.za
www.un.org/esa/dsd/agenda21/
Epstein, Helen, The Invisible Cure: Africa, the West, and the Fight Against AIDS (Penguin Books, 2007)
Fassin, Didier, When Bodies Remember: Experiences and Politics of AIDS in South Africa (University of California Press, 2007)
Mandela, Nelson, Long Walk to Freedom: The Autobiography of Nelson Mandela (Abacus, 1995)
Nolen, Stephanie, 28 Stories of AIDS in Africa (Portobello Books, 2007)
Orbinsky, James, An Imperfect Offering: Dispatches from the Medical Frontline (Rider & Co., 2008)
Otter, Steven, Khayelitsha: uMlungu in a Township (The Penguin Group South Africa, 2007)
Tutu, Desmond, God Has a Dream: A Vision of Hope for Our Time (Rider & Co., 2004)
Tutu, Desmond, No Future Without Forgiveness: A Personal Overview of South Africa's Truth and Reconciliation Commission (Rider & Co., 1999)
Wooten, James T., We Are All the Same: The Story of a Boy's Courage and a Mother's Love (Penguin Press, 2004)
Worden, Nigel, The Making of Modern South Africa: Conquest, Apartheid, Democracy (Wiley Blackwell, 1994)

United States - Maria Gunnoe

www.appalachianvoices.org
www.appalachiarising.org
www.earthjustice.org
www.epa.gov
www.facesofcoal.org
www.ilovemountains.org
www.auroralights.org
www.mtrstopshere.org
www.ohvec.org
www.restoringeden.org

www.sierraclub.org
www.southwings.org
www.thelastmountainmovie.com
Ahern, M.M., et al., The association between mountaintop mining and birth defects among live births in central Appalachia, 1996–2003. Environ. Res. (2011), doi:10.1016/j.envres.2011.05.019
Abramson, Rudy, and Jean Haskell (editors), Encyclopedia of Appalachia (University of Tennessee Press, 2006)
Biggers, Jeff, Reckoning at Eagle Creek: The Secret Legacy of Coal in the Heartland (The Nation / Basic Books, 2010)
Butler, Tom and George Wuerthner (editors), Plundering Appalachia: The Tragedy of Mountaintop-Removal Coal Mining (Earth Aware Editions, 2009)
Caudill, Harry, Night Comes to the Cumberlands: A Biography of a Depressed Area (Little, Brown and Co., 1963)
Goodell, Jeff, Big Coal: The Dirty Secret Behind America's Energy Future (Mariner Books, 2007)
House, Silas, and Jason Howard (editors), Something's Rising: Appalachians Fighting Mountaintop Removal (University Press of Kentucky, 2009)
Howard, Jason (editor), We All Live Downstream: Writings about Mountaintop Removal (Motes Books, 2009)
Kahn, Kathy, Hillbilly Women (Avon Books, 1985)
Kennedy, Robert, Jr., Crimes against Nature: How George W. Bush and His Corporate Pals Are Plundering the Country and Hijacking Our Democracy (HarperCollins, 2004)
Pancake, Ann, Strange As This Weather Has Been (Shoemaker & Hoard, 2007)
Pooley, Eric, The Climate War: True Believers, Power Brokers, and the Fight to Save the Earth (Hyperion, 2010)
Reece, Erik, Lost Mountain: A Year in the Vanishing Wilderness: Radical Strip Mining and the Devastation of Appalachia (Riverhead Books, 2006)
Shapiro, Tricia, Mountain Justice: Homegrown Resistance to Mountaintop Removal, for the Future of Us All (AK Press, 2010)
Stewart Burns, Shirley and Mari-Lynn Evans and Silas House (editors), Coal Country: Rising Up Against Mountaintop Removal Mining (Sierra Club Books, 2009)

Venezuela - Liliana Ortega

www.chavez.org.ve
www.cidh.oas.org
www.cofavic.org
www.derechos.org.ve
www.gumilla.org.ve
www.sinergia.org.ve
http://venezuelanalysis.com
Los Grupos Parapoliciales en Venezuela (Cofavic, 2005; only available in Spanish)
Chávez, Hugo and Martha Harnecker, Understanding the Venezuelan Revolution: Hugo Chávez Talks to Marta Harnecker (Monthly Review Press, 2005)
Galeano, Eduardo, Open Veins of Latin America: Five Centuries of the Pillage of a Continent (Monthly Review Press, 1973)
Golinger, Eva, The Chávez Code: Cracking US Intervention in Venezuela (Pluto Press, 2007)
Gott, Richard, Hugo Chávez and the Bolivarian Revolution (Verso, 2000)
Martinez, Carlos, Michael Fox and JoJo Farrell (editors): Venezuela Speaks! Voices from the Grassroots (PM Press, 2010)
Wilpert, Gregory, Changing Venezuela by Taking Power: The History and Policies of the Chávez Government (Verso, 2007)

Western Sahara - Aminatou Haidar

www.fishelsewhere.eu
www.hrw.org
www.independentdiplomat.org
www.sandblast-arts.org
www.securitycouncilreports.org
www.un.org/en/peacekeeping/missions/minurso/
www.upesonline.info
www.vest-sahara.no
www.wsrw.org

Arts, Karin and Pedro Pinto Leite (editors), International Law and the Question of Western Sahara (International Platform of Jurists for East Timor, 2007)

Damis, John, Conflict in Northwest Africa: The Western Sahara Dispute (Hoover Institution Press, 1983)

Hodges, Tony, Western Sahara: The Roots of a Desert War (Lawrence Hill & Company, 1983)

Human Rights Watch, Human Rights in Western Sahara and in the Tindouf Refugee Camps: Morocco/Western Sahara/Algeria (2008)

Jensen, E., Western Sahara: Anatomy of a Stalemate (Lynne Rienner Publishers, 2005)

Pazzanita, Anthony G. and Tony Hodges, Historical Dictionary of Western Sahara (The Scarecrow Press, Inc., 1994)

Ross, Carne, Independent Diplomat: Despatches from an Unaccountable Elite (Hurst & Company, 2007)

Shelley, Toby, Endgame in the Western Sahara: What Future for Africa's Last Colony? (Zed Books, 2004)

United Nations Security Council, Report of the Secretary-General on the situation concerning Western Sahara, 14 April 2011 (S/2011/249)

Acknowledgements

First of all, I would like to thank the contributors for their time and their hospitality. This book could not have been realized without their cooperation, and the book is essentially their merit. Secondly, I would like to thank all staff at the supporting or sympathizing organizations and all those who have helped and facilitated compiling these chapters in many ways over the years from 2008 through 2011.

Rebiya Kadeer; East Turkestan / Germany / United States / Belgium: Alim Seytoff, Henryk Szadiewski and Ms. Amy Reger of the Uyghur Human Rights Project (UHRP) in Washington DC; Dolkun Isa, staff and supporters at the World Uyghur Congress (WUC) in Munich and Washington DC; Congressional Executive Commission on China (CECC) in Washington DC; the 2010 joint conference of the World Uyghur Congress and members of the European Parliament, sponsored by the National Endowment for Democracy at the European Parliament (Brussels).

Soe Myint; Burma / India / Norway: staff at Mizzima in New Delhi; Khin Maung Win and staff at Democratic Voice of Burma (DVB) in Oslo.

Martin Macwan; India: Staff and students at Navsarjan Trust. Special thanks to Manjula Pradeep, director. Special thanks also to the villagers of Kheecha (Gujarat).

Khassan Baiev; Chechnya / Russia / United States: Nicholas Daniloff and Ms. Ruth Daniloff (Boston); Doctors Without Borders (Boston); International Committee for the Children of Chechnya; special thanks to Ms. Maryam Baiev.

Aminatou Haidar; Western Sahara / Belgium / Spain / The Netherlands: Javier Lachica of the Western Sahara Resource Watch (Sevilla, Spain); representatives of the Collective of Sahrawi Human Rights Defenders (CODESA) and the Sahrawi Association of Victims of Grave Human Rights Violations Perpetrated by the Moroccan State

(ASVDH); Frank Ruddy (Washington DC); the European Parliament for hosting the conference Fishing in the Sahara in Brussels; Stichting Zelfbeschikking West-Sahara (Rotterdam); Fish Elsewhere Campaign; Ms. Sara Eyckmans, European Coordinator of the Western Sahara Resource Watch (Belgium).

Samuel Kofi Woods; Liberia / The Netherlands / United States: Kenneth Y. Best of the Liberian Observer (Monrovia); Ms. Mary H. Moran (Colgate University, New York).

Vuyiseka Dubula; South Africa: staff at Treatment Action Campaign (TAC) in Khayelitsha near Cape Town; Con and Marion Cloete of Botshabelo (near Magaliesberg, Johannesburg).

Maria Gunnoe; United States: Ohio Valley Environmental Coalition, Ms. Terri Blanton of Kentuckians for the Commonwealth; Larry Gibson of Keeper of the Mountains; Ken Hechler; Jack Spadaro; and various persons participating in the conference Voices of Appalachia and Appalachia Rising (25-27 September 2010); Ms. Liz Judge of Earth Justice; Ms. Sandra Diaz of Appalachian Voices and Restoring Eden (Christians for Environmental Stewardship).

Pablo Fajardo; Ecuador / United States: Amazon Defense Coalition (Quito, Ecuador); Amazon Watch (United States); Ms. Karen Hinton of Hinton Communications (Washington DC); Steven Donziger (New York); Ms. Suzana Sawyer (San Francisco).

Liliana Ortega; Venezuela: Ms. Yris Medina, Ms. Hilda Páez, Ms. Maritza Romero, Ms. Elisa Ruiz, and other staff members of the Committee of Family Members of Victims (COFAVIC, Caracas).

Sheila Watt-Cloutier; Nunavut / Canada: Ms. Rian van Bruggen (Department of Health and Social Services, Government of Nunavut in Iqaluit); Ms. Sandra Inutiq (Nunavummiut Makitagunarningit); Natan Obed (Nunavut Tunngavik); Ms. Terry Rahbek-Nielsen (University of Calgary Press).

International: Representatives of the Unrepresented Nations and Peoples Organization (UNPO, The Hague); Ms. Kenneth van Toll of Freevoice (Hilversum, Netherlands); Mamatjan Juma, Jilili Musha and Gulgehra Keyum of Radio Free Asia (United States); Any Kultalahti (Amnesty International, London). Special thanks to the Royal Library and the Peace Palace Library in The Hague (Netherlands); Ms. Laura Spann (Amnesty International USA); the International Human Rights Film Festival (Geneva); Ms. Nanda Ramanathan; Ms. Milene J. Fernandez, Ms. Pia Boonstra and Ms. Marjon van Opijnen.

Special thanks to all those who chose to remain anonymous.

Last but not least, thanks to all staff at PixelPerfect Publications, The Hague.

Arne Peter Braaksma

Colophon

Human Dignity
Eleven Defenders of Human Rights *at Close Range*

© 2015 Arne Peter Braaksma / PixelPerfect Publications, The Hague, the Netherlands

Cover photo of Aminatou Haidar by Sofia Moro http://sofiamoro.com

ISBN Book   9789491833250
ISBN Ebook 9789491833267

PixelPerfect Publications
Bankastraat 107b
2585 EK The Hague
The Netherlands

info@pixelperfectpublications.com
www.pixelperfectpublications.com